T0304876

THE VIRAGO BOOK OF
FRIENDSHIP

Also by Rachel Cooke

Her Brilliant Career
Kitchen Person

THE VIRAGO BOOK OF
FRIENDSHIP

EDITED BY

RACHEL COOKE

virago

VIRAGO

First published in Great Britain in 2024 by Virago Press

3 5 7 9 10 8 6 4

A CIP catalogue record for this book
is available from the British Library.

ISBN 978-0-3490-1843-0

Typeset in Perpetua by M Rules
Printed and bound in Great Britain by
Clays Ltd, Elcograf S.p.A.

Papers used by Virago Press are from well-managed forests
and other responsible sources.

Virago Press
An imprint of
Little, Brown Book Group
Carmelite House
50 Victoria Embankment
London EC4Y 0DZ

The authorised representative
in the EEA is
Hachette Ireland
8 Castlecourt Centre
Dublin 15, D15 XTP3, Ireland
(email: info@hbgi.ie)

An Hachette UK Company
www.hachette.co.uk

www.virago.co.uk

For Rachel Kitt
and in memory of CC

If one could be friendly with women, what a pleasure – the relationship so secret & private compared with relations with men. Why not write about it? Truthfully?

Virginia Woolf
The Diary of Virginia Woolf, 1 November, **1924**

Our subterranean grapevine, which men, like fools, call gossip, has always been efficient.

Robin Morgan, 'Letter to a Sister Underground'
(1970)

Harriet had long ago discovered that one could not like people any the better merely because they were ill, or dead – still less because one had once liked them very much.

Dorothy L. Sayers, *Gaudy Night* **(1935)**

'What a cow!' Kate said.

Shirley Conran, *Lace* **(1982)**

Contents

Introduction 1

1 Definitions 25

2 Childhood 35

3 First Encounters 93

8 Shifting Sands 265

Virginia Woolf ∼ *Stella Gibbons* ∼ *Lizzie Stewart*
Henry James ∼ *Rose Tremain* ∼ *Jami Attenberg*
Nella Larsen ∼ *Jane Austen* ∼ *Lore Segal*
Beatrice Webb ∼ *Lorrie Moore* ∼ *Vera Brittain*
Winifred Holtby

9 Old Friends 305

Jackie Kay ∼ *E. M. Delafield* ∼ *Carol Shields*
Margaret Drabble ∼ *Amanda Craig* ∼ *Barbara Pym*
Samuel Richardson ∼ *Geoffrey Chaucer* ∼ *Toni Morrison*
Katherine Philips

10 Goodbyes 327

Mary McCarthy on Hannah Arendt
Rachel Cooke on Carmen Callil ∼ *Anne Sexton on Sylvia Plath*
Anne Preston on Hilary Mantel ∼ *Edith Simcox on George Eliot*
Virginia Woolf on Katherine Mansfield
Anne Thackeray Ritchie on Margaret Oliphant ∼ *Helen Garner*
Elizabeth Bishop on Marianne Moore
Anne Stevenson on Frances Horovitz ∼ *Charlotte Brontë*

Introduction

M Y OLDEST FRIEND has the same name as me: Rachel. But I call her Kitty, a variation on her surname. We have been close for more than forty years, and this book, an anthology of writing devoted to friendship between women, is dedicated to her, the constancy of our relationship being, after so long, a given (though this is not to suggest I take it for granted, because I don't). She and I will, I believe, know each other now until one of us finds ourself at the other's funeral, where she will, perhaps, be required to tell funny stories to a crowd of unfamiliar people (it's a long time since we knew all the same people, driving our parents mad with our gossip). Kitty, if you're reading this, please don't bring up that school trip to Normandy during which I famously disgraced myself.

We were fourteen when we met at our Sheffield comprehensive, having arrived there from different primary schools, current best friends in tow. I wonder now that we found each other, because the school was unimaginably vast. But then I remember that it was the 1980s. Our teachers were often on strike: lessons began with a long wait for substitute staff to turn up, and in those minutes, the gossip, like the bad behaviour, was frantic, everyone squeezing in as much as they could before the door opened and some slightly desperate figure tried to bring us to attention. Stuck in the same stream for maths, we spoke in those snatched moments about make-up and music – and also, of course, about boys: about who we liked, and who we thought liked us, and which of these creatures we might nonchalantly pass in the corridor when the bell rang, or stand next to in the lunch queue, our trays awaiting our daily ration of sausage rolls, chips and baked beans. And somehow, we never ran out of things to say: when the day was done we would go home, and promptly ring each other. Telephones were – you'll have heard this before – in the hall in those days. There was no privacy. Your brother would make annoying noises to distract you. Your mum would walk past, clicking her tongue in irritation, a finger tapping the face of her wristwatch. But we were not to be put off. The daily unpicking – Who did Mrs Kirkpatrick single out in double French? What outrage did Jez Jenkins commit in netball? – was as vital as air. We could wring drama from anything, though very often no squeezing was required. A certain Miss X appeared to be dating both a physics teacher and the hairy bloke who taught geography. A boy in history kept falling asleep, the result of his addiction to glue. Most sensationally of all, there were the sex lives of those girls who were so much more daring and sought after than us. Their daily soap operas, loudly and melodramatically performed, began with that staple of *Just Seventeen*'s problem page, the love bite (if a girl wore a polo neck, she was semaphoring a bruise). They ended, when we were not quite sixteen, with one girl falling pregnant. This wasn't what we wanted for ourselves, and as she paraded her bump we must have resembled a pair of tricoteuses at the guillotine.

Friendship is lots of things, but when you're young it's a way of making sense of the adult world (for me, this was what it had in common with reading novels). My conversations with Kitty, rapt and ceaseless, helped me to discern character; to make up my mind about people; to learn about such things as trust and reliability. She and I were like-minded when it came to our friends and acquaintances: we saw them in a similar way, which is interesting to me now because we were not similar at all. While she was mostly sensible, I was inclined to rash behaviour. As we got older, I was always in love, or pining, or broken-hearted – and she would listen, and laugh at the way I embellished things, and hazard caution (because boys were complete idiots). And when I got drunk, as I sometimes did then at parties and on school trips, it was Kitty who'd hold my hair when I threw up, who'd administer the Alka-Seltzer and who, on one shameful occasion, would travel with an unconscious me in an ambulance to hospital. (I loved her for the fact that she dealt with the midnight arrival of the parental hounds of hell, though she'd done nothing wrong at all herself.)

We went to college in the same city, so we still saw each other fairly often. And in the long holidays, we sank straight back into the old routines, as springy as moss: weeknights were for the pub and TV soaps, Saturdays were for dancing (if we went to the library in between times, there would always be a bag of sweets on the desk between us). After we graduated, she returned to Sheffield to teach and I went to London to become a journalist, at which point the threads that bound us should have frayed – we were moving, rapidly, in different directions. Yet this never really happened. If we began to meet less often, ours was – and is – a bond that could survive long silences. We resume where last we left off. There are friends Kitty sees a lot more than me these days, and vice versa. But I maintain that I still know her as well as, and probably better than, anyone – and she me. This may be a delusion, of course. But if it is, I don't care. This is my psychic ballast. Think of your friends. Who among them could you call in the middle of the night, and know they would listen and try to help, and not be angry with you for having woken them up? She is that person, for me.

Four decades. There have been weddings and funerals. Looking back, though, one memory still stands out. In my thirties, a man left me suddenly; we had just bought a house together, and this came as a terrible shock. The first person I rang was Kitty, and as soon as she possibly could, she came to London to see me. Full of gratitude, I remember that I went to St Pancras Station to meet her. I also remember that of the two of us, she was the more tearful. 'Oh, my poor friend,' she said, putting her arms around me. We stood like that for a while, quite oblivious to the swirling crowd, and I began to feel better then and there: a leaking boat that had managed somehow to come into harbour.

* * *

In October 2022, another friend of mine, the publisher Carmen Callil, died at the age of eighty-four, after a short illness. I was sad, because I loved her and she made life, whenever we were together, such amazing fun.* But in the run-up to her funeral I suffered for another reason, too. As plans for a send-off were made, I found myself on the outside of things, and this brought me to realise that I had been less close to her than I'd imagined – or, to be more accurate, that she had many, many friends who were just as dear to her as I was, and some a great deal *more* dear. About this, I was upset and confused, as well as embarrassed and a bit jealous, too. In life, Carmen had, everyone agreed, a genius for friendship; those who knew her felt special, singled out; we basked in the beam of her attention, like seals on a rock. In death, though, things got hierarchical. Finding myself lower down the ladder than I might have wanted to be it was hard not to feel bruised. Everything seemed different, somehow: up for reassessment. It was as if I had been handed a new version of an old photograph; the parts of it that, unbeknownst to me, had been cropped, were now fully restored, and I could only wonder at what I had missed, at what Carmen had failed to tell me.

Her funeral took place in the November and, that December, I began reading *Between Friends*, a new collection of the letters of Vera Brittain and Winifred Holtby.† I didn't expect this book, long and loquacious, to speak to how I was feeling then; I predicted mild literary gossip and shingled hair. But I was wrong. It was just what I needed. If friendship is beautiful, it's also intensely complicated – and

---

* The piece I wrote for the *Observer* when the news of her death was announced is collected in the last chapter of this book: 'Goodbyes'.
† Edited by Elaine and English Showalter, some of these letters appear in Chapter 8: 'Shifting Sands'.

now I remembered this. Outwardly, of course, Brittain and Holtby's famous and celebrated friendship was mutually supportive, tender and generous. The two women met as undergraduates at Oxford; one fateful day, Holtby all but crashed into the room where they were both to have a tutorial. After university, they shared a flat in Bloomsbury; a blue plaque now marks the spot. When Brittain later married and had children, Holtby moved in with the family, taking over the childcare when her friend had to travel, which she did often. Most famously of all, Brittain would memorialise Holtby in *Testament of Friendship*, a book she wrote after Winifred's tragic death from kidney failure in 1935 at the age of just thirty-seven.

But as the letters make plain, a lot was happening beneath the surface of their relationship – and sometimes just above it, too. They were very different in character. Holtby, who was the younger, was tall and fair and gregarious; she had a kind of inner confidence, perhaps because her mother had always encouraged her education (Brittain's had not). During the First World War, she had interrupted her degree to serve as a nurse, but she had enjoyed the experience; in those years, she suffered no tragic personal losses. Brittain, on the other hand, was small and dark and deeply serious; in the war, she lost both her fiancé, Roland Leighton, and her brother, Edward. Like Holtby, she was fiercely ambitious – they both longed to be writers – but Brittain's determination was edged with a certain neediness. Perhaps with good reason, she seemed to fear abandonment.

When Holtby moved in with Brittain and her husband, Gordon Catlin, she did so perfectly happily – and Brittain accepted it almost as her due. Stella Benson, a novelist friend of Holtby's, regarded Brittain as a 'bloodsucker', but if she – Winifred – ever felt this herself, she never let on. Human beings (I think) may be divided, roughly speaking, into drains and radiators. Holtby was a radiator, warm and encouraging, while Brittain was a drain, more prone both to complaining and to offering 'honest' criticism, though she would doubtless have been affronted to receive any in return. At moments, to use a very twenty-first century term, there's something of the frenemy about Brittain. In a letter of 1921, she prefaces some compliments she wants to pay her friend by noting that Mrs Leighton (the late Roland's mother) had said Holtby was 'not in the least pretty'. She struggles to hide her envy of the fact that, in the race to be published first, Holtby is over the finishing line even as she is still waiting for the starting pistol. She also has a patronising idea of what she believes Holtby needs in life (less than her). Having lost her virginity to Catlin, Brittain writes to say that for Holtby, once would be enough, sex-wise. When I first read this, I wondered if it was just a rather cack-handed attempt to make Holtby feel better about her marriage by suggesting that sex was no great shakes. But there's no getting away from it. The assumptions she makes about Holtby's capacity for desire, born perhaps of wishful thinking (don't ever leave me), are distinctly mean-spirited.

But as I've already written, friendship is complex. At other times, their affection is tangible, as toasty as a hissing gas fire. It's inspiriting to read the letters in which, as they're finally getting started on adulthood proper, they set out their aspirations for what lies ahead. They have so many ideas about how life should be lived. In the end, they are – and they know they are – the best thing for each other: plump with questions, eager to listen, genteel disclosure their lingua franca. Can a man ever offer the same understanding to a woman as a member of her own sex? The answer must be no. As Brittain writes of her own kind and clever husband: 'He never says "Tell me some more!"' It is about talking, and listening, and talking again. It's about giving your whole self, not just nodding your head as you keep half an eye on a phone or a book or a newspaper.

Can the value of a friendship be measured? What effect might it have on our physical and mental health? In Brittain and Holtby's time, it would have been strange to talk in these terms. Just finish that letter, dear, and run to catch the post. But friendship is increasingly the focus of research by social psychologists, anthropologists, geneticists and neuroscientists, and thanks to this it can now be said with certainty that the number and quality of our friendships may have a bigger influence on our happiness, health and mortality risk than anything else in our life except for giving up smoking. Robin Dunbar,* Emeritus Professor of Evolutionary Psychology at the University of Oxford, reports in his book *Friends: Understanding the Power of Our Most Important Relationships*, that when we are lonely, and have no one to talk to or touch, our endorphin system is activated less often; endorphins are the

---

* Dunbar is the psychologist who first suggested there may be a cognitive limit to the number of people with whom one can maintain stable social relationships. Research he conducted in the nineties suggested that most human beings typically have 150 friends-in-general (people who know us on sight, and with whom we have a history), of whom just five can usually be described as intimate.

brain's painkillers, and thanks to this, we're more susceptible to everyday bruising. No wonder, then, that an impoverished social life has a marked impact on anxiety and depression. What's more surprising, perhaps, is that it also plays a part in cognitive decline, increasing the risk of dementia.

On paper, the cure for this appears straightforward: a matter of picking up the phone. But better not leave it too long. As Dunbar also notes, friendship is a matter of investment, if not hard work. Like a garden without water, it 'dies fast' when neglected. The Covid-19 pandemic was the loneliest time in my life – and in most people's, I would imagine; the technology at our disposal, we soon learned, was no substitute for flesh-and-blood encounters. However, longing did not inevitably translate into increased ardour, commitment or time spent. All of us know that the months of lockdown led to a great sloughing off of friends and acquaintances; that we allowed silence to fall, and then to continue long after we were released from captivity. To be positive about this, perhaps it made us realise who we really valued; we grasped which relationships were most important, and seized the moment for a diary cull. To be negative, it shrank our world, whether through laziness, or something more sad and dangerous.

Dunbar's book was published during the pandemic; we'll doubtless have to wait a while for the social scientists to determine Covid-19's long-term effects, both on our networks and our mental health. And he doesn't have much to say, either, about the way technology has changed our connections, for better or worse. On this score, I have many questions. Have mobile phones and social media made us closer, or pushed us further apart? Is a text message any kind of substitute for the calls that people, especially the young, are increasingly reluctant to make? Do messaging apps create a false sense of security, encouraging us to imagine all our friends are safely in our pockets? And what about the agony that comes with such technology? Aren't read messages and blue ticks just latter-day instruments of torture? The hours we waste wondering why someone hasn't replied to an email! Throw a party nowadays, and the person you forgot to invite will inevitably see it on Facebook. I wonder, too, about the performative element of Instagram. Is it harder for people who post a lot, and always on the bright side, to be honest with those they know in real life? Do they feel they must keep up appearances? And if they do, where does this leave those who care about them?

Opposed as I am to gender stereotypes, I would say that this territory is particularly vexed for women – and in this, at least, Dunbar backs me. Do women really have more friends than men, and are their relationships with them more intense? It seems that the answer to both questions is yes. While men's perception of intimacy is primarily based, at least according to one study, on little more than frequency of contact, women have very high expectations of their relationships, especially in respect of reciprocity (mutual support) and communion (self-disclosure). Such expectations bring with them the danger of disappointment, the possibility of hurt – and it may be, too, that our society sets women against one another at moments; if the patriarchy encourages solidarity, it also sows division. But do we *envy* men the seeming straightforwardness of their relationships? No, I don't believe that we do. Whenever a man tells me what he and his friends talk about on their nights out – 'music, football, books . . .' – I'm not envious; I'm amazed, though I really should know better by now.

In the end, though, Dunbar and his colleagues can only take us so far. Science can't see deep inside friendship, a relationship that is as abstract as it is tangible. It can't explain, or even fully describe, both its intensity and its singular ease; its reliance on such ineffable things as chemistry, timing, temperament and taste; above all, the way it can wax and wane. Clever people in white coats may be able to record an image of a brain that is grieving a lost friend, or in the midst of an agonising argument with one, but they cannot reach the emotional roots of such losses; life's endless human drama. For some of us, in certain cases, this may be a job for the therapists. Really, though, it is the work of art: of novels and plays and poetry, of films and television series. Thinking about Carmen, the greatest reader I've ever known, and about Vera Brittain and Winifred Holtby, two writers she happened to publish, I began to feel the twitch of an idea. What if I looked at women's friendship through the medium of an anthology, examining it from all sides, through the eyes of all manner of writers? Suddenly, it was so obvious. This was the only thing to do. What pleased me about the thought was that such an investigation would be, in itself, both an act of friendship – I could dedicate it to Carmen – *and* a token of it. Here was a book, full of all the lovely, impossible, unsayable things, that one friend might be moved to give to another in recognition of their bond.

* * *

But here's the rub. Perhaps this wasn't only going to be a mere matter of raiding my bookshelves. Sometimes, I would tell women friends what I was working on, and almost without exception they would say: 'Oh, I've got loads of ideas. Let me have a think and I'll give you a list.' I soon learned not to get my hopes up. If they came back to me at all, it was inevitably to ask if I had thought of including Jane Eyre's friendship with Helen Burns. (Yes, I had! Poor Helen's death was the very first piece I picked out, typing it into a file on my computer with tears rolling down my cheeks.) Mostly, though, they didn't come back to me. 'It's more difficult than I thought,' said one. She had spent her entire career in publishing, and I was caught, on hearing this, between disbelief, and fear that I had unwittingly bitten off more than I could chew.

As friendship has moved centre stage in our culture – the result both of feminism and, I think, of capitalism – it has become the central subject of ever greater numbers of novels. The shift towards this began slowly, after the Second World War, with books like Stella Gibbons' *Westwood*, Rona Jaffe's *The Best of Everything* and, of course, Mary McCarthy's bestselling *The Group*, about the lives of eight women friends following their college graduation, and – since Helen Fielding's *Bridget Jones's Diary* and Candace Bushnell's *Sex and the City* in the nineties – the numbers have increased exponentially. Go back a bit further, however, and the relative paucity – the paucity, full stop – of fully realised and articulated friendships between women in literature strikes you with some force and, in my case, a certain amount of embarrassment. As Vera Brittain writes: 'From the days of Homer on, the friendships of men have enjoyed glory

and acclamation, but the friendships of women, in spite of
Ruth and Naomi, have usually been not merely unsung, but
mocked, belittled and falsely interpreted.'* How had I come
somehow to forget that while male relationships have always
been central to storytelling, women's have been neglected?
Isn't my beloved old paperback of *A Room of One's Own*, in
which Virginia Woolf writes of her struggle to remember
'any case in the course of my reading where two women are
represented as friends',† scribbled all over with grey pencil?
Don't I know very well that even in modern novels the love
plot tends to push women's other (because seemingly lesser)
relationships from the text? I can only imagine that the wish
was the mother of the thought: that I longed so much for this
anthology to exist, I had convinced myself I could conjure it
into being, no matter what. Like Mr Micawber, I thought, in
spite of all evidence to the contrary, that something would
turn up.

But now, I was excited. How good it would be to do something that was entirely new. Not since 1991 (I discovered)
had a serious anthology dedicated to the subject of friendship been published: *The Oxford Book of Friendship*, which
was edited by the poet, D. J. Enright, and the academic,
David Rawlinson (two men). When I opened this volume
up, it was almost comical to find only a single, brief chapter
devoted to women's friendships with one another – though

---

*   In *Testament of Friendship*.
†   'They are confidantes, of course, in Racine and the Greek tragedies. They
are now and then mothers and daughters. But almost without exception they
are shown in their relation to men. It was strange to think that all the great
women of fiction were, until Jane Austen's day, not only seen by the other
sex, but seen only in relation to the other sex.' (*A Room of One's Own*, 1928).

it would also have been difficult for its editors to expand it: of a list of authors more than three hundred strong, only forty-nine of the names belong to women writers. Was this bias or was it, as the editors insisted, because while they could 'pick and choose among friendships between men, examples of friendship between women . . . we had to seek out'? In the past, Enright and Rawlinson note, women have written less about friendship because they have written less about anything; or less of it survived.* Many months on from reading their words, I understand why they struggled pre the eighteenth century (and I'm grateful to them for sending me to two writers whose work I didn't know well: Henry Handel Richardson and Christina Stead). However, I'm also struck by how much of the material in my book, some of it very well known, *was* available to them in 1991. To take one example, they quote from Virginia Woolf's *Diary* just once; the name Katherine Mansfield, with whom Woolf had a famously spiky and tangled friendship, does not appear at all.

This anthology, then, tells two stories. The first (and least important) has to do with literature. The second is about friendship between women, and what it means, and how it changes over the course of a life. To begin with the first of these narratives, we start with Naomi and Ruth in the Bible, and from there move swiftly through the centuries: here is Geoffrey Chaucer's Wife of Bath laughingly describing her cherished gossip of a friend, and here is Celia in Shakespeare's

---

* Here they quote Anne Elliot in Jane Austen's *Persuasion*: 'If you please, no reference to examples in books. Men have had every advantage of us in telling their own story . . . the pen has been in their hands.'

As You Like It, quite determined that she and Rosalind will go on sharing confidences, no matter the danger involved ('. . . do not seek to take your change upon you,/To bear your griefs yourself and leave me out'). As you will have noticed, these are all male writers (let us assume the Book of Ruth is the work of a man). But then comes Katherine Philips (1632–64), otherwise known as the Matchless Orinda: a less daring writer than her great contemporary, Aphra Behn, but for our purposes the only choice. Philips' poems celebrate platonic love between women, a relationship she regards as nothing less than a commingling of souls. I hadn't read her before, and I fell in love with her bright, near-numinous appropriation of hitherto male forms to exalt the sacrament that is a shared secret.

After this – slim pickings! – we arrive at the eighteenth century, during which the novel begins its irresistible rise. This particular century presents a paradox. In *Clarissa* (1748), Samuel Richardson puts female friendship centre stage. Anna Howe loves the book's eponymous heroine with all her heart: 'Nay, she *is* my soul'; theirs is a relationship that, according to Janet Todd, the great feminist scholar of the period, will become 'the pattern in life and literature'. But on the other hand, Richardson also gives full and frank expression to the views of men about female friendships. 'Verily, Jack, these vehement friendships are nothing but chaff and stubble, liable to be blown away by the very wind that raises them,' Lovelace writes to Belford.

Apes! mere apes of *us*! they think the word *friendship* has a pretty sound with it; and it is much talked of; a fashionable word: And so, truly, a single woman, who thinks she has a Soul, and knows that she wants something, would be thought to have found a fellow-soul for it in her own Sex. But I repeat, that the word is a *mere* word, the thing a *mere* name with them; a cork-bottomed shuttlecock, which they are fond of striking to and fro, to make one another glow in the frosty weather of the Single State; but which, when a *man* comes in between the pretended *inseparables*, is given up, like their Music, and other maidenly amusements . . .*

Later, Colonel Morden writes to Belford to say that he believes Clarissa and Anna's friendship to be a remarkable exception to the general rules. What might those rules be? In short, that friendship is 'too fervent a flame for female minds to manage', that it is always superseded by marriage, and that no woman is capable of maintaining two of the close kind at the same time.

In her book, *Women's Friendship in Literature*, Todd writes that she hopes to prove Virginia Woolf wrong by showing that there are indeed strong 'friendly' ties between women in writing from this period. But, in truth, even she struggles with this project. So powerful is the romance element of most stories of the time that any bonds women do form with each other rarely outlast (let alone outgun) the privileged male–female relation. I reread some of the texts she cites – Mary Wollstonecraft's gloomy *Mary, A Fiction* and John Cleland's ribald *Fanny Hill* – and found them wanting for my purposes; like one of their heroines, I struggled to find a true

---

* Samuel Richardson, *Clarissa, Volume 6.*

'friend for my heart' for inclusion here. Only when I reached the novels of Jane Austen, the century having turned, did I find myself, if not spoiled for choice, then on more certain ground: Catherine Morland and Isabella Thorpe, Elizabeth Bennet and Charlotte Lucas, Emma Woodhouse and Harriet Smith. Austen's modernity in the matter of friendship still amazes; she knows all about what twenty-first century readers would call the toxic friend. In this book, I have included in its entirety the chapter in which Emma advises Harriet to refuse Mr Martin's proposal of marriage, and I make no apology for it.

On we go. The nineteenth century is ever transfixing to me, and never more so, perhaps, than in terms of women's lives. Victorian women wore jewellery made from the hair of their female friends; a few exchanged rings and vows, left property to each other on their deaths, and lived together in marriage-like partnerships that were accepted, even exalted, by family, wider society and the church (some may have been in sexual relationships with each other, but we cannot – and must not – assume that all of them were). Companion culture was central to the lives of Victorian women, and would play into the ideal of companionate (heterosexual) marriage we find in later novels; it helped them to cultivate feminine virtues; it was also a form of grace. But there is a gap between these facts and the century's fiction. To find the fullest descriptions of female friendship, you have to look at letters, diaries and other forms of life writing, and perhaps you need to read, too, the rather strange popular guidance manuals of the time, like those by Sarah Stickney

Ellis* (though she should also be treated with caution: I doubt any of her readers took too seriously her advice to women not to tell friends their secrets). The multifarious and often deeply peculiar ways in which women who were essentially powerless sought some manner of control over their lives through their friendships is fascinating. As Laura Marcus writes, women could touch their friends but not their lovers and, thanks to this, all manner of strange practices ensued (not just caressing but smacking, too).† Yet there is a sweetness and an effervescence here that we in the twenty-first century recognise. The words 'love' and 'like', for instance, were interchangeable, much as they are today. 'Oh, my little woman,' wrote Jane Carlyle in 1862, to her friend Mrs Mary Austin, after a recent visit to see her.‡ 'How glad I was to recognise your face through the glass of the carriage window, all dimmed with human breath! And how frightened I was the train would move, while you were clambering up like a school-boy to kiss me!' (Jane had been married to the historian, Thomas Carlyle, since 1826.) Infatuations were commonplace, whether erotic or not. One of the most famous is that of Edith Simcox, the writer and labour activist, with George Eliot: an enduring crush that seems rather to have amused the great novelist and the man with whom she lived, George Henry Lewes.

In novels of the time, however, such relationships may be found less often, if at all. The marriage plot – in the case

---

* Ellis is the author of, among other works, *The Daughters of England: Their Position in Society, Character and Responsibilities* (1842).
† In *Between Women: Friendship, Desire and Marriage in Victorian England* (2007).
‡ *Letters and Memorials of Jane Carlyle*, ed. Thomas Carlyle and others.

of *Middlemarch*, the remarriage plot – maintains a stranglehold on Victorian fiction; readers were (and are) in its thrall. 'There is no happiness in love, except at the end of an English novel,' says the narrator of Anthony Trollope's *Barchester Towers*. I roamed the Georges Eliot and Gissing, and Thomas Hardy.* As I've already written, I went to *Jane Eyre* before I made for any library. But it is *Shirley*, a less well known novel of Charlotte Brontë's, that in the end includes the fullest fictional account of friendship between women, as you will discover (*Shirley*, incidentally, was a favourite book of Carmen's; I read it for this anthology in the old edition, bound in leather the colour of black pudding, that she gave me one Christmas Day). Let us here also note that in William Makepeace Thackeray's *Vanity Fair*, Becky Sharp's considerable character flaws are attributed to the fact that 'she had never mingled in the society of women' (Sharp, like the novel's narrator, is cynical about female friendship, believing it to be little more than a decorous concealment for feminine rivalry).

Leaving the Victorians behind, I felt myself out of the woods at last: the going would henceforth be easier. Politics (suffrage) and the First World War (spinsters) were rich ground for friendship, and for writing about it. The Second World War arrives, and stays are loosened: women, now wearing trousers, embark on collective adventures in bombed-out cities and far-off billets; some of them keep frank and saucy diaries under the auspices of Mass

---

* I longed to include Charles Dickens, who gave us Joe Gargery, one of the sweetest friends in all literature. But Dickens cannot do women.

Observation. I know the fifties, betwixt and between, very well; another book of mine is all about them. So I was ready with my Elizabeth Taylor and my Elizabeth Jenkins. The sixties arrive, and with those rackety years, second-wave feminism. I combed Robin Morgan's furious compendium of 1970, *Sisterhood is Powerful*, trying (and failing) to find good accounts of the bonds formed in consciousness-raising groups, and then I turned to Marilyn French, writing in the seventies but looking back to those times. After this, I found myself surrounded by the writing of my own lifetime; here were books I read when they were first published, like Margaret Drabble's *The Radiant Way* (1987), in which a group of university friends reach middle age. And then, finally, I arrived in the present day: the age of ghosting and frenemies; of lonely cubicles in even lonelier offices; a time when old age – extreme old age – is commonplace, and women may find themselves losing friends they've had for seventy years.

So much reading. I tried hard to be a friend to every book that passed by my desk: to see interest or beauty in it even when it frustrated me by refusing to deliver what I was after. It was a joyous experience, and a profound one – enriching in the fullest sense. My plan had worked. Here was friendship scrutinised from every angle, and with this came an uncommon amount of wisdom. *The Virago Book of Friendship* contains more than one letter to – and from – an agony aunt, and I'm very glad that it does. I wanted it to be capacious and eclectic, attentive to many different modes. But in the end, the true – the utmost – sagacity belongs to the novelists and the poets. If there is sometimes bitterness and heartbreak in their stories and poems, there is also reassurance and consolation.

* * *

This book has the shape of a human life. It begins with childhood and school: our earliest efforts at friend-making and breaking. And, yes, *Anne of Green Gables* is here. It then looks at the kind of first encounters that take place in adulthood: the human collisions born of college or university, a new job, a chance conversation at a party. One chapter is devoted to old friends, another to fallings-out, yet another to change: to the effects on friendship of new and unwelcome shifts and imbalances, of altered circumstances. It contemplates (though not for too long) the flip side of friendship, which is not enmity, but loneliness, and celebrates solidarity in all its guises, and it ends with loss, the moment of goodbye.

I've chosen to look only at women's friendships with other women. Lots of us have brilliant male friends, but that bond is for another book. I haven't included sisters, cousins (with one exception) or friends who may also be lovers; I longed to extract Tove Jansson's brief but radical novel, *Fair Play*, about two women living and working side by side, but in the end I concluded that they are life partners, not pals. The book gathers together more than one hundred authors, the vast majority of them women; this was an important (feminist) aspect of the project for me. But I believe in the imagination – that the writer may be anyone they like on the page. A small number of men, then, do appear in its pages, and I do not begrudge them their entry (step forward, Henry James). As I've already said, I wanted to include lots of different kinds of writing, and this may be the first traditional literary anthology to embrace graphic novels, which I know, as one who loves them, to be capable of doing all the things regular novels can, and more. I've also added – I couldn't resist – a strip from *Bunty*, the comic for girls I adored as a child.

I'm not omnipotent. There will be things I've missed, or perhaps for which I couldn't secure – or afford – the rights. Though I've read widely, this book inevitably reflects my tastes, my passions, my fervent interests; if it represents the work of a year, it's also the result of a life spent with books. Which brings me to my final point. Books are, in themselves, another kind of friend, quiet and constant.* My hope is that this one will be a good and constant companion to many readers down many years: a source of warmth, wit and camaraderie in moments dark and bright.

---

* The elision of books and friends makes me think of a letter from Charlotte Brontë to Elizabeth Gaskell, on 5 July 1853. 'Thank you for your letter,' she wrote. 'It was as pleasant as a quiet chat, as welcome as spring showers, as reviving as a friend's visit, in short, it was very like a page of *Cranford*.'

NOW IT CAME to pass in the days when the judges ruled, that there was a famine in the land. And a certain man of Bethlehem-Judah went to sojourn in the country of Moab, he, and his wife, and his two sons.

And the name of the man was Elimelech, and the name of his wife Naomi, and the name of his two sons Mahlon and Chilion . . .

And Elimelech Naomi's husband died; and she was left, and her two sons.

And they took them wives of the women of Moab; the name of one was Orpah, and the name of the other Ruth: and they dwelled there about ten years.

And Mahlon and Chilion died also both of them; and the woman was left of her two sons and her husband.

Then she arose with her daughters in law, that she might return from the country of Moab: for she had heard in the country of Moab how that the Lord had visited his people in giving them bread.

Wherefore she went forth out of the place where she was, and her two daughters in law with her; and they went on the way to return unto the land of Judah.

And Naomi said unto her two daughters in law, Go, return each to her mother's house: the Lord deal kindly with you, as ye have dealt with the dead, and with me.

The Lord grant you that ye may find rest, each of you in the house of her husband. Then she kissed them; and they lifted up their voice, and wept.

And they said unto her, Surely we will return with thee unto thy people.

And Naomi said, Turn again, my daughters: why will ye go with me? Are there yet any more sons in my womb, that they may be your husbands?

Turn again, my daughters, go *your* way; for I am too old to have an husband. If I should say, I have hope, *if* I should have an husband also tonight, and should also bear sons;

Would ye tarry for them till they were grown? would ye stay for them from having husbands? nay, my daughters; for it grieveth me much for your sakes that the hand of the Lord is gone out against me.

And they lifted up their voice, and wept again: and Orpah kissed her mother in law; but Ruth clave unto her.

And she said, Behold, thy sister in law is gone back unto her people, and unto her gods: return thou after thy sister in law.

And Ruth said, Intreat me not to leave thee, or to return from following after thee: for whither thou goest, I will go; and where thou lodges, I will lodge: thy people shall be my people, and thy God my God.

Where thou diest, will I die, and there will I be buried: the Lord do so to me, and more also, if ought but death part thee and me.

When she saw that she was steadfastly minded to go with her, then she left speaking unto her.

So they two went until they came to Bethlehem.

Ruth 1: 1–19

1

DEFINITIONS

Nature assigns the Sun –
That – is Astronomy –
Nature cannot enact a Friend –
That – is Astrology.

**Emily Dickinson, 'Nature Assigns
the Sun' (1875)**

Vivian Gornick ⁓ Marilynne Robinson ⁓ Elena Ferrante
Nancy Mitford ⁓ Colette ⁓ Sue Limb ⁓ Dorothy L. Sayers
Mary Wollstonecraft ⁓ Elizabeth Bowen ⁓ Anaïs Nin

Friendship is as difficult to capture in words as romantic love, not least because it is just as complicated, piercing the heart in most, if not all, of the same ways. Aristotle believed that friendship enables us to enjoy a kind of supplementary life, an awareness of the existence of others that makes us more fully aware of our own place in the world. But as alluring as this sounds – empathy as a portal to gratitude – there is a lot more to it than this, good and bad. This book examines friendship between women and all its attendant complications, through some of the best and most beautiful writing there has ever been on the subject, from cradle to grave. But since we must begin somewhere, let us start by trying – and perhaps failing – to set our terms . . .

THERE ARE TWO categories of friendship: those in which people enliven one another and those in which people must be enlivened to be with one another. In the first category one clears the decks to be together; in the second one looks for an empty space in the schedule.

Vivian Gornick, *The Odd Woman and the City: A Memoir* (2015)

HAVING A SISTER or a friend is like sitting at night in a lighted house. Those outside can watch you if they want, but you need not see them. You simply say, 'Here are the perimeters of our attention. If you prowl around under the windows till the crickets go silent, we will pull the shades. If you wish us to suffer your envious curiosity, you must permit us not to notice it.' Anyone with one solid human bond is that smug, and it is the smugness as much as the comfort and safety that lonely people covet and admire.

Marilynne Robinson, *Housekeeping* (1980)

I'VE OCCASIONALLY BEEN told by women I know that I'm a good friend. I'm pleased, and don't dare say that, in general, I tend not to put next to the word 'friend' adjectives that refer to a hierarchy of feelings or reliability. They seem pointless to me. I would never say, for example, 'she's my best friend', for I would have to deduce from it that I have friends I like less; others I don't trust so much; others with whom I feel less kinship. And if I did, it would occur to me to wonder: why do I consider myself the friend of these women? Why do I consider them my friends?

The word 'friend', in the presence of hierarchies of this type, isn't apt. Maybe we should acknowledge that a bad friend, an unreliable friend, isn't a friend. Maybe, to be clear, even if it's painful, we should learn to say not 'a friend' but 'a woman I spend time with, or have spent time with'. The problem is that it comforts us to have many friends – it makes us feel popular, loved, less alone. We therefore prefer to describe as 'friends' women with whom we have little or nothing in common, but with whom, if necessary, we fill a void: we spend an afternoon in a cafe, we drink a glass of wine, talking about nothing in particular. Never mind if later, at the first opportunity, we call them gossips, snakes, sour, touchy. The fact is that a woman friend is as rare as a true love. The Italian word for 'friendship', *amicizia*, has the same root as the verb 'to love', *amare*, and a relationship between friends has the richness, the complexity, the contradictions, the inconsistencies of love. I can say, without fear of exaggeration, that love for a woman friend has always seemed of a substance very similar to my love for the most important man in my life.

Elena Ferrante, the *Guardian*, trans. Ann Goldstein (2018)

⌒

FRIENDSHIP IS SOMETHING to be built up carefully, by people with leisure. It is an art, nature does not enter into it.

Nancy Mitford, *The Pursuit of Love* (1945)

⌒

ONE'S OWN BEST self. For centuries, this was the key concept behind any essential definition of friendship: that one's friend is a virtuous being who speaks to the virtue in oneself. How foreign is such a concept to the children of the therapeutic culture! Today we do not look to see, much less affirm, our best selves in one another. To the contrary, it is the openness with which we admit to our emotional incapacities – the fear, the anger, the humiliation – that excites contemporary bonds of friendship. Nothing draws us closer to one another than the degree to which we face our deepest shame openly in one another's company . . . What we want is to feel known, warts and all: the more warts the better. It is the great illusion of our culture that what we confess to is who we are.

Vivian Gornick, *The Odd Woman and the City: A Memoir* (2015)

⌒

M Y TRUE FRIENDS have always given me that supreme proof of devotion, a spontaneous aversion to the man I loved.

Colette, *Break of Day* (1928)

A T THE MOMENT, I feel I am deep in several continuing conversations, conducted by letter and phone and at occasional meetings. For example, I try to encourage one friend to recover from a failed marriage and from the shattering cruelties she has suffered. When at last she falls in love again, I rejoice, I meet him, I tell her he is indeed splendid, and will still be splendid to the dispassionate observer long after Eros's sleepless fevers have given way to dozy domesticity. At the same time I warn her not to give up her work or friends or home altogether on the tide of this first fine careless rapture. In the past, she helped me through similar experiences: mourned with me the end of a relationship, though carefully reminding me that there were good reasons why it had to end, and so on. The peculiar nature of female friendship, for me, is this mixture of sympathy and instruction: of a loving heart and a shrewd eye. And above all it offers an endless patience and curiosity, so that feelings that may be buried and yet irritating can be brought to light, explored, and, one hopes, dispersed.

Some men may enjoy this kind of laundering of the soul with their close friends, but I suspect it is as rare in the male world as it is commonplace in the female. Our friends see us at our most vulnerable, know us intimately over the years, and best understand whether what we are currently saying or doing is making sense. In other words, I think female friends help us to cultivate our integrity and guard against losing our way. This is, of course, most likely to happen under the influence of Eros. One of the useful enigmas of falling in love is that one's female friends remain undecided. They provide footholds of sound sense to help one away from disaster. They patiently endure all the significant details of the affair, providing encouragement, solace and congratulation where needed ... they must accept that their newly-enamoured friend will perforce spend less time with them. I think most of us understand this mechanism, though it is still hard when one woman gets married leaving her girl friend still single and feeling bereft and neglected. But as we get older, a new truth breaks in upon us – that after all, female friendship and love between man and woman are very different things, and that whilst any number of Eros's arrows fall away into the dust, their darts spent, and their feathers frazzled, female friendship endures. Eros makes the heart bound: we rush to our mirrors and see a special face there: captivated, captivating. We open ourselves with careful artifice, aching to be more fascinating than we are, and inspired by adrenalin, achieving it. Friendship, in contrast, cares not if we have combed our hair, or if we feel dull and uninspired. In friendship we open ourselves with careless honesty. If our lover's laugh is irritating, it is a moment of intense, though infinitesimal damage. Our friend's laugh is welcome whatever its sound. Friendship escapes the desperate distorting appetites of Eros, and survives.

Sue Limb, 'Female Friendship', collected in *The Dialectics of Friendship*, ed. Roy Porter and Sylvana Tomaselli (1989)

'A LITTLE *change of companionship* is good for *everybody*. I've known so many *happy friendships* spoilt by people seeing *too much* of one another.'

'They couldn't have been *real* friendships, then,' asserted the girl, dogmatically. 'Mary and I are *absolutely* happy together.'

'Still,' said Miss Climpson, 'if you don't mind an *old woman* giving you a word of warning, I should be inclined not to keep the bow *always* bent. Suppose Miss Whittaker, for instance, wanted to go off and have a day in Town on her own, say – or go to stay with friends – you would have to learn not to mind that.' 'Of course I shouldn't mind. Why—' she checked herself. 'I mean, I'm quite sure that Mary would be every bit as loyal to me as I am to her.'

'That's right,' said Miss Climpson. 'The longer I live, my dear, the more *certain* I become that *jealousy* is the most *fatal* of feelings. The Bible calls it "cruel as the grave", and I'm sure that is so. *Absolute* loyalty, without jealousy, is the essential thing.'

'Yes. Though naturally one would hate to think that the person one was really friends with was putting another person in one's place . . . Miss Climpson, you do believe, don't you, that a friendship ought to be "fifty-fifty"?'

'That is the ideal friendship, I suppose,' said Miss Climpson, thoughtfully, 'but I think it is a *very rare thing*. Among women, that is. I doubt very much if I've ever seen an example of it. *Men*, I believe, find it easier to give and take in that way – probably because they have so many outside interests.'

'Men's friendships – oh yes! I know one hears a lot about them. But half the time, I don't believe they're *real* friendships at all. Men can go off for years and forget all about their friends. And they don't really confide in one another. Mary and I tell each other all our thoughts and feelings. Men seem just content to think each other good sorts without ever bothering about their inmost selves.'

'Probably that's why their friendships last so well,' replied Miss Climpson. 'They don't make such demands on one another.'

Dorothy L. Sayers, *Unnatural Death* (1927)

FRIENDSHIP IS A serious affection; the most sublime of all affections, because it is founded on principle, and cemented by time. The very reverse may be said of love. In a great degree, love and friendship cannot subsist in the same bosom; even when inspired by different objects they weaken or destroy each other, and for the same object can only be felt in succession. The vain fears and fond jealousies, the winds which fan the flame of love, when judiciously or artfully tempered, are both incompatible with the tender confidence and sincere respect of friendship.

Mary Wollstonecraft, *A Vindication of the Rights of Men* **(1790)**

I NTIMACIES BETWEEN WOMEN often go backwards, beginning in revelations and ending in small talk.

Elizabeth Bowen, *The Death of the Heart* **(1938)**

W HAT I CANNOT love, I overlook. Is that real friendship?

Anaïs Nin, *The Diary of Anaïs Nin,* **Volume 1:** *1931–1934*

2
CHILDHOOD

Make friends, make friends,
Never, never break friends . . .

Children's playground rhyme (traditional)

⌣

Antonia White ⌢ *Winifred Holtby* ⌢ *Margaret Atwood* ⌢ *L. M. Montgomery*
Emilia McKenzie ⌢ *Cathy & Claire* ⌢ *Frances Hodgson Burnett*
Curtis Sittenfeld ⌢ *The Four Marys* ⌢ *Toya Wolfe* ⌢ *Enid Blyton*
Elizabeth Jane Howard ⌢ *Charlotte Brontë* ⌢ *Hilary Mantel*
Zadie Smith ⌢ *Muriel Spark*

In his long poem *In and Out*, Daryl Hine writes that the friendships of youth are more instant than Nescafé – and it's true that some young people do make friends (and break them) with a speed that is dizzying. But not everyone is so lucky, or so adept. Childhood can also be lonely: shyness is a curse, cliques tricky to break into. Questions of coolness – who's in, who's out – have been a hallmark of novels about school for a century at least.

The literature of childhood, for those who like to read, can play a potent role in our first encounters. Expectations of friendship are often stoked by a beloved book: the girl who reads L. M. Montgomery's *Anne of Green Gables* at the right (I mean the most susceptible) moment will end up longing for her own Diana Barry. But we may also turn to books for company, especially if things at school are difficult. As Lucy Mangan writes in her memoir, *Bookworm*, who needs flesh-and-blood pals when everyone at Malory Towers is at your beck and call? Either way, our earliest friendships remain vivid to us long into adulthood, whether we recall them fondly, or with a certain queasiness. The writing on the following pages encompasses both the agony and the ecstasy of first friend-ship, and the wistfulness that almost inevitably accompanies remembrances of childhood. I couldn't resist including a favourite strip from a comic I loved as a ten-year-old, one my father dutifully used to roll up like a sausage and post to me every week when I was living abroad with my mother. Like so many girls, I was only ever at boarding school in my dreams.

THROUGHOUT EACH DAY, Nanda watched herself with the utmost scruple. She examined her conscience minutely every night, and made passionate acts of contrition for every fault. She gave up sugar in her tea and forced herself to eat the things she hated most to the very last scrap. Even the saintly Madeleine was impressed by her zeal and smiled approvingly as she gave her a second helping of particularly nasty cabbage. Having read somewhere of a Jesuit novice who mortified one of his senses every day, she tried to imitate him. On Monday she mortified her eyes by shutting her book at the most interesting place and not reading another word. On Tuesday, she stuffed her fingers in her ears while the organ played at benediction. On Wednesday, she refused to smell flowers and made herself sniff a particularly nauseating mixture of ink and liquorice powder. On Thursday, she put salt instead of sugar on her rhubarb to mortify her sense of taste. And on Friday, after much thought, she managed to penalise her sense of touch by scraping her finger-nails against the rough serge of her apron and putting burrs against her skin under her vest.

Among the First Communicants was a girl of twelve years old named Léonie de Wesseldorf. Léonie was half French and half German by birth; she belonged to a very old and very wealthy family whose name, to Catholic ears, had something of the glamour of Medici or Gonzaga. Nanda's private image of Léonie de Wesseldorf was of a young prince, pale and weary from a day's ride, with his lovelocks carelessly tied back in a frayed ribbon. Léonie wore a black uniform instead of a blue one, being in mourning for some ambassadorial uncle, and the dusty coat she wore in the garden had the name of Paquin on its torn lining. In her unfeminine, unchildish way, she was exceedingly handsome, yet her deeply cut mouth and beautiful shallow brows seemed like the stamp of a medal rather than the changing growth of a face. Her red, unformed hands did not seem to belong to the pale, haughty head. Nanda, always reverent towards the people she liked, looked at Léonie's hands as little as possible; they embarrassed her like a deformity. Her feeling for Léonie was one of pure admiration, the feeling of page for prince, too cold and absolute to be called love. It would not have mattered if Léonie had never spoken or even looked at her, provided Nanda could bind herself to her by a private allegiance. Léonie was invincibly lazy. She would let herself be beaten in arguments or work by Nanda or others far stupider, but every now and then she would say something startling or write a sentence so shapely and mature that the nuns would find it hard to believe she was not quoting. Her mind, like her face, seemed to have been handed down to her full-grown, a blade of old, finely tempered steel, that she carried as carelessly as her shabby Paquin coat.

Nanda and Léonie studied their catechism side by side for three weeks and were bracketed top of the test in Christian Doctrine which the First Communicants had to pass. Monica, with much difficulty, managed to obtain the necessary forty marks out of a hundred, though she was very shaky on the subject of Transubstantiation.

The day after the Christian Doctrine examination, while the band of First Communicants was walking round the inner garden, cutting flowers for the altar, Léonie dropped behind the rest and beckoned to Nanda. For a few minutes they strolled in silence, Léonie with her handsome chin in the air and her hands deep in her pockets. It was early summer, and the small, secluded garden, far away from the playgrounds, was spicy with the smell of azaleas. Nanda was glad that it was not Wednesday and that she need not stop her nose. The warmth playing on her skin made her feel quite dizzy with happiness; she wanted to tear off her thick serge and shake her hair loose from its plait. Léonie, who was always cold, huddled her smart, disreputable coat around her so tightly that its seams showed white in the sunshine.

'Well, Nanda, my child, what do you make of all this?'

'All what?'

'Oh, the Catholic Church, your First Communion, und so weiter.'

Léonie had a very grown-up voice; husky and rather harsh but extremely attractive. When she sang, it cleared and sweetened, and its rich, coppery ring cleaved straight to the heart of the note.

Nanda knitted her eyebrows and did not answer. Léonie helped her.

'Do you really believe all the things in the catechism, for example?'

'Why, of course.'

'You mean you want to believe them? Being a convert, you have to make an effort . . . more effort than I, for example. And so you come to believe them better than I.'

'But don't you . . .'

'Believe them? I don't know. They're too much part of me. I shall never get away from them. I don't want to, even. The

Catholic Church suits me much too well. But it's fun some-times to see what a little needle-point the whole thing rests on.'

Nanda's world was spinning round her.

'Léonie, what on earth do you mean?'

'Well, for example, there's no rational proof of the exist-ence of God. Oh, I know there are four the Jesuits give you. But not one that would really hold water for a philosopher.'

'But, Léonie, that's sheer blasphemy,' said Nanda stoutly.

'Not necessarily. It doesn't affect the goodness of the beliefs one way or the other. After all, there's no rational proof that you exist yourself.'

This had never occurred to Nanda. For quite fifty yards she walked in deep thought. Then she burst out:

'Good heavens . . . it's quite true. There isn't. Léonie, how awful.'

'*I* think it's rather amusing,' said Léonie, beginning to whistle.

Antonia White, *Frost in May* (1933)

THE TERM AFTER Clare's arrival Muriel lay in bed staring at the faint blur against the wall where Clare lay asleep. The room was dark and still, but near the pale translucent panels of the window the curtains stirred as though moved by the breathing of the seven girls.

The miracle that had led Clare to her on that first day still endured. Clare and Muriel slept in the same room. Of course that did not mean that they were friends. Clare had immediately marched with her cheerful serenity right into the most exclusive circle of the elect, of 'Them'. But to see Clare was an education; to speak with her a high adventure. To sleep in the same room with her, to see her bath-salts and her powder, only permitted at Heathcroft because she was her father's daughter, to touch her underclothing, embroidered in a Belgian convent – this was to live perpetually on the threshold of a marvellous world, removed by millions of miles from school or Marshington.

She was wonderful, this Clare Duquesne. At night Muriel would raise her head above the bed-clothes and try to tell herself that this was really true, that the world was large enough to hold people so different as Clare and Muriel. Muriel, for all her brave dreams, knew herself to be one of those whose eager, clutching hands let slip prizes, friendships and achievement, as quickly as they grasp them. But Clare, lazy, careless, happy Clare, laughed when she made mistakes, was amused by her arithmetic, hopelessly confused by her premature acquaintance with the metric system, cared nothing for her erratic spelling, and swung up her average of weekly marks by her staggering proficiency in languages. Her supremacy at singing and dancing cost her no more effort than the wearing of fine raiment cost the lilies of the field. Her French and German were more fluent than her clipped, accentuated English. She could swear in Spanish, order a dinner in Dutch, and write a love-letter in Italian. Impish as a street-urchin, sophisticated as a cocktail, fearless of life, loved by it and its lover, judging no man as no man judged her, she dazzled Heathcroft as a glorious, golden creature not wrought from common clay.

Muriel's heart went out to her in a great wave of adoration. Passionate emotion, stronger than any she had known, even on the hushed silver morning of her First Communion, filled her small body like a mighty wind.

'Oh, I would die for her,' she breathed ecstatically. 'O God, if you've planned anything awful to happen to Clare, let it happen to me instead. I could bear anything for her, even if she never knew how I cared. But do let me know her. Let me get to be her friend!'

Forlorn hope, thought Muriel next day, preparing reluctantly for the school walk. As usual the time was trapping her, and she had no partner. Life at Heathcroft being organised upon the partner system, this was Muriel's daily and hourly terror – to have no one to walk with, to be driven as an enforced intruder to walk with the last couple in the crocodile, to feel the checked resentment of the juniors upon whom she was thus imposed.

She stood in front of the small glass, pushing the elastic of her sailor hat beneath her long, brown plait, and thinking, 'Well, there's one thing about Connie coming here next term. I'll never have to walk alone again.' Which just showed how little at this time she knew her Connie.

Then she heard Clare's voice.

'Will you not walk with me, Muriel?'

Muriel gasped. She could not believe that Clare had spoken. But there was no other Muriel in the school, and no other voice like Clare's. Yet, Clare, who could walk with 'Them', surely she would never ask Muriel? They never walked with those who were not of the elect. They would not so imperil their dignity. But, of course, Clare never bothered about her dignity. Years afterwards, when Muriel referred to 'Them', Clare asked with interest, 'Who were "They"?' But when Muriel said, 'Oh, you, and Rosalie and Cathie and Patricia. All the people who counted.' Then Clare laughed. 'Oh, was I one? How perfectly thrilling! And I never knew. What things we miss!' But now Muriel only blushed and asked: 'I beg your pardon?'

'I haven't got a partner,' Clare said. 'Will you walk with me?'

Muriel, blushing and palpitating, answered, 'If you like.' Always, when she was profoundly moved, she became a little stiffer and more prim, not gauche, but prim, like a Victorian teapot, or a bit of sprigged muslin.

Clare never noticed. She was arranging her blue serge coat with the air of a mannequin trying on a Paris model.

'Would you mind holding my collar straight?' she asked.

They took their place in the crocodile.

All the way along the Esplanade Clare chattered. Muriel at the time was too much bewildered by her strange good fortune to remember everything that Clare was saying, but she retained a glowing impression of Clare skating outside a gay hotel in Switzerland, of Clare in a box at the Comédie Française, listening to one of her father's plays, of Clare crossing the Irish Channel in a ship, and being sea-sick all the way. It was perhaps the most unquestionable proof of Clare's attraction that even her sea-sickness became distinguished.

Before Muriel had said three words, the girls had reached the cliffs beyond the Esplanade. Beyond the asphalt and clipped box hedges of the Promenade, the cliffs sprawled untidily. They were not even real cliffs, but ragged slopes, overgrown with coarse grass and tamarisk, sprinkled with yarrow, and patched with stunted bushes of rusty gorse. Far below the tide crept up in circles, flat as paper, and washed back, dragging with white sickles at the shelving sand. The place had a deserted look, and Clare was bored.

'What shall we do now?' she asked obligingly, when Miss Reeve gave the order to break rank.

She waited for Muriel to entertain her.

'Oh, I'll do anything you like,' said Muriel fatally.

They strolled along the winding path. Abruptly to their right rose a steep rock, witness of the time before the landslide, when the cliffs had been cliffs. For fifteen feet it frowned above the way to the sands. Clare stood still, gazing at it in contemplative silence. Then she had an idea.

'Muriel,' she suggested, 'do let's see if we can climb that rock. No one can see us now. Miss Reeves's miles away. I'll go first. Come on, do.'

Clare was like that. She never noticed natural things except as a potential background to her own action. But, having decided to act, she was prompt. She tore off her gloves and faced the rock. Muriel stood, suddenly smitten dumb by an agony of apprehension. But without looking back, Clare began to climb. Agile as a cat, she scrambled with firm hand-grips and burrowing toes, clutching at the sheer side of the rock and chuckling to herself.

'Clare! You can't. You'll fall. You'll be killed.'

Muriel meant to cry out all these things, but somehow she said nothing. She only stood at the bottom of the rock while a sick numbness robbed her of her strength.

Then Clare was up. She swung herself easily on to the

summit of the rock. Her figure was outlined against a windy sky. Her laughing face looked down at Muriel.

'It's glorious up here,' she called. 'But what a wind! I say, do come on, Muriel!'

Before she had thought what she was doing, Muriel began to climb.

'Whatever I do, I mustn't funk in front of Clare,' she thought.

Her fingers tore at the sharp ledges of the rock. Her toes slipped on the uneven surface. She grasped at a brittle root of broom. It came away in her hand. She almost fell. Unused to climbing, blind with fear, she hardly saw the places for her hands to hold.

Clare, completely oblivious of her distress, stared calmly out to sea.

'Oh, Muriel, there's such a big steamer on the horizon. Do hurry up and tell me where it's going.'

But Muriel could not hurry. She was beyond hope, beyond sight, almost beyond fear. For she had just remembered Freddy Mason's stories of the Ladder, and how the men carrying sacks up it had overbalanced and fallen to their doom, far in the yard below.

Her grasp loosened. Rock and sky swung round her. Her feet slipped on the narrow ledge.

She must not fail Clare; here was the time to test her courage.

Fear swooped upon her, tore her fingers from the rock, poured drops of perspiration on her forehead.

'Clare!' shrieked a voice that was not surely hers. 'Clare, I'm slipping!'

Clare's round face appeared between the edge of the rock and the reeling sky. Clare's voice remarked imperturbably:

'Oh, well, if you do fall you haven't far to go, so it won't hurt. But hold on a bit and I'll give you a hand.'

She came over the edge again. Her solid, shapely ankles were on a level with Muriel's hat, her eyes. A firm hand reached down for Muriel's clutching, sticky one.

'That's all right. Come along. You've got a great dab of mud on your nose, Muriel.'

She never faltered. Somehow they both scrambled over the edge. Muriel flung herself down on the short turf, too sick and humiliated to notice even Clare.

She had disgraced herself. She had failed. Her cowardice was flagrant. Far from conducting herself heroically, she had risked Clare's own safety because she was afraid. Far more than her nerve had failed then. Her confidence in her whole personality was shaken. Black with the unlit blackness of youth, the future stretched before her.

'Muriel,' – when Clare pronounced her name it sounded warm and golden – 'do you not think that the girls here are like children?'

Muriel opened her eyes and stared as if to discover some connection between this remark and her own disgraceful exhibition of childishness. But there was none. Clare, astounding, incalculable Clare, had not even noticed the tragedy of Muriel. She had taken it for granted that if you couldn't climb, you couldn't, and that was your affair. She continued meditatively:

'You must know what I mean, for you are different.' Oh, glorious triumph! Mrs Hancock forgotten, Muriel glowed at the delightful thought that she was different. 'Have you not observed? How many of them have had *affaires de cœur*? But very few!'

'*Affaires de cœur?*' It is hard to grope with a meagre French vocabulary when one has just emerged from one physical and two spiritual crises. Affaires! Muriel's knowledge of Marshington phraseology assisted her. *De Cœur* – of the heart. Of course.

'Why, Clare, you can't mean being in love!'

'And why not?' asked Clare serenely. 'I have had five affairs. There was the student at the Sorbonne, and the man who played with Mamma in New York, and my cousin Michael at Eppleford, and, and—'

'But were you in love with them?'

'My dear child, no! Why should I be?'

'Then, how?'

'Dear me, chérie, have you never observed that I am very attractive?'

Her laugh rang out, merry and spontaneous.

'What a solemn face! Muriel, do you ever smile? No, no, I shan't fall in love for years. Perhaps never. But crowds and crowds of men will fall in love with me. That's why Félix decided that I had better come to school. "They're beginning too soon," he said. "You mustn't cut out your mother yet, child." And he sighed. He's terribly sentimental, my Félix. I'm sure I didn't mind. On the whole it bores me. Men in love are so terribly alike, I think, don't you?'

Fascinating, incredible conversation!

'Of course, really, I'm rather grateful to Félix,' Clare continued sagely. 'It's no use getting it all over too soon. And of course one day one might go too far, and really I don't want to marry yet, however rich he was. What do you think?'

'But, Clare, do – do men fall in love with all women if we let them?'

'Why, of course. Else why be a woman?' Clare responded with tranquility. 'Of course there are some, poor dears, like Miss Reeve, I suppose, and most schoolmistresses, and missionaries, and things, but they are hardly women, are they?'

'I – I don't know. I—'

Somehow, it must be confessed, Muriel had always thought of these unfortunates as women. That merely showed her terrible simplicity. With a sigh, she pondered over her ignorance of Life.

'Oh, Muriel, do look at Miss Reeve coming up the path!' Clare darted forward and peered over the edge of the rock. The young lady from the Swiss hotel, the sophisticated philosopher on Life, had vanished. The Irish urchin, impish, grinning, disreputable, took her place. 'Do just watch her hat bobbing along the path! It's as round as a soup plate. Why do people wear such hats? It should be forbidden by law. Here, hand me one of those little stones. Quick!'

Unthinking and hypnotised, Muriel obeyed.

Plop! went the stone, right into the middle of Miss Reeve's round hat. Clare was back behind the rock.

'Oh, Clare, she'll see you,' agonised Muriel.

Clare chuckled. 'She won't. I never get found out.'

But for once she was wrong. Her crimson scarf, blown by the wind, waved a bright pennon from the rock. Nobody else at Heathcroft wore such a scarf.

'Clare Duquesne, Clare Duquesne!' Miss Reeve's shrill voice was ripped to ribbons of sound by the wind.

Clare leant down, smiling benignly upon the furious lady on the path. 'You called?' she inquired politely.

'What are you doing there? Come down! How dare you?'

'How dare I come down? Well, it does look rather steep. I'm not sure that we can this way,' pondered Clare, her head on one side.

'Don't deliberately misunderstand me. Who threw that stone?'

'The stone?' Clare's innocent voice repeated, but Muriel knew that the situation was growing serious. With the ardent heroism of a martyr, she flung herself into the breach – in other words, her head appeared over the rock by the side of Clare. Desire to serve her beloved had vanquished fear, hesitation and conscientiousness.

'It wasn't Clare's fault, Miss Reeve,' she called. 'We were trying to get to the other path, and – and I slipped, and that set some stones rattling down, and Clare came to stop me falling, and I do hope that nobody's hurt.'

Relieved to find that this was not a situation requiring to be dealt with by a major punishment, an embarrassing ordeal at the best of times, devastating when the culprit was Clare Duquesne, Miss Reeve contented herself with a haughty stare.

'I do not think that you two have been behaving very nicely. It is not ladylike to climb these high rocks, and I am sure that it is dangerous. Please come down at once, both of you.'

It was impossible to scold two heads detached from bodies, appearing from the sky like cherubs from a Christmas card cloud. Muriel and Clare withdrew.

Safely back behind the rock, Clare chuckled delightedly.

'I didn't know you had it in you, Muriel; that was quite magnificent.'

But Muriel, to her own surprise as much as Clare's, suddenly began to cry, aloud and helplessly, like a little child.

'But, Muriel, chérie, what is the matter?'

'I don't know. I'm so sorry to be so stupid. I think – I – you know, I didn't mean to tell a lie. It just came out.'

'You? What? Is that all? But you didn't. We were going to the lower path – sometime. And that stone was loosened with your foot. And you did slip. That wasn't a lie. It was a stroke of genius.'

Then, with a sudden access of delighted interest, Clare turned upon Muriel.

'My dear, is it possible that you have a temperament? And I never guessed it. But how very odd. I should not have thought it somehow. It just shows that you never can tell. And I have been so bored with these suet dumplings of girls.' Them! The elect and sacred 'Them' suet dumplings! Muriel forgot her tears. 'Although I, thank heaven, I have no temperament myself. That is why Félix says that I shall never be a singer.'

She flashed her dazzling smile upon the embarrassment of Muriel, who, resolutely determined to acquire a temperament – whatever this might be – immediately, was returning thanks to a benevolent providence who sends success to people in spite of their own failures.

Winifred Holtby, *The Crowded Street* **(1924)**

G RACE WAVES. AFTER a moment Carol waves too. The
third girl doesn't wave. They stand among the asters and
goldenrod, waiting as I go towards them. The apple trees are
covered with scabby apples, red ones and yellow ones; some
of the apples have fallen off and are rotting on the ground.
There's a sweet, cider-y smell, and the buzz of drunken yel-
lowjackets. The apples mush under my feet.

Grace and Carol are browner, less pasty; their features
are further apart, their hair lighter. The third girl is the
tallest. Unlike Grace and Carol, who are in summer skirts,
she wears corduroys and a pullover. Both Carol and Grace
are stubby-shaped, but this girl is thin without being fragile:
lank, sinewy. She has dark-blonde hair cut in a long pageboy,
with bangs falling half into her greenish eyes. Her face is
long, her mouth slightly lopsided; something about the top
lip is a little skewed, as if it's been cut open and sewn up
crooked.

But her mouth evens out when she smiles. She has a smile
like a grown-up's, as if she's learned it and is doing it out of
politeness. She holds out her hand. 'Hi, I'm Cordelia. And
you must be . . .'

I stare at her. If she were an adult, I would take the hand,
shake it, I would know what to say. But children do not shake
hands like this.

'Elaine,' Grace says.

I feel shy with Cordelia. I've been riding in the back of
the car for two days, sleeping in a tent; I'm conscious of my
grubbiness, my unbrushed hair. Cordelia is looking past me
to where my parents are unloading the car. Her eyes are
measuring, amused. I can see, without turning around, my

father's old felt hat, his boots, the stubble on his face, my brother's uncut hair and seedy sweater and baggy knees, my mother's grey slacks, her man-like plaid shirt, her face blank of make-up.

'There's dog-poop on your shoe,' Cordelia says.

I look down. 'It's only a rotten apple.'

'It's the same color though, isn't it?' Cordelia says. 'Not the hard kind, the soft squooshy kind, like peanut butter.' This time her voice is confiding, as if she's talking about something intimate that only she and I know about and agree on. She creates a circle of two, takes me in.

Margaret Atwood, *Cat's Eye* (1988)

'MARILLA,' SHE DEMANDED presently, 'do you think that I shall ever have a bosom friend in Avonlea?'

'A—a what kind of friend?'

'A bosom friend – an intimate friend, you know – a really kindred spirit to whom I can confide my inmost soul. I've dreamed of meeting her all my life. I never really supposed I would, but so many of my loveliest dreams have come true all at once that perhaps this one will, too. Do you think it's possible?'

'Diana Barry lives over at Orchard Slope and she's about your age. She's a very nice little girl, and perhaps she will be a playmate for you when she comes home. She's visiting her aunt over at Carmody just now. You'll have to be careful how you behave yourself, though. Mrs Barry is a very particular woman. She won't let Diana play with any little girl who isn't nice and good.'

Anne looked at Marilla through the apple blossoms, her eyes aglow with interest.

'What is Diana like? Her hair isn't red, is it? Oh, I hope not. It's bad enough I have red hair myself, but I positively couldn't endure it in a bosom friend.'

'Diana is a very pretty little girl. She has black eyes and hair and rosy cheeks. And she is good and smart, which is better than being pretty.'

Marilla was as fond of morals as the Duchess in Wonderland, and was firmly convinced that one should be tacked on to every remark made to a child who was being brought up.

But Anne waved the moral inconsequently aside and seized only on the delightful possibilities before it.

'Oh, I'm so glad she's pretty. Next to being beautiful oneself – and that's impossible in my case – it would be best to have a beautiful bosom friend. When I lived with Mrs Thomas she had a bookcase in her sitting room with glass doors. There weren't any books in it; Mrs Thomas kept her best china and her preserves there – when she had any preserves to keep. One of the doors was broken. Mr Thomas smashed it one night when he was slightly intoxicated. But the other was whole and I used to pretend that my reflection in it was another little girl who lived in it. I called her Katie Maurice, and we were very intimate. I used to talk to her by the hour, especially on Sunday, and tell her everything. Katie was the comfort and consolation of my life. We used to pretend that the bookcase was enchanted and that if I only knew the spell I could open the door and step right into the room where Katie Maurice would have taken me by the hand and led me out into a wonderful place, all flowers and sunshine and fairies, and we would have lived there happy for ever after. When I went to live with Mrs Hammond it just broke my heart to leave Katie Maurice. She felt it dreadfully, too, I know she did, for she was crying when she kissed me goodbye through the bookcase at Mrs Hammond's. But just up the river a little way from the house there was a long green little valley, and the loveliest echo lived there. It echoed back every word you said, even if you didn't talk a bit loud. So I imagined that it was a little girl called Violetta and we were great friends and I loved her almost as well as I loved Katie Maurice – not quite, but almost, you know. The night before I went to the asylum I said good-bye to Violetta, and oh, her good-bye came back to me in such sad, sad tones. I had become so attached to her that I hadn't the heart to imagine a bosom friend at the asylum, even if there had been any scope for imagination there.'

L. M. Montgomery, *Anne of Green Gables* (1908)

IN THE BEGINNING

MY FAMILY MOVED AROUND A LOT WHEN I WAS A CHILD.

Dad (English) →

← Äiti / Mum (Finnish)

Me →

← Younger Brother

Naf Naf

Chicago Bulls

EVERYWHERE WE WENT I MANAGED TO FIND MYSELF A SPECIAL FRIEND BEFORE INEVITABLY MOVING AWAY.

LIKE JOHN IN NEW JERSEY, WHO HAD THE SAME BIRTHDAY AS ME.

Michael Jackson

sluurp

OR EMMA, THE GIRL NEXT DOOR WHEN WE LIVED IN NORTH WALES.

Making a city for TROLLS

IN 1997, WE WERE LIVING IN ISTANBUL, WHERE I WENT TO AN AMERICAN INTERNATIONAL SCHOOL.

School = portakabins

I LOVED IT THERE. MY BEST FRIEND WAS A GIRL CALLED SOO-JIN WHO DREW AMAZING COMICS.

BUT THAT SUMMER, AS I TURNED 13, WE MOVED BACK TO THE UK.

HOME WAS NOW A TOWN NEAR LONDON. IT WAS A WEIRD REVERSE CULTURE SHOCK, ESPECIALLY AT MY NEW SCHOOL.

SUDDENLY I FOUND MYSELF IN A HIERARCHICAL, INTENSELY COMPETITIVE ALIEN WORLD.

I HAD NO IDEA WHERE I WOULD FIT IN AND FIND FRIENDS.

I WAS TOO MUCH OF A WEIRDO FOR THE SHINY ALPHAS.

BUT I WASN'T COOL ENOUGH FOR THE EDGY REBELS, EITHER.

EVENTUALLY I FOUND SOME NICE GIRLS TO HANG OUT WITH.

THEY WERE FRIENDLY, BUT WE DIDN'T HAVE MUCH IN COMMON.

LET'S DO S CLUB 7 DANCE ROUTINES!

There also seemed to be an unspoken rule to never get too serious or intense about anything, and we definitely never discussed our *feelings*. Like most teenagers, I had a <u>lot</u> of feelings to discuss.

I GUESS I WAS LUCKY I DIDN'T GET BULLIED FOR BEING AN OUTSIDER, BUT I PINED AFTER MY OLD LIFE. IT FELT LIKE SOME-THING IMPORTANT WAS MISSING.

TIME PASSED, AND I STARTED TO NOTICE AN INTRIGUING GIRL...

CHARLOTTE

LUNCHTIME CLUB (1999)

IN YEAR 10, I ATE LUNCH IN THE LOCKER ROOM MOST DAYS, WITH OTHER CANTEEN AVOIDERS.

"LUNCHTIME CLUB" WAS ME, CHARLOTTE, MEERA, AND NADIA, EATING AND CHATTING.

I GOT TO KNOW C A BIT, MOSTLY JUST JOKING AROUND.

...AND THEN MY BROTHER AND I SPEWED BLACKCURRANT MUNCH BUNCH ALL OVER THE CAR!

SOMETIMES IT GOT MORE SERIOUS, AND C ALWAYS HAD AN OPINION.

THEY REMOVED THE COLOR PURPLE FROM THE SCHOOL LIBRARY! THAT'S CENSORSHIP!

awkward silence

SCHOOL WAS MOSTLY BORING OR STRESSFUL, BUT MAYBE THINGS WOULD BE BETTER WITH THE RIGHT FRIENDSHIP?

angel of hope

I SENSED C WAS A KINDRED SPIRIT, AND I WANTED MORE...

IF ONLY IT COULD BE JUST ME AND HER ON OUR OWN!

BONDING (1999)

WE ALSO TALKED ABOUT HOME AND LIFE IN GENERAL.

SO YEAH, THAT'S WHY I'M SEEING THE THERAPIST.

STUFF WE'D NEVER FELT ABLE TO SHARE WITH OTHER PEOPLE.

Other people ?!

ER... OK THEN?

FREAK!

LOSER!

I THINK AT THE TIME THERE WAS MORE OF A STIGMA AROUND "MENTAL HEALTH." WE CALLED THESE CHATS "THE CONFESSIONS."

I PROMISE I'LL NEVER TELL ANYONE.

IN THE EVENINGS WE WROTE LETTERS AND SENT EMAILS.

WE BOTH HAD A FLAIR FOR THE DRAMATIC BUT IT WAS SINCERE.

"Lessons seem like an inconvenience because they keep tearing us from one another..."

WE SWAPPED MIXTAPES, TOO.

Mix for Emilia- Side A

Manic Street Preachers: "Sou

Jeff Buckley: "Grace"

Hole: "Pretty on the Inside"

My Vitriol: "Always"

Suede: "Animal Nitrate"

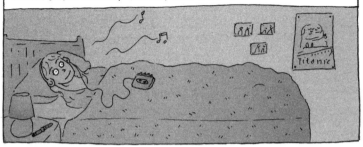

Emilia McKenzie, *But You Have Friends* **(2023)**

*D*ear Cathy & Claire
— I don't think it matters what sort of clothes you wear and what sort of music you like — but all my friends seem to think it does. They say I don't look right when I wear a long skirt and like different music from them. They all wear tartan, and talk about nothing else but the Bay City Rollers.

I don't want to be like this. I like being different and doing what I want to do. I don't want to be influenced by other people but sometimes I can't help it. I know I shouldn't take any notice of other people, but sometimes it's difficult. Have you any suggestions on how I can just forget about what my friends do and say?

— You're doing quite well as it is! Of course you've every right to dress the way you want and act the way you want! Don't let yourself be bothered by other people — you're an individual, after all. In a way, these other girls are probably jealous of your individuality and independence — you don't need to follow fashions and trends to give you confidence. Your friends will eventually accept you and stop trying to change you — so don't worry about them. You're obviously happy the way you are, so just keep on being yourself!

Cathy & Claire, 'My Friends Don't Understand Me', *Jackie: Dear Cathy & Claire,* by Lorna Russell (2006)*

---

* *Jackie* was a popular magazine for teenage girls, published weekly from 1964 until 1993, when it closed. Cathy & Claire was the title of its problem page, which received up to 400 letters a week from readers, often on what were considered then to be controversial subjects (for instance, heavy petting).

O N THAT FIRST morning, when Sara sat at Miss Minchin's side, aware that the whole schoolroom was devoting itself to observing her, she had noticed very soon one little girl, about her own age, who looked at her very hard with a pair of light, rather dull, blue eyes. She was a fat child who did not look as if she were in the least clever, but she had a good-naturedly pouting mouth. Her flaxen hair was braided in a tight pigtail, tied with a ribbon, and she had pulled this pigtail around her neck, and was biting the end of the ribbon, resting her elbows on the desk, as she stared wonderingly at the new pupil. When Monsieur Dufarge began to speak to Sara, she looked a little frightened; and when Sara stepped forward and, looking at him with the innocent, appealing eyes, answered him without any warning, in French, the fat little girl gave a startled jump, and grew quite red in her awed amazement. Having wept hopeless tears for weeks in her efforts to remember that 'la mere' meant 'the mother', and 'le pere', 'the father' – when one spoke sensible English – it was almost too much for her suddenly to find herself listening to a child her own age who seemed not only quite familiar with these words, but apparently knew any number of others, and could mix them up with verbs as if they were mere trifles.

She stared so hard and bit the ribbon on her pigtail so fast that she attracted the attention of Miss Minchin, who, feeling extremely cross at the moment, immediately pounced upon her.

'Miss St John!' she exclaimed severely. 'What do you mean by such conduct? Remove your elbows! Take your ribbon out of your mouth! Sit up at once!'

Upon which Miss St John gave another jump, and when

Lavinia and Jessie tittered she became redder than ever – so red, indeed, that she almost looked as if tears were coming into her poor, dull, childish eyes; and Sara saw her and was so sorry for her that she began rather to like her and want to be her friend. It was a way of hers always to want to spring into any fray in which someone was made uncomfortable or unhappy.

'If Sara had been a boy and lived a few centuries ago,' her father used to say, 'she would have gone about the country with her sword drawn, rescuing and defending everyone in distress. She always wants to fight when she sees people in trouble.'

So she took rather a fancy to fat, slow, little Miss St John, and kept glancing towards her through the morning. She saw that lessons were no easy matter to her, and that there was no danger of her ever being spoiled by being treated as a show pupil. Her French lesson was a pathetic thing. Her pronunciation made even Monsieur Dufarge smile in spite of himself, and Lavinia and Jessie and the more fortunate girls either giggled or looked at her in wondering disdain. But Sara did not laugh. She tried to look as if she did not hear when Miss St John called 'le bon pain,' 'lee bong pang'. She had a fine, hot little temper of her own, and it made her feel rather savage when she heard the titters and saw the poor, stupid, distressed child's face.

'It isn't funny, really,' she said between her teeth, as she bent over her book. 'They ought not to laugh.'

When lessons were over, and the pupils gathered together in groups to talk, Sara looked for Miss St John, and finding her bundled rather disconsolately in a window-seat, she walked over to her and spoke. She only said the kind of thing little girls always say to each other by way of beginning an acquaintance, but there was something friendly about Sara, and people always felt it.

'What is your name?' she said.

To explain Miss St John's amazement one must recall that a new pupil is, for a short time, a somewhat uncertain thing; and of this new pupil the entire school talked the night before until it fell asleep quite exhausted by excitement and contradictory stories. A new pupil with a carriage and a pony and a maid, and a voyage from India to discuss, was not an ordinary acquaintance.

'My name's Ermengarde St John,' she answered.

'Mine is Sara Crewe,' said Sara. 'Yours is very pretty. It sounds like a story book.'

'Do you like it?' fluttered Ermengarde. 'I – I like yours.'

Miss St John's chief trouble in life was that she had a clever father. Sometimes this seemed to her a dreadful calamity. If you have a father who knows everything, who speaks seven or eight languages, and has thousands of volumes which he has apparently learned by heart, he frequently expects you to be familiar with the contents of your lesson books at least; and it is not improbable that he will feel you ought to be able to remember a few incidents of history and to write a French exercise. Ermengarde was a severe trial to Mr St John. He could not understand how a child of his could be a notably and unmistakably dull creature who never shone in anything.

'Good heavens!' he had said more than once, as he stared at her, 'there are times when I think she is as stupid as her Aunt Eliza!'

If her Aunt Eliza had been slow to learn and quick to forget a thing entirely when she had learned it, Ermengarde was strikingly like her. She was the monumental dunce of the school, and it could not be denied.

'She must be *made* to learn,' her father said to Miss Minchin.

Consequently, Ermengarde spent the greater part of her life in disgrace or in tears. She learned things and forgot them; or, if she remembered them, she did not understand them. So it was natural that, having made Sara's acquaintance, she should sit and stare at her with profound admiration.

'You can speak French, can't you?' she said, respectfully.

Sara got on to the window-seat, which was a big, deep one, and, tucking up her feet, sat with her hands clasped round her knees.

'I can speak it because I have heard it all my life,' she answered. 'You could speak it if you had always heard it.'

'Oh no, I couldn't,' said Ermengarde. 'I NEVER could speak it!'

'Why?' inquired Sara, curiously.

Ermengarde shook her head so that the pigtail wobbled.

'You heard me just now,' she said. 'I'm always like that. I can't SAY the words. They're so queer.'

She paused a moment, and then added with a touch of awe in her voice, 'You are CLEVER, aren't you?'

Sara looked out of the window into the dingy square, where the sparrows were hopping and twittering on the wet, iron railings and the sooty branches of the trees. She reflected a few moments. She had heard it said very often that she was 'clever', and she wondered if she was – and IF she was, how it had happened.

'I don't know,' she said. 'I can't tell.'

Then, seeing a mournful look on the round, chubby face, she gave a little laugh and changed the subject.

'Would you like to see Emily?' she inquired.

'Who is Emily?' Ermengarde asked, just as Miss Minchin had done.

'Come up to my room and see,' said Sara, holding out her hand.

They jumped down from the window-seat together, and went upstairs.

'Is it true,' Ermengarde whispered, as they went through the hall – 'is it true that you have a playroom all to yourself?'

'Yes,' Sara answered. 'Papa asked Miss Minchin to let me have one, because – well it was because when I play I make up stories and tell them to myself, and I don't like people to hear me. It spoils it if I think people listen.'

They had reached the passage leading to Sara's room by this time, and Ermengarde stopped short, staring, and quite losing her breath.

'You MAKE up stories!' she gasped. 'Can you do that – as well as speak French? CAN you?'

Sara looked at her in simple surprise.

'Why, anyone can make up things,' she said. 'Have you never tried?'

She put her hand warningly on Ermengarde's.

'Let us go very quietly to the door,' she whispered, 'and then I will open it quite suddenly; perhaps we may catch her.'

She was half laughing, but there was a touch of mysterious hope in her eyes which fascinated Ermengarde, though she had not the remotest idea what it meant, or whom it was she wanted to 'catch,' or why she wanted to catch her. Whatsoever she meant, Ermengarde was sure it was something delightfully exciting. So, quite thrilled with expectation, she followed her on tiptoe along the passage. They made not the least noise until they reached the door. Then Sara suddenly turned the handle, and threw it wide open. Its opening revealed the room quite neat and quiet, a fire gently burning in the grate, and a wonderful doll sitting in a chair by it, apparently reading a book.

'Oh, she got back to her seat before we could see her!' Sara explained. 'Of course they always do. They are as quick as lightning.'

Ermengarde looked from her to the doll and back again.

'Can she – walk?' she asked breathlessly.

'Yes,' answered Sara. 'At least I believe she can. At least I PRETEND I believe she can. And that makes it seem as if it were true. Have you never pretended things?'

'No,' said Ermengarde. 'Never. I – tell me about it.'

She was so bewitched by this odd, new companion that she actually stared at Sara instead of at Emily – notwithstanding that Emily was the most attractive doll person she had ever seen.

'Let us sit down,' said Sara, 'and I will tell you. It's so easy that when you begin you can't stop. You just go on and on doing it always. And it's beautiful. Emily, you must listen. This is Ermengarde St John, Emily. Ermengarde, this is Emily. Would you like to hold her?'

'Oh, may I?' said Ermengarde. 'May I, really?' She is beautiful!' And Emily was put into her arms.

Never in her dull, short life had Miss St John dreamed of such an hour as the one she spent with the queer new pupil before they heard the lunch-bell ring and were obliged to go downstairs.

Sara sat upon the hearth-rug and told her strange things. She sat rather huddled up, and her green eyes shone and her cheeks flushed. She told stories of the voyage, and stories of India; but what fascinated Ermengarde the most was her fancy about the dolls who walked and talked, and who could do anything they chose when the human beings were out of the room, but who must keep their powers a secret and so flew back to their places 'like lightning' when people returned to the room.

'WE couldn't do it,' said Sara, seriously. 'You see, it's a kind of magic.'

Once, when she was relating the story of the search for Emily, Ermengarde saw her face suddenly change. A cloud seemed to pass over it and put out the light in her shining eyes. She drew her breath in so sharply that it made a funny, sad little sound, and then she shut her lips and held them tightly closed, as if she was determined either to do or NOT to do something. Ermengarde had an idea that if she had been like any other little girl, she might have suddenly burst out sobbing and crying. But she did not.

'Have you a – a pain?' Ermengarde ventured.

'Yes,' Sara answered, after a moment's silence. 'But it is not in my body.' Then she added something in a low voice which she tried to keep quite steady, and it was this: 'Do you love your father more than anything else in the whole world?'

Ermengarde's mouth fell open a little. She knew that it would be far from behaving like a respectable child at a select seminary to say that it had never occurred to you that you COULD love your father, that you would do anything

69

desperate to avoid being left alone in his society for ten minutes. She was, indeed, greatly embarrassed.

'I – I scarcely ever see him,' she stammered. 'He is always in the library – reading things.'

'I love mine more than all the world ten times over,' Sara said. 'That is what my pain is. He has gone away.'

She put her head quietly down on her little, huddled-up knees, and sat very still for a few minutes.

'She's going to cry out loud,' thought Ermengarde, fearfully.

But she did not. Her short, black locks tumbled about her ears, and she sat still. Then she spoke without lifting her head.

'I promised him I would bear it,' she said. 'And I will. You have to bear things. Think what soldiers bear! Papa is a soldier. If there was a war he would have to bear marching and thirstiness and, perhaps, deep wounds. And he would never say a word – not one word.'

Ermengarde could only gaze at her, but she felt that she was beginning to admire her. She was so wonderful and different from anyone else.

Presently, she lifted her face and shook back her black locks, with a queer little smile.

'If I go on talking and talking,' she said, 'and telling you things about pretending, I shall bear it better. You don't forget, but you bear it better.'

Ermengarde did not know why a lump came into her throat and her eyes felt as if tears were in them.

'Lavinia and Jessie are "best friends",' she said rather huskily. 'I wish we could be "best friends". Would you have me for yours? You're clever, and I'm the stupidest child in the school, but I – oh, I do so like you!'

'I'm glad of that,' said Sara. 'It makes you thankful when you are liked. Yes. We will be friends. And I'll tell you what,' – a sudden gleam lighting her face – 'I can help you with your French lessons.'

Frances Hodgson Burnett, *A Little Princess* **(1905)**

IN LATIN CLASS, Martha told me Conchita had gone to the infirmary before breakfast. She was not at lacrosse practice, and then she wasn't there again the next day, either. During this time, Martha and I consulted each other frequently, or at least I consulted Martha. The first thing I'd done after leaving Conchita sitting outside on Sunday evening was call Martha from the pay phone in Broussard's. (If I went to their dorm, of course, I risked running into Conchita.) It had been strange – the truth was, it had been exciting – to need to talk on the phone to someone who was also on campus.

'She's definitely angry,' Martha told me on Monday, and when I said, 'At both of us or at me?' Martha replied, 'Mostly at you. She's being irrational because she feels hurt, but she'll get over it.' As usual, because she was Martha, this did not sound callous.

After Conchita missed a second practice, I went to the infirmary to find her, and the nurse said she'd returned to her dorm. Standing outside her door, I could hear music that I thought might be Dylan. I knocked, and Conchita called, 'Come in.'

Clearly, she'd expected someone else – when she saw that

it was me, she drew her lips together and furrowed her eyebrows, like a child making a mad face.

I gestured toward the stereo. 'Good song.'

'What do you want?'

'I was worried about you.'

'Before or after you stole my best friend? But the real question is if you were using me to get to Martha all along or if you just took an opportunity when you saw it.'

'Conchita.' I didn't mean to, but I actually smiled.

She glared at me.

'We're not on a soap opera,' I said. 'Stealing friends isn't something that happens in real life.'

'How would you know? You didn't have any friends before me.'

'That's not true.' I thought of Sin-Jun. Then I thought of Heidi and Alexis, whom I hadn't spoken to since the night of the dangling pillowcase; I was pretty sure they didn't count.

'I over-estimated you,' Conchita said. 'I thought you were smart and neat. But really you're shallow and conformist. You don't have an identity, so you define yourself by who you spend time with, and you get nervous that you're spending time with the wrong people. I feel sorry for Martha because I bet she has no idea what you're like. If Aspeth Montgomery told you she wanted to be your roommate next year, you would drop Martha in a minute.'

Again, listening to Conchita's analysis, I felt the sting of truth, and that old relief, a relief bordering on gratitude, that someone recognized me.

Curtis Sittenfeld, *Prep* (2005)

20

★ A Royal Invitation for Mary Radleigh. ★

73

The Four Marys, *Bunty,*
D. C. Thomson (20 January 1979)*

* *Bunty* was a British comic for girls, published between 1958 and 2001. The Four Marys, set in a boarding school called St Elmo's, was its longest-running story.

———

I LET GO OF both ends of the rope and ran after her. I caught up with her on the stairway landing between the third and fourth floors, and shouted, 'What's your name?'

She turned around, raised her hands up as high as her ears, and backed up against the cinder block wall. Her eyes popped as wide as they could go. I took a step back and said, 'My name is Fe Fe.' Then I asked her again, this time slower, and not so loud. She let her shoulders ease a little, and her eyes went back to normal.

'Tonya.'

I looked down the stairs and saw Precious's and Stacia's faces. Stacia, a puddle of attitude, had her neck all stuck out and a hand on one of her hips. Precious just seemed confused about why I'd dashed up the stairs after a girl we didn't know.

All the signs were there, that this was a terrible idea, but I ignored them, and asked Tonya, 'You want to play rope with me and my friends?' Her eyes widened again, but this time, out of shock.

Stacia had heard enough and stomped away from the stairs, audibly sharing her disgust at what I'd just asked Tonya. Precious remained, understanding what I was about to do.

The year before, I'd invited Stacia to join our little duo. In the building, it had been Precious and me for most of our lives. Our other friends were kids we saw in specific places, like at school or the girls that Precious saw on the weekends

75

at church. For as long as I'd known her, Precious had a sweet spirit, and made friends easily, so even though Stacia was a Buchanan, and we had all heard that they were bullies, Precious didn't mind playing with Stacia.

Stacia was different: very territorial of her people and things. Tonya moved toward me, and when she was inches away, I could smell her, a combination of soured milk and armpit funk. She had a shiny jelly stain on her T-shirt.

We walked back into the square, where Stacia and Precious huddled together, whispering. I raised my voice, smothering them out. 'This Stacia. That's Precious. This Tonya.' The tension made the square seem cramped, and I tried my best to get everybody's mood back up.

'Stacia, can you pick the next song?' I knew it would be something vulgar.

'Tonya, you can get on the end, it's Precious's turn.' And for a second, they'd forgotten that I'd pulled in a new girl without asking if it was cool.

It was a kind of betrayal to open up a friendship, something so private and special, and walk a stranger in like that; Stacia's facial expression and body language confirmed this very notion. I didn't know that things wouldn't ever smooth over, that it would be so hard to fold in Tonya. In fact, the day our crew grew to four, that's when everything terrible started. It was like Tonya was the catalyst for the summer's events. I'd blame Stacia, but sometimes I wonder if Tonya was the real omen. I feel bad for thinking this way, but I can't help it.

With four people, we could play Beat, competing to see who jumped the longest, and wouldn't have to turn the rope.

Days later, when Stacia got in my face about inviting 'that dirty girl' to play with us, this was the reason that I gave, but truthfully, it had little to do with jumping rope. Tonya reminded me of Stacia when I met her, a kid with no friends. My heart went out to her, this lonely-looking girl; I wanted to help her. If I told that to Stacia, I knew she wouldn't care. That summer, Stacia watched Tonya go up and down the stairs too. Sometimes, Stacia would roll her eyes at her or just make a face as if she'd tasted something awful. This may be why, before today, Tonya stopped looking at us at all and passed by our double Dutch game without a glance.

Toya Wolfe, *Last Summer on State Street* (2022)

D ARRELL SOON BEGAN to settle down. She learnt the names not only of the North Tower girls in her form, but of every girl there, from the head girl, Pamela, down to Mary-Lou, the youngest but one in the first form. Darrell herself was the youngest girl in North Tower, she found, but she felt that Mary-Lou was very much younger.

Mary-Lou was a scared mouse of a girl. She was frightened of mice, beetles, thunderstorms, noises at night, the dark, and a hundred other things. Poor Mary-Lou, no wonder she had big scared eyes. Darrell, not easily scared of anything, laughed when she saw poor Mary-Lou rush to the other side of the dormy because she saw an earwig on the floor.

There were ten girls in the first-form dormy at North Tower. Katherine, the quiet head girl. Alicia, the talkative, unruly-tongued monkey. The three new girls, Darrell, Gwendoline and Sally. Mary-Lou, with her big scared eyes, always ready to shy back like a nervous horse at anything unexpected.

Then there was clever Irene, a marvel at maths and music, usually top of the form – but oh, how stupid in the ordinary things of life. If anyone lost her book, it was Irene. If anyone went to the wrong classroom at the wrong time, it was Irene. It was said that once she had gone to the art room, thinking that a painting lesson was to be taken there, and had actually sat there for half an hour, apparently waiting for Miss Linnie to come. What she thought had happened to the rest of the class no one knew.

'But *how* could you sit there all that time and not even *wonder* why nobody came?' said Katherine, in amazement. 'What were you thinking of, Irene?'

'I was just thinking of a maths problem that Potty set us, that's all,' said Irene, her eyes shining through her big glasses. 'It was rather an interesting one, and there were two or three ways of getting it right. You see—'

'Oh, spare us maths out of school!' groaned Alicia. 'Irene, I think you're bats!'

But Irene wasn't. She was a most intelligent girl who, because her mind was always so deeply at work at something, seemed to forget the smaller everyday things of life. She had a sense of fun too, and when she was really tickled she came out with a tremendous explosive giggle that startled the class and made Miss Potts jump. It was Alicia's delight to provoke this explosion sometimes, and upset the class.

The other three girls in the form were Jean, a jolly,

shrewd girl from Scotland, very able at handling money for various school societies and charities; Emily, a quiet, studious girl, clever with her needle, and one of Mam'zelle's favourites because of this; and Violet, a shy, colourless child, very much left out of things because she never seemed to take any interest in them. Half the form never even noticed whether Violet was with them or not.

That made up the ten girls. Darrell felt that she had known them for years after she had lived with them only a few days. She knew the way Irene's stockings always fell down in wrinkles. She knew the way Jean spoke, clipped and sharp, in her Scots accent. She knew that Mam'zelle disliked Jean because Jean was scornful of Mam'zelle's enthusiasm and emotions. Jean herself never went into ecstasies about anything.

Darrell knew Gwendoline's sighs and moans over everything, and Mary-Lou's scared exclamations of fear at any insect or reptile. She liked Katherine's low, firm voice, and air of being able to cope with anything. She knew a great deal about Alicia, but then so did everyone, for Alicia poured out everything that came into her head: she chattered about her brothers, her mother and father, her dogs, her work, her play, her knitting, her opinion of everything and everybody under the sun.

Alicia had no time at all for airs and graces, pretences, sighs, moans or affectations. She was as downright as Darrell, but not so kind. She was scornful and biting when it pleased her, so that girls like Gwendoline hated her, and those like scared Mary-Lou feared her. Darrell like her immensely.

She's so lively, she thought to herself. *Nobody could be dull with Alicia. I wish I was as interesting as she is. Everyone listens when*

79

*Alicia speaks, even when she says something unkind. But nobody
pays much attention when I want to say something. I do really like
Alicia, and I wish she hadn't got Betty for a friend. She's just the
one I would have chosen.*

Enid Blyton, *First Term at Malory Towers* (1946)

I THINK I SPENT about a year alone with Miss Cobham
before the appearance of fellow pupils. This began one
morning when I came downstairs to hear my mother on the
telephone saying, 'That will be splendid, then. They can
leap along together.' Somehow, from the tone of her voice,
I could tell that she was talking about me, but 'leap along'?,
'*they*'? – it all sounded more embarrassing even than it was
mysterious.

'What were you talking about?'

'A neighbour up the road has a daughter your age and she
would like to join the classes with Miss Cobham. Won't that
be nice?'

I wasn't sure that it would. All my terror of people my
own age who weren't my cousins repossessed me and I
didn't reply. Over the ensuing weekend, I tried to come to
terms with the idea: she would only be one, after all. Miss
Cobham would always be present; there wasn't much that
one girl could do to me. And we were certainly not going to
stop reading Shakespeare, whatever this girl thought about
it. Nobody had asked me if I wanted to do lessons with
other people, and nobody had asked me what I felt about it.

In between my Saturday ride in the Row before breakfast – my best treat of the week – my visits to the nursery to play with Colin, my long morning of reading in the battered old leather armchair by the dining-room window, my nervy hours of piano practice, I struggled with the way I could be ambushed by decisions and events over which I had not the slightest control. And then, out of the blue, I wondered how *she*, the new girl, was feeling about it. Probably not good. It was far worse for her: I was in my own house and she had that, plus Miss Cobham and me, to contend with. It was up to me to be nice to her unless or until she was horrible to me, whereupon I'd stop at once.

I need not have worried about Carol joining the class. In no time it was as though she'd always been there. She loved our Shakespeare reading and got on at once with Miss Cobham. I know now that she and I had met when we were about seven or eight, but I don't remember that. We were both about twelve when she joined the class, and she became my best friend. We spent as much time together as possible, rang each other up every day, went to tea with each other, and spent hours in Ladbroke Square to which she had a key. She lived two blocks away from me, so that frequent meeting was easy.

Her family always seemed to me rather glamorous. Her father was head of advertising in England for Shell, and was the first person to use painters to produce posters: Carol would talk about Barnett Freedman and Ted McKnight Kauffer and other painters she knew. Her mother was small, dark and very attractive; always beautifully dressed as though she was just going to a party. I particularly remember her lying on a sofa in a mysteriously dusky drawing room, wearing a black dress with an enormous dark red velvet sash, with one lamp illuminating her novel. She wore the newest scents; Tweed was a favourite. Some of this grooming had brushed off on Carol, who was always immaculately dressed and learned early the trick of making quite ordinary clothes look special. She taught me to wash my hair with egg yolks, and we made face cream of the whites. She also had a dachshund called Vernon and, not being allowed a dog, I envied her. Like me, she had a much younger brother in the care of a large kindly nurse, but Carol didn't lead a nursery life: she had her own room on a floor above where tea on a tray was sent to us . . .

It was with Carol I had been acting pieces that I'd either written or learned by heart or improvised, and she was a wonderfully appreciative audience. It was with her that I learned I could make people laugh, and this gave me a streak of hitherto unknown confidence. Sometimes she'd say: 'Oh, Jane, don't be so silly!' We called each other 'my dear', I think because we thought that this was what grown-ups did. She was less than a year older than I, but those months gave her the lien on authority. I admired her appearance. She had a beautiful complexion, small but very lively brown eyes, and silky hair that curled naturally. I was pasty and my hair was lamentably straight and that was absolutely not the thing to have in those days.

Elizabeth Jane Howard, *Slipstream* (2002)

Having invited helen and me to approach the table, and placed before us each a cup of tea, with one delicious but thin morsel of toast, she got up, and unlocked a drawer, and taking from it a parcel wrapped in paper, disclosed presently to our eyes a good-sized seed-cake.

'I meant to give each of you some of this to take with you,' said she; 'but as there is so little toast you must have it now,' and she proceeded to cut slices with a generous hand.

We feasted that evening as on nectar and ambrosia; and not the least delight of the entertainment was the smile of gratification with which our hostess regarded us, as we satisfied our famished appetites on the delicate fare she liberally supplied. Tea over and the tray removed, she again summoned us to the fire; we sat one on each side of her, and now a conversation followed between her and Helen, which it was indeed a privilege to be admitted to hear.

Miss Temple had always something of serenity in her air, of state in her mien, of refined propriety in her language, which precluded deviation into the ardent, the excited, the eager: something which chastened the pleasure of those who looked on her and listened to her, by a controlling sense of awe; and such was my feeling now; but as to Helen Burns, I was struck with wonder.

The refreshing meal, the brilliant fire, the presence and kindness of her beloved instructress, or perhaps more than all these, something in her own unique mind, had roused her powers within her. They woke, they kindled; first, they glowed in the bright tint of her cheek, which till this hour I had never seen but pale and bloodless; then they shone in the liquid lustre of her eyes, which had suddenly acquired a beauty more singular than that of Miss Temple's – a beauty neither of fine colour, nor long eyelash, nor pencilled brow, but of meaning, of movement, of radiance. Then her soul sat on her lips, and language flowed, from what source I cannot tell. Has a girl of fourteen a heart large enough, vigorous enough, to hold the swelling spring of pure, full, fervid eloquence? Such was the characteristic of Helen's discourse on that, to me, memorable evening; her spirit seemed hastening to live within a very brief span as much as many live during a protracted existence.

They conversed of things I had never heard of; of nations and times past; of countries far away; of secrets of nature discovered or guessed at; they spoke of books; how many they had read! What stores of knowledge they possessed! Then they seemed so familiar with French names and French authors; but my amazement reached its climax when Miss Temple asked Helen if she sometimes snatched a moment to recall the Latin her father had taught her; and taking a book from a shelf, bade her read and construe a page of Virgil; and Helen obeyed, my organ of veneration expanding at every sounding line. She had scarcely finished ere the bell announced bed-time; no delay could be admitted; Miss Temple embraced us both, saying as she drew us to her heart:

'God bless you, my children!'

Helen she held a little longer than me: she let her go more reluctantly; it was Helen her eye followed to the door; it was for her she a second time breathed a sad sigh; for her she wiped a tear from her cheek.

On reaching the bedroom, we heard the voice of Miss Scatcherd; she was examining drawers; she had just pulled out Helen Burns's, and when we entered Helen was greeted with a sharp reprimand, and told that tomorrow she should have half-a-dozen of untidily folded articles pinned to her shoulder.

'My things were, indeed, in shameful disorder,' murmured Helen to me, in a low voice; 'I intended to have arranged them, but I forgot.'

Next morning, Miss Scatcherd wrote in conspicuous characters on a piece of pasteboard the word 'Slattern', and bound it like a phylactery round Helen's large, mild, intelligent and benign-looking forehead. She wore it till evening, patient, unresentful, regarding it as a deserved punishment. The moment Miss Scatcherd withdrew after afternoon school, I ran to Helen, tore it off, and thrust it into the fire; the fury of which she was incapable had been burning in my soul all day, and tears, hot and large, had continually been scalding my cheek; for the spectacle of her sad resignation gave me an intolerable pain at the heart.

Charlotte Brontë, *Jane Eyre* **(1847)**

I N MY FIRST year exams I performed with competence in each subject, and was placed fifteenth in a class of thirty-four girls. I was very satisfied with my modest success; it was unlikely to tempt fate, unlikely to attract envy or spite. But then in my second year – in spite of myself, it seemed – I was placed near the top of the class. A year later, only Julianne and I were serious contenders for the Third-Year

Prize. She began to notice me, her blue eyes sliding dubiously over me from beneath the lemony froth of her fringe.

Julianne was a doctor's daughter. She was tall, strong, athletic and fast. She never minded what she said and she never minded what she did. If this were a school story for girls, of the kind that have gone out of fashion now, I would be telling you that she was the most popular girl in the form. In fact, I have to report that she was not particularly popular at all. She never exerted herself on anyone's behalf, never exerted herself on her own. Her academic successes came to her without apparent effort; on the tennis court, she would skid to retrieve a wayward ball and thump it down in an unreachable corner of the far court, without loss of poise or loss of breath. Julianne was perhaps too sardonic to wish to be a leader, too deep: that is what I think now. Nothing about her – her beauty, her confidence, her brilliance – did I admire. To begin admiring Julianne would have been to dig myself a bottomless pit. I did not think there was any hope for me if once I fell into it.

Hilary Mantel, *An Experiment in Love* (1995)

IF ALL THE Saturdays of 1982 can be thought of as one day, I met Tracey at ten a.m. on that Saturday, walking through the sandy gravel of a churchyard, each holding our mother's hand. There were many other girls present but for obvious reasons we noticed each other, the similarities and the differences, as girls will. Our shade of brown was exactly the same – as if one piece of tan material had been cut to make us both – and our freckles gathered in the same areas, we were of the same height. But my face was ponderous and melancholy, with a long, serious nose, and my eyes turned down, as did my mouth. Tracey's face was perky and round, she looked like a darker Shirley Temple, except her nose was as problematic as mine, I could see that much at once, a ridiculous nose – it went straight up in the air like a little piglet. Cute, but also obscene: her nostrils were on permanent display. On noses you could call it a draw. On hair she won comprehensively. She had spiral curls, they reached to her backside and were gathered into two long plaits, glossy with some kind of oil, tied at their ends with satin yellow bows. Satin yellow bows were a phenomenon unknown to my mother. She pulled my great frizz back in a single cloud, tied with a black band. My mother was a feminist. She wore her hair in a half-inch Afro, her skull was perfectly shaped, she never wore make-up and dressed us both as plainly as possible. Hair is not essential when you look like Nefertiti. She'd no need of make-up or products or jewellery or expensive clothes, and in this way her financial circumstances, her politics and her aesthetic were all perfectly – conveniently – matched. Accessories only cramped her style, including, or so I felt at the time, the horse-faced seven-year-old by her side. Looking across at Tracey I diagnosed the opposite problem: her mother was white, obese, afflicted with acne. She wore her thin blond hair pulled back very tightly in what I knew my mother would call a 'Kilburn facelift'. But Tracey's personal glamour was the solution: she was her own mother's most striking accessory. The family look, though

not to my mother's taste, I found captivating: logos, tin
bangles and hoops, diamanté everything, expensive trainers
of the kind my mother refused to recognise as a reality in the
world – 'Those aren't shoes.' Despite appearances, though,
there was not much to choose between our two families. We
were both from the estates, neither of us received benefits.
(A matter of pride for my mother, an outrage to Tracey's:
she had tried many times – and failed – to 'get on the dis-
ability'.) In my mother's view it was exactly these superficial
similarities that lent so much weight to questions of taste. She
dressed for a future not yet with us but which she expected
to arrive. That's what her plain white linen trousers were
for, her blue-and-white striped 'Breton' T-shirt, her frayed
espadrilles, her severe and beautiful African head – everything so plain, so understated, completely out of step with
the spirit of the time, and with the place. One day we would
'get out of here', she would complete her studies, become
truly radical chic, perhaps even spoken of in the same breath
as Angela Davis and Gloria Steinem . . . Straw-soled shoes
were all a part of this bold vision, they pointed subtly at
the higher concepts. I was an accessory only in the sense
that in my very plainness I signified admirable maternal
restraint, it being considered bad taste – in the circles to
which my mother aspired – to dress your daughter like a
little whore. But Tracey was unashamedly her mother's
aspiration and avatar, her only joy, in those thrilling yellow
bows, a frou-frou skirt of many ruffles and a crop top revealing inches of childish nut-brown belly, and as we pressed up
against the pair of them in this bottleneck of mothers and
daughters entering the church I watched with interest as

Tracey's mother pushed the girl in front of herself – and in front of us – using her own body as a means of obstruction, the flesh on her arms swinging as she beat us back, until she arrived in Miss Isabel's dance class, a look of great pride and anxiety on her face, ready to place her precious cargo into the temporary care of others. My mother's attitude, by contrast, was one of weary, semi-ironic servitude, she thought the dance class ridiculous, she had better things to do, and after a few further Saturdays – in which she sat slumped in one of the plastic chairs that lined the left-hand wall, hardly able to contain her contempt for the whole exercise – a change was made and my father took over. I waited for Tracey's father to take over, but he never did. It turned out – as my mother had guessed at once – that there was no 'Tracey's father', at least not in the conventional, married sense. This, too, was an example of bad taste.

*

At this stage Tracey and I were not friends or enemies or even acquaintances: we barely spoke. Yet there was always this mutual awareness, an invisible band strung between us, connecting us and preventing us from straying too deeply into relations with others. Technically, I spoke more to Lily Bingham – who went to my school – and Tracey's own standby was sad old Danika Babić, with her ripped tights and thick accent, she lived on Tracey's corridor. But though we giggled and joked with these white girls during class, and although they had every right to assume that they were our focus, our central concern – that we were, to them, the good friends we appeared to be – as soon as it came to break-time and squash and biscuits Tracey and I lined up next to each

other, every time, it was almost unconscious, two iron filings
drawn to a magnet.

Zadie Smith, *Swing Time* **(2016)**

S ANDY STRANGER HAD a feeling at the time that they were
supposed to be the happiest days of her life, and on her
tenth birthday she said so to her best friend Jenny Gray who
had been asked to tea at Sandy's house. The speciality of the
feast was pineapple cubes with cream, and the speciality of
the day was that they were left to themselves. To Sandy the
unfamiliar pineapple had the authentic taste and appearance
of happiness and she focused her small eyes closely on the
pale-gold cubes before she scooped them up in her spoon,
and she thought the sharp taste on her tongue was that of a
special happiness, which was nothing to do with eating, and
was different from the happiness of play that one enjoyed
unawares. Both girls saved the cream to the last, then ate it
in spoonfuls.

'Little girls, you are going to be the crème de la crème,'
said Sandy, and Jenny spluttered her cream into her
handkerchief.

'You know,' Sandy said, 'these are supposed to be the
happiest days of our lives.'

'Yes, they are always saying that,' Jenny said. 'They say,
make the most of your schooldays because you never know
what lies ahead of you.'

'Miss Brodie says prime is best,' Sandy said.

'Yes, but she never got married like our mothers and fathers.'

'They don't have primes,' said Sandy.

'They have sexual intercourse,' Jenny said.

The little girls paused, because this was still a stupendous thought, and one which they had only lately lit upon; the very phrase and its meaning were new. It was quite unbelievable. Sandy said, then, 'Mr Lloyd had a baby last week. He must have committed sex with his wife.' This idea was easier to cope with and they laughed screamingly into their pink paper napkins. Mr Lloyd was the art master to the senior girls.

'Can you *see* it happening?' Jenny whispered.

Sandy screwed her eyes even smaller in the effort of seeing with her mind. 'He would be wearing his pyjamas,' she whispered back.

The girls rocked with mirth, thinking of one-armed Mr Lloyd, in his solemnity, striding into school.

Then Jenny said, 'You do it on the spur of the moment. That's how it happens.' Jenny was a reliable source of information, because a girl employed by her father in his grocery shop had recently been found to be pregnant, and Jenny had picked up some fragments of the ensuing fuss. Having confided her finds to Sandy, they had embarked on a course of research, which they called 'research', piecing together clues from remembered conversations illicitly overheard, and passages from the big dictionaries.

'It all happens in a flash,' Jenny said. 'It happened to Teenie when she was out walking at Puddocky with her boyfriend. Then they had to get married.'

'You would think the urge would have passed by the time

she got her *clothes* off,' Sandy said. By 'clothes', she definitely meant to imply knickers, but 'knickers' was rude in this scientific context.

'Yes, that's what I can't understand,' said Jenny.

Sandy's mother looked round the door and said, 'Enjoying yourselves, darlings?' Over her shoulder appeared the head of Jenny's mother. 'My word,' said Jenny's mother, looking at the tea table, 'they've been tucking in!'

Sandy felt offended and belittled by this; it was as if the main idea of the party had been the food.

'What would you like to do now?' Sandy's mother said.

Sandy gave her mother a look of secret ferocity which meant: you promised to leave us all on our own, and a promise is a promise, you know it's very bad to break a promise to a child, you might ruin all my life by breaking your promise, it's my birthday.

Sandy's mother backed away, bearing Jenny's mother with her. 'Let's leave them to themselves,' she said. 'Just enjoy yourselves, darlings.'

Muriel Spark, *The Prime of Miss Jean Brodie* **(1961)**

3

FIRST ENCOUNTERS

The real marriage of true minds is for any two people to possess a sense of humour or irony pitched in exactly the same key, so that their joint glances on any subject cross like interarching searchlights.

Edith Wharton, *A Backward Glance* **(1934)**

Melissa Bank ∼ Michèle Roberts ∼ Helen Garner ∼ Charlotte Brontë
Anthony Quinn ∼ George Eliot ∼ Hilary Mantel ∼ Zoë Heller
Emma Cline ∼ Jane Austen ∼ Mona Awad ∼ Margaret Drabble
Shirley Hazzard ∼ Emily Gould ∼ Christina Stead ∼ Sigrid Nunez
Dorothy Whipple ∼ Virginia Woolf

After school, the big, wide world. One thing that may mark out a good friend (as opposed to a mere acquaintance) is that we can almost always remember how, when and where we first met them. My closest friend from college days – we've known each other for more than thirty years now – appeared in a doorway in the middle of my first term at university. She was holding a clipboard, and announced she was casting a play. I had no ambitions as an actor, but I recall her officious manner very well, and have teased her regularly about it in the decades since. I didn't *know* she would be my friend then, but I *wanted* her to be; I resolved, somehow, to inch inside her glamorous orbit. Many of the first encounters in this chapter similarly take place when a young woman is far from home for the first time. Others occur at work, where we spend so much of our lives, and must find a friend if we want to survive. I believe in the idea of seduction when it comes to friends, of spells being cast – and one way to make this happen is through food. In Dorothy Whipple's 1930 novel, *High Wages*, a lonely older and rather rich woman, Mrs Briggs, makes a friend of Jane, a lowly shop girl, with rock buns and parkin, tinned peaches and soft peaks of whipped cream. Elma Stuart, a woodcarver and nutritionist who was what we would describe now as a fan of George Eliot, made a friend of the writer via letters and thoughtful presents, including an 'exquisite' shawl, sent to her before they had even met. Their friendship lasted until Eliot's death in 1880, and they now lie side by side in Highgate Cemetery in London.

V ENICE LAMBOURNE WAS famous the way a beautiful girl can be in a small circle of places and parties, but hardly anyone knew her. *Knockout* was the word people used to describe Venice, and *bombshell*, and she did seem to stir violence; men could seem almost angry at her for being so pretty.

I met Venice when we were both eighteen. She was my roommate. This was at Rogers, the not-very-good school in Klondike, New York . . . Venice said the reason she was there was that her SATs had somehow not arrived at the better schools she'd applied to; she said that her application to Rogers consisted of one phone call her uncle placed to the admissions committee. I doubted the story, as I did almost every story Venice told, but it turned out to be true – or true enough.

Venice didn't arrive until the night before classes started, hours after the last parents had kissed their freshman sons and daughters good-bye and gotten into station wagons headed homeward for Darien, Connecticut, or Katonah, New York, or, in my parents' case, Surrey, Pennsylvania. Venice pulled up in a cab and carried her sole suitcase inside.

She knocked on what at that moment became our door and walked into what still felt to me like my room.

She was very thin and very tall – five foot ten in flat shoes. She almost always wore flats, one pair until they wore out, and then she'd get another. She didn't have many things – not many clothes or many possessions, either; she believed in owning only perfect things or, as she said, 'one perfect thing'.

Her hair was blond and straight, and she tucked it behind her ears; she had blue eyes that you noticed partly because her brows were so dark and thick.

She said, 'I'm Venice Lambourne,' and when she shook my hand her formality unnerved me so much that I answered as I'd been instructed to as a child: 'How do you do?' Then I said, 'I'm Sophie Applebaum.'

She told me that she'd been traveling and was exhausted; she'd come all the way from Antibes.

I hadn't heard of Antibes but vaguely remembered a movie called *Raid on Entebbe*, and was it in Israel or somewhere in Africa? Was Israel in Africa?

'Wow,' I said, and then suggested that maybe she wanted to check in with our resident adviser, a button-nosed teddy bear named Betsy, who'd been worried.

This Venice seemed not to hear. 'I need a drink,' she said.

When I told her about the soda machine in the basement, she turned and looked at me as though I was the last and possibly longest leg of her trip.

She'd passed a bar that she said was close and open. 'Those might be its only virtues,' she said, 'but they are the only virtues I care about at the moment.'

I hesitated; with the lack of self-knowledge I'd exhibit for years to come, I'd signed up for an eight o'clock class.

I told her that the bar was called the Pines, and it was the college bar; basically, the only bar, but fine; I was hoping that if I talked long enough, she'd realize how tired she was.

She raised her thick eyebrows, asking why I was talking about a bar we should be walking to, and I said, 'I have an eight o'clock class.'

She said, 'I don't even know what I'm taking,' and won.

It took her about thirty seconds to get ready. She didn't change her clothes – a robin's-egg-blue boatneck, white capris, and black flats, each a perfect thing – and didn't wear make-up, herself a perfect thing. All she did was wash her face.

As we were leaving the room, she noticed my fiddle in its case.

'Do you play the violin?'

'I fiddle,' I said, and I felt the way I sometimes had when I was little and needed to defend my younger brother from someone older than both of us and hoped I could.

Sort of jokey, she said, 'Will you fiddle for me some time?'

'Probably not,' I said.

*

Our resident adviser invited Venice and me into her homey room, saying, 'I just want to have a little chat.' She asked if we wanted tea or coffee, and she also had hot chocolate and chicken noodle soup. 'I'll have some soup,' I said. 'Thanks.'

Venice gave me a look: *Let's not make this any longer than it has to be.* She said, 'Nothing for me, thanks.'

Betsy plugged in her hot pot. She asked how we were liking Rogers, and who our favorite professors were. She was a nice girl from Syracuse, and you could tell that she took her job as resident adviser seriously.

She handed me the mug of soup; it was hot, and I blew on it.

She said, 'You guys are spending an awful lot of time together.' She was struggling. 'You know, this is the time for making new friends,' she said. 'Meeting everybody.'

We both said we'd made other friends, which was a little truer for me than for Venice.

Betsy said, 'I just want to make sure you're open to other relationships.'

I said, 'I'm open.'

Venice couldn't make herself say words like these, but she nodded and widened her eyes to convey openness.

Betsy said, 'College is when you make the friendships that will last for the rest of your life.' She looked miserable saying this.

She went from cliché to cliché, as though stepping from one flat stone to the next across a roiling river, until finally Venice said, 'I think I understand what you're trying to say,' though neither of us did.

A few days later we found out: there was a rumor that Venice and I were lesbians.

It didn't bother Venice at all, and I tried to act nonchalant, too. I asked if she wasn't afraid the rumor would prevent some hypothetical man from hypothetically falling in love with her.

She said the rumor wasn't going to prevent anyone from anything, just the opposite: According to Georges, ninety percent of men had lesbian fantasies.

I said, 'But what if he's in the other ten percent?'

She said, 'The other ten percent are gay.'

Then Venice met Hugh, and that was that.

Melissa Bank, *The Wonder Spot* (2005)

I CONTINUED TO MAKE new friendships. I met Frances Wood, who was an Assistant Keeper at the British Museum, rapidly becoming an expert on Chinese culture. She and her boyfriend drove me home from one party. We stopped in Kentish Town for fish and chips. Frances fizzed with energy and wit. She was beautiful, with silky black hair and rosy cheeks, fiercely intelligent, funny. In her company I felt real; ordinary; able to enjoy myself.

Frances was the queen of the flat, and I her handmaiden. This was a role I had played before and would play again vis-à-vis charismatic, powerful women who stood in, on one level, as mother-figures, however un-maternal (in the conventional sense) they actually were. I admired Frances. Sometimes I envied her. Sometimes I wanted to fight her.

Michèle Roberts, *Paper Houses* (2007)

NICOLA LIVED BEYOND the northern beaches of Sydney on a hillside that could be reached only by boat. For years she had chugged back and forth in a tinny between a Palm Beach jetty and the landing below her house, a ten-minute ride in fine weather. She would collect me from my car on the Palm Beach side, urge me down the white wooden ladder with the groceries, and make the outboard roar with one yank of the cord. Away we bounced. She sat at the tiller, erect and handsome as a duchess, in loose garments that the wind ballooned and rippled, her silver hair streaming flat against her skull.

Under her practical and good-humoured command, skimming across the water and hauling the bags up the steep bush track to the house, I was safe. On her territory I deferred to her and obeyed her. She knew about ticks and leeches, snakes, goannas; the names of birds and their habits; the movements of the moon; how to save water; how to manage an outdoor fire. She was older, taller, braver, and more free: she had taught herself to live alone.

The first time I went to stay a weekend, she dared me to climb the bush-choked escarpment that soared up behind her shack to Kuringai Chase. We clawed our way to the top, grunting and cursing, and hauled ourselves, two filthy, panting hags, out of the scrub on to a track along which at that moment came strolling a city couple in pale, freshly ironed sporting clothes, with a shih tzu trotting on a leash. All afternoon we lay on our beds and read mighty works of literature, shouting to each other analytical or admiring remarks.

That night we took the bottle of Stoly down the rough path to the landing where, sitting on our jackets in the dark, we launched the long conversation that would become our friendship. She told me about the only man she had lived with, Hamish, whose children she loved and was still in touch with, but who had been a brute to her; and an Aboriginal bloke who, in the days when she was doing a lot of acid and having a sort of crack-up in a rainforest, had wandered in from nowhere and saved her from starving herself to death.

When she was about seven, she said, a neighbour in his twenties had come over the fence one afternoon while she was playing in the yard. 'He ran away. I picked myself up and hid at the top of the back steps. I stayed out there till it got dark and I could hear my mother and my sister calling me. I knew I could never, ever tell anyone what had happened. And I never did.'

I was already half drunk. I said, 'Fuckin' animal. Is he still alive?'

She shrugged.

'Don't you want to hunt him down and bash the shit out of him? I'll help you. We can look in the electoral rolls.'

She uttered a laugh of good-natured scorn. We hunched on the end of the old timber wharf. Masts were jingling. On the black, restless water of the inlet, boats' riding lamps were laying down what she said a poet had called 'stacked saucers of light'.

Helen Garner, *The Spare Room* (2008)

IN CAROLINE, MISS Keeldar had first taken an interest because she was quiet, retiring, looked delicate, and seemed as if she needed some one to take care of her. Her predilection increased greatly when she discovered that her own way of thinking and talking was understood and responded to by this new acquaintance. She had hardly expected it. Miss Helstone, she fancied, had too pretty a face, manners and voice too soft, to be anything out of the common way in mind and attainments; and she very much wondered to see the gentle features light up archly to the réveillé of a dry sally or two risked by herself; and more did she wonder to discover the self-won knowledge treasured, and the untaught speculations working in that girlish, curl-veiled head. Caroline's instinct of taste, too, was like her own: such books as Miss Keeldar had read with the most pleasure were Miss Helstone's delight also. They held many aversions too in common, and could have the comfort of laughing together over works of false sentimentality and pompous pretension.

Few, Shirley conceived, men or women have the right taste in poetry: the right sense for discriminating between what is real and what is false. She had again and again heard very clever people pronounce this or that passage, in this or that versifier, altogether admirable, which, when she read, her soul refused to acknowledge as anything but cant, flourish and tinsel, or at the best, elaborate wordiness; curious, clever, learned perhaps; haply, even tinged with the fascinating hues of fancy, but, God knows, as different from real poetry as the gorgeous and massy vase of mosaic is from the little cup of pure metal; or, to give the reader a choice of similes, as the milliner's artificial wreath is from the fresh gathered lily of the field.

Caroline, she found, felt the value of the true ore, and knew the deception of the flashy dross. The minds of the two girls being toned in harmony, often chimed very sweetly together.

Charlotte Brontë, *Shirley* **(1849)**

STEPHEN SAID HE had some errands to run, so he would meet them at the restaurant. After he had gone Freya enlisted Nancy's help in taking down the black out curtains in the two bedrooms. As they struggled with the dusty folds of dark serge drooping over their shoulders, Nancy said with a laugh, 'It's like getting lost inside a nun's skirts.'

'Not an experience I'm familiar with,' said Freya, archly. 'Were they beastly to you at convent school?'

'There were one or two it was best to avoid, but most of them were all right. And I'm grateful to Sister Philomena, and Mrs Eagle – they encouraged me to apply to Oxford.'

'Mrs Eagle? On a wing *and* a prayer, then.'

Nancy stopped, and smiled at her. 'I'd never thought of – that's so funny!'

Freya shrugged, wondering why, if it was so funny, she hadn't actually laughed. When they'd first met yesterday she was worried that Nancy had no sense of humour at all. But after last night, when they had guffawed at almost everything, she had felt an enormous sense of relief: you couldn't really be friends with someone if you didn't make them laugh.

Anthony Quinn, *Freya* (2016)

Blackbrook, Bickley, Kent, September 17, 1873

My dear Mrs Stuart,

The lovely shawl is come in safety.* I suppose that Wordsworth would have rebuked me for calling a shawl 'lovely'. But I think the word is allowable in this case, where

---

* Since 1870, Elma Stuart had been sending George Eliot presents, mostly of her own making. They would meet for the first time on 3 October 1873.

the exquisite texture seems to my imagination to hold much love in its meshes. It is really just the sort of garment I delight to wrap myself in – the utmost warmth compatible with the utmost lightness being my ideal of clothing for my feeble body. Thanks, dear Friend. You have made many pretty epochs for me since that epoch of your first letter, when, as Clotilde de Vaux said of her friend, 'J'ai eu le bonheur de vous acquérir' . . .

I confess I tremble a little at the prospect of your seeing me in the flesh. At present I have the charms of a 'Yarrow Unvisited'. As to the portrait, I am not one bit like it – besides it was taken eight years ago. Imagine a first cousin of the old Dante's – rather smoke-dried – a face with lines in it that seem a map of sorrows. These portraits seen beforehand are detestable introductions, only less disadvantageous than a description given by an ardent friend to one who is neither a friend nor ardent. But it would be sad if one's books were not the best of one, seeing that they reach farther and last (it is to be hoped) longer than the personality they went out from.

I need say no more now, since we shall soon see you. Only let me thank you once more for all the sweet affection you have manifested towards me, and the valued words you have written me about your own experience so far as it has drawn your heart towards me. Such things are among my reasons for being glad that I have lived. Mr Lewes and I are keeping a warm welcome for you. We have often observed that Solomon's wise admonition is rarely applied except by those who are the least in danger of being wearisome. The real bore, alas, never dreads boring you. In expectation

Yours maternally

M. E. Lewes

Blackbrook, Bickley, Kent, October 4, 1873

My dear Elma,

Here is the shabby little lock of hair. I want also to say that I love you the better for having seen you in the flesh, and shall always (for the brief time that I shall last) be with motherly interest

Your affectionate Friend

M. E. Lewes

George Eliot, collected in *Selections from George Eliot's Letters*, **ed. Gordon S. Haight (1985)**

KARINA ARRIVED AT Tonbridge Hall two days after Julianne, and was billeted as arranged in Room C21, with a girl called Lynette Segal, who was a third-year student at the School of East European Studies. We met Lynette just after Karina's installation, when she tapped at our door after dinner.

I liked her even before she spoke: she was pale, neat and delicate, with a brunette's glitter and many gold rings. Her eyes were the colour of blackberries. They fell first on the skull on our bookshelf. She said simply, 'I admire.'

Julianne, sprawled on her bed, looked up. 'Oh, we do have taste.'

Lynette stood uncertainly, poised almost on her toes.

'My room-mate says she knows you.'

I nodded.

'So I said I'd ask you round for coffee.'

'And *petits fours*?' Julianne asked.

Lynette rose a little, as if poised for a balletic spring.

'Bendicks Bittermints,' she offered.

Julianne uncoiled her legs. 'I admire,' she murmured.

'Oh, but you must do *something*,' Lynette said. She gave a little sideways hop. 'Or you would die.'

Julianne stood up. Pointed to me. 'May the prole come too? Only half a mint for her, mind!'

Lynette said to me, 'How very short your hair is! But it shows off your beautiful eyes.'

I could see that Julianne had also fallen in love. I think women carry this faculty into later life: the faculty for love, I mean. Men will never understand it till they stop confusing love with sex, which will be never. Even today, there are ten or twenty women I love: for a turn of phrase or wrist, for a bruised-looking ankle where the veins have blossomed out, for a squeeze of the hand or for a voice on the end of a phone. I would no more go to bed with any of them than I would drown myself; and drowning is my most feared form of death. Perhaps I love too easily; I can say Lynette has left a mark on my heart.

Hilary Mantel, *An Experiment in Love* (1995)

I TOOK SHEBA'S FAILURE to forge an instantaneous friendship as an encouraging sign. In my experience, newcomers – particularly female ones – are far too eager to pin their colours to the mast of any staffroom coterie that will have them. Jennifer Dodd, who used to be my closest friend at the school, spent her first three weeks at St George's buried in the welcoming bosoms of Mary Horsely and Diane Nebbins. Mary and Diane are two hippies from the Maths department. They both carry packets of 'women's tea' in their handbags and use jagged lumps of rock crystal in lieu of anti-perspirant. They were entirely ill-suited – temperament-wise, humour-wise, world view-wise – to be Jennifer's friends. But they happened to get to her first and Jennifer was so grateful for someone being nice to her that she cheerfully undertook to ignore their soy milk mumbo-jumbo. I dare say she would have plighted her troth to a Moonie during her first week at St George's, if the Moonie had been quick enough off the mark.

Sheba displayed no such new-girl jitters and for this I admired her. She did not exempt me from her general aloofness. Owing to my seniority at St George's and the fact that I am more formal in manner than most of my colleagues, I am used to being treated with a certain deference. But Sheba seemed to be oblivious of my status. There was little indication, for a long time, that she really *saw* me at all. Yet, in spite of this, I found myself possessed by a strange certainty that we would one day be friends.

Early on, we made a few tentative approaches to one another. Somewhere in her second week, Sheba greeted me in the corridor. (She used 'Hello', I was pleased to note, as opposed to the awful mid-Atlantic 'Hiya' that so many of the staff favour.) And another time, walking from the arts centre after an assembly, we shared some brief, rueful comments about the performance that had just taken place. My feelings of connection to Sheba did not depend upon these minute exchanges, however. The bond that I sensed, even at that stage, went far beyond anything that might have been expressed in quotidian chit-chat. It was an intuited kinship. An unspoken understanding. Does it sound too dramatic to call it spiritual recognition? Owing to our mutual reserve, I understood that it would take time for us to form a friendship. But when we did, I had no doubt it would prove to be one of uncommon intimacy and trust – a relationship *de chaleur* as the French say.

Zoë Heller, *Notes on a Scandal* (2003)

IT WASN'T THAT I couldn't remember my life before Suzanne and the others, but it had been limited and expected, objects and people occupying their temperate orbits. The yellow cake my mother made for birthdays, dense and chilly from the freezer. The girls at school eating lunch on the asphalt, sitting on their overturned backpacks. Since I'd met Suzanne, my life had come into sharp, mysterious relief, revealing a world beyond the known world, the hidden passage behind the bookcase. I'd catch myself eating an apple, and even the wet swallow of apple could incite gratitude in me. The arrangement of oak leaves overhead condensing with a hothouse clarity, clues to a riddle I hadn't known you could try to solve.

Emma Cline, *The Girls* (2016)

A T M---- WE arrived in a few hours; and on sending in our names were immediately admitted to Sophia, the Wife of Edward's freind*. After having been deprived during the course of 3 weeks of a real freind (for such I term your Mother) imagine my transports at beholding one, most truly worthy of the Name. Sophia was rather above the middle size; most elegantly formed. A soft languor spread over her lovely features, but increased their Beauty. – It was the Charectarestic of her Mind. – She was all Sensibility and Feeling. We flew into each other's arms and after having exchanged vows of mutual Freindship for the rest of our Lives, instantly unfolded to each other the most inward secrets of our Hearts. – We were interrupted in the delightfull Employment by the entrance of Augustus (Edward's freind), who was just returned from a solitary ramble.

Never did I see such an affecting Scene as was the meeting of Edward and Augustus.

'My Life! my Soul!' (exclaimed the former) 'My Adorable Angel!' (replied the latter) as they flew into each other's arms. It was too pathetic for the feelings of Sophia and myself – We fainted alternately on a sofa.

Jane Austen, *Love and Freindship* (1790)

---

* Misspellings as in the original.

W<small>E CALL THEM</small> Bunnies because that is what they call each other. Seriously. Bunny.

Example:

Hi, Bunny!

Hi, Bunny!

What did you do last night, Bunny?

I hung out with you, Bunny. Remember, Bunny?

That's right, Bunny, you hung out with me and it was the best time I ever had.

Bunny, I love you.

I love you, Bunny.

And then they hug each other so hard I think their chests are going to implode. I would even secretly hope for it from where I sat, stood, leaned, in the opposite corner of the lecture hall, department lounge, auditorium, bearing witness to four grown women – my academic peers – cooingly strangle each other hello. Or good-bye. Or *just because you're so amazing, Bunny.* How fiercely they gripped each other's pink-and-white bodies, forming a hot little circle of such rib-crushing love and understanding it took my breath away. And then the nuzzling of ski-jump noses, peach fuzzy cheeks. Temples pressed against temples in a way that made me think of the labial rubbing of the bonobo or the telepathy of beautiful, murderous children in horror films. All eight of their eyes shut tight as if this collective asphyxiation were a kind of religious bliss. All four of their glossy mouths making squealing sounds of monstrous love that hurt my face.

I love you, Bunny.

I quietly prayed for the hug implosion all year last year. That their ardent squeezing might cause the flesh to ooze from the sleeves, neck holes, and A-line hems of their cupcake dresses like so much inane frosting. That they would get tangled in each other's *Game of Thrones* hair, choked by the ornate braids they were forever braiding into each other's heart-shaped little heads. That they would choke on each other's blandly grassy perfume.

Never happened. Not once.

They always came apart from these embraces intact and unwounded despite the ill will that poured forth from my staring eyes like so much comic-book-villain venom. Smiling at one another. Swinging clasped hands. Skins aglow with affection and belonging as though they'd just been hydrated by the purest of mountain streams.

Bunny, I love you.

Completely immune to the disdain of their fellow graduate student. Me. Samantha Heather Mackey. Who is not a Bunny. Who will never be a Bunny.

I pour myself and Ava more champagne in the far corner of the tented green, where I lean against a white Doric pillar bedecked with billowing tulle. September. Warren University. The Narrative Arts department's annual welcome back *Demitasse*, because this school is too Ivy and New England to call a party a party. Behold the tiger-lily-heavy center-pieces. Behold the Christmas-lit white gauze floating everywhere like so many ghosts. Behold the pewter trays of salmon pinwheels, duck-liver crostini topped with little sugared orchids. Behold the white people in black discussing grants they earned to transla. poets no one reads from the French. Behold the lavish tent under which the overeducated mingle, well versed in every art but the one of conversation.

THE VIRAGO BOOK OF FRIENDSHIP

Smilingly oblivious to the fact that they are in the mouth of hell. Or as Ava and I call it, the Lair of Cthulhu. Cthulhu is a giant squid monster invented by a horror writer who went insane and died here. And you know what, it makes sense. Because you can feel it when you're walking down the streets beyond the Warren Bubble that this town is a wrong town. Something not quite right about the houses, the trees, the light. Bring this up and most people just look at you. But not Ava. Ava says, *My God, yes. The town, the houses, the trees, the light – it's all fucked.*

I stand here, I sway here, full of tepid sparkling and animal livers and whatever hard alcohol Ava keeps pouring from her Drink Me flask into my plastic cup. 'What's in this again?' I ask.

'Just drink it,' she says.

I observe from behind borrowed sunglasses as the women whom I must call my colleagues reunite after a summer spent apart in various trying locales such as remote tropical islands, the south of France, the Hamptons. I watch their fervent little bodies lunge for each other in something like rapture. Nails the color of natural poisons digging into each other's forearms with the force of what I keep telling myself is feigned, surely feigned, affection. Shiny lips parting to call each other by their communal pet name.

'Jesus, are they for real?' Ava whispers in my ear now. She has never seen them up close. Didn't believe me when I first told her about them last year. Said, *There is no way grown women act like that. You're making this up, Smackie.* Over the summer, I started to think I had too. It is a relief in some ways to see them now, if only to confirm I am not insane.

'Yes,' I say. 'Too real.'

I watch her survey them through her fishnet veil, her David Bowie eyes filled with horror and boredom, her mouth an unimpressed red line.

'Can we go now?'

'I can't leave yet,' I say, my eyes still on them. They've pulled apart from one another at last, their twee dresses not even rumpled. Their shiny heads of hair not even disturbed. Their skins glowing with health insurance as they all crouch down in unison to collectively coo at a professor's ever jumping shih tzu.

'Why?'

'I told you, I have to make an appearance.'

Mona Awad, *Bunny* (2019)

⌒

ESTHER, LIZ AND Alix, who in Jane Austen's day would never have met at all, met in Cambridge in 1952. Just before Christmas, when they were up for interview from their respective schools. Alix was applying to read English Literature, Liz to read Natural Sciences (with a view to medicine) and Esther to read Modern Languages. This should have safely prevented any rapport between them, but did not. There were, it is true, many awkwardnesses in their first communications, for none of them was much used to speaking to strangers, but this lack of practice was balanced by a strong desire on the part of all three of them to enter upon a new life in which speaking to strangers was possible.

Otherwise, each had separately recognised, the future was circumscribed. Somehow, haltingly, over dinner in Hall (chicken, leeks and tinned spaghetti, a mixture delicious to each after years of post-war whale meat and school meals) they lurched into conversation, having found themselves for no good reason sitting together: Liz and Alix discovered that both came from Yorkshire and that neither played lacrosse, nor had ever seen it played, and Esther joined the discussion by volunteering that she had herself managed to avoid playing netball for the past three years on the grounds that she was too small. 'I said I was unfairly handicapped, and they let me do extra Latin instead,' she said. The fact that both Liz and Alix seemed to accept that extra Latin might be preferable to netball indicated that a further interchange might be possible, and they continued to talk, through the fruit tart and custard, of the nature of intellectual and physical education, of matter and spirit, of Descartes (brought up by Alix) and of schizophrenia (brought up by Liz). The matter was abstract, for none of them knew anything other than abstractions, and the tone lofty. It was what they had expected of University, but had not hoped so soon to find. Esther, at the end of the meal, expressed her satisfaction with her new companions by inviting them to go with her to visit a friend already attending the college, an Old Girl of her school. They accepted with alacrity the prospect of a glimpse of the world inside, and all three of them went along dark portrait-hung corridors and up panelled staircases to the room of one Flora Piercy, a second year History student of considerable sophistication, who offered them a glass of wine. Had they known how rare such a commodity was in a woman's college at that date, they might have been even more astonished, but in a sense, looking round Flora's room, with its bright scatter cushions and Picasso prints and posters for plays at the ADC, with its invitations on the mantelpiece, with its gas fire and clutter of shoes, with its romantic piles of what looked like lecture notes and essays, with its candle in a pewter stick and its wilting rose in a vase, they were beyond astonishment. The glass of wine went quickly to each head, for Alix's family were teetotal, and Liz's alcohol consumption to that date comprised perhaps three glasses of brown sherry and one (celebrating her A levels with her teacher) of Liebfraumilch: Esther seemed better connected with drink as with friends, but even she became confiding under the mild influence. They shared their dreams and aspirations, encouraged by the benevolent, admonitory, tutelary spirit of ample broad-faced Flora. 'I would like,' said Liz Ablewhite, after midnight, staring into the white flaming chalky cracked pitted flaring columns of the gas fire, 'to make sense of things. To understand.' By things, she meant herself. Or she thought she meant herself. 'I would like,' said Alix, 'to change things.' By things, she did not mean herself. Or thought she did not mean herself. 'You reach too high,' said Esther. 'I wish to acquire interesting information. That is all.'

Margaret Drabble, *The Radiant Way* (1987)

By these means, I was able to meet Gioconda occasionally in the centre of town. Standing up at a counter we would have coffee, fierce black coffee, a spoonful apiece, served in tiny cold cups that were always wet from the draining board. Or she would take me, on some general's behalf, to a source of tablecloths, or gloves, or tortoise-shell boxes. We made an expedition of that kind one bitter day towards the end of that year, when the Colonel sent me out to find him a genuine Christmas tree to replace the miniature nylon one that had been issued to him. I don't suppose the colonel's commission was as hilarious as it appeared to us, but I remember that Gioconda and I went together to the Via For, where the trees were sold, giggling all the way like schoolgirls and wiping away tears of joy. The slain trees, niggard and meridional, lay about in dismal heaps in a little park there, and we walked round in the cold examining them. A merchant heating his hands over an improvised brazier was astounded by our request for a better specimen, flinging his hands apart then quickly re-aligning them over the coals. He reminded us this was not Canada and advised me to take what was going – which I did, lugging it back to Bagnoli in the Vehicle.

I had not had a female friend since childhood, and novelty made this one the more singular. Perhaps it was something the same for her. At her house, from time to time, I was to meet women she had gone to school with, a relative who lived at Vico Equense, two plump girls, twin sisters, with a curious English name that derived from the Napoleonic wars. She might recount to me a conversation she had had at some dinner party or on the telephone, but the very diversity of these connections suggested that she had no single close friend – no friend, in fact, closer than I.

Shirley Hazzard, *The Bay of Noon* **(1970)**

WHEN BEV FIRST started making friendship advances toward Amy, she was so dogged that Amy thought Bev might want to sleep with her.

Bev wanted *something*, that much was clear. She had been hired at the office where Amy worked a year after Amy started there. Amy had the best prospects for advancement in the editorial department, and all the other assistants knew it. She was the protégée of an editor who was on a hot streak; his books were bestsellers, and his anointed former assistants had all gone on to great things – i.e., they had become full editors before their thirtieth birthdays, which in book publishing was the greatest thing anyone could realistically hope for.

Bev was meek and put-upon; her office clothes were poly-blend jackets and skirts from the part of H&M where you went when, broke, you had to try to dress for the job you wanted. Amy wore Marc by Marc Jacobs blouses (so coveted, in the early aughts) with short sleeves that showed her tattoos. She'd been Bev exactly one year earlier, and for this reason she avoided her as much as possible.

Bev either didn't notice or did notice and still blithely persisted in her attempts to cultivate Amy's friendship. 'Hey,' she said one day while waiting outside Amy's boss's office for his signature on a form attached to a clipboard – Amy's boss was, as usual, on the phone – 'You seem like you might like Sleater-Kinney. I have an extra ticket to the show at Roseland on Thursday. Do you want to go?'

'Um, I have to check,' said Amy, thinking fast. 'My boyfriend and I might be doing something that night.' This was unlikely; Amy's boyfriend at the time was a pot-dealing sometimes musician, and the things they did together didn't tend to require advance planning, because they mostly involved sitting on the couch, smoking joints, and watching pirated DVDs.

'Relax, Amy, I'm not gay,' Bev said, and Amy looked up from her screen, where she'd been pretending to check her Outlook calendar. She was shocked by Bev's perceptiveness. 'I just like Sleater-Kinney. It's possible to like them and be heterosexual. It's not like I invited you to see Tegan and Sara.'

In spite of herself, in spite of her overwhelming desire to maintain her place in the office hierarchy, Amy laughed. 'Okay. Well, but I hope we can still go to the Michigan Womyn's Music Festival Together,' she said, and Bev cracked up. They kept making jokes, eventually devolving into one of those punchy overcaffeinated office gigglefests, until the marketing director, who *was* gay, came out of her office and shot them a dirty look that was kind of a joke but was still mortifying, and then a second later Amy's boss came to the door of his office and, without really looking at either of them, made it clear that he needed Amy to do something other than sit on her ass and chat with Bev. Bev, for her part, grabbed the clipboard off the edge of Amy's cube and rushed into his office, hurriedly explaining its importance. After he'd signed it, Bev scurried back out of his office, but not before depositing the Sleater-Kinney ticket, which she'd had in her blazer pocket the whole time, in Amy's in-box, as if it were just another interoffice form or letter to file.

*

It was nine o'clock. Without quite realizing what she was doing, she dialed Bev's number. They weren't yet the kind of friends who called each other out of the blue for no reason, so Amy was relieved when Bev picked up.

'Hi! How did the move go? You must be exhausted.'

'Oh, the movers did most of it. I just carried the little stuff, the breakable stuff. The real nightmare is unpacking, of course.'

'Want me to come over and help?'

'No! I mean, don't help. I don't want to do any more tonight, and I wouldn't inflict that on you. But do come over! I mean, if you want.'

Fifteen minutes later, Bev was standing at Amy's door with a bottle of wine and a paper bag full of take-out sushi. 'I had just ordered this, but I always order enough for two people,' she explained. Her hair was in shiny plaits, making her look even more innocent than usual, like a milkmaid on an antique can label. Amy felt a pang of gratitude so extreme that tears briefly, unnoticeably came to her eyes.

They ate the sushi and drank the wine on a little ledge of roof they could crawl to from Amy's fire escape, which the broker who'd shown Amy the apartment had described as a 'deck'. Rotting fallen leaves clotted one corner and made the hot summer air smell more like the woods and less like car exhaust. They balanced the plastic trays of spicy tuna rolls on their laps and looked out at the cars on the BQE and, beyond that, the storage warehouses, the Navy Yard, and, across the East River, Manhattan, just visible between the nearby buildings, skyscrapers with all their lights on, wastefully twinkling.

Soon the sushi was gone and they were on their third plastic cups of wine. Amy felt almost too tired to talk, so she listened to Bev, who was telling her about the last terrible thing her boss had done:

'It wasn't even that she claimed credit for my work. I mean, that's what I'm there for, I'm her assistant. It was that she wanted me to continue the fiction when we weren't even in the meeting anymore, when we were just alone in her office. She wanted me to congratulate her on the great idea she'd had for the subtitle! If I felt like being really self-destructive, I'd have called her out on it, but it's just not worth it. She'd just pretend she had no idea what I was talking about, and then she'd be angry at me for a week and take it out on me by deliberately leaving me off some crucial scheduling email, then having a screaming fit when she arrived at the wrong restaurant to have lunch with Marcia Gay Harden or whatever C-lister she's currently courting.'

'I think you should call her out on it, regardless of the consequences. If you don't assert yourself, if you just keep being the world's best assistant, you'll never get promoted,' Amy said.

'If my boss despises me, I'll never get promoted.'

'Ahh, a catch-twenty-two.'

Bev pulled out a pack of Camel Lights, Amy's favorite brand of cigarettes. Neither of them really smoked, but when Bev pretend smoked, she bought Parliaments. The Camels were another kind gesture on her part, like the wine and the sushi. They lit cigarettes and smoked with exaggerated seriousness, enjoying the ritual of the burst of flame, the first puff of smoke dissipating into the night air.

'I have something I need to ask you, and I'm afraid it'll be awkward,' Bev said, speaking quickly. They were still facing the highway, not looking at each other, but Amy snuck a glance at Bev's face. Bev seemed tense but resolute.

'Okay, what is it?'

'Well, you know, growing up where I did, I was often considered kind of an odd duck. I mean, I wasn't a total social reject. I always had a couple of people to, like, eat lunch with in the cafeteria, but I definitely never had a best friend, and I'm not sure how it works.'

'How what works?'

'Like, becoming best friends. Do you have to say something, confirming that you're best friends?'

'Are you asking me whether we're best friends?'

'Well, yeah. I assume you've had a best friend before, so you know, generally, how it goes.'

Amy thought about it for a second. 'I've had close friends, for sure. But mostly I've had boyfriends. You always think they're your best friend, but that's obviously bullshit.'

'Yeah. If you're having sex with someone, they're not your best friend.'

Their cigarettes were almost done; Amy poured a little bit of wine into one of the empty plastic soy sauce cups and stubbed hers out in this makeshift ashtray so as not to further befoul her new deck. 'Is this . . . are we having the DTR conversation?'

'The . . . wait, let me guess what it stands for. Determining . . . No. Defining? Defining The Relationship?'

'Yeah!' said Amy.

'Yeah, we are. Sorry, I just . . . Look, it's okay if you don't feel the same way. But you're my best friend. And I guess I just wanted you to know that. No pressure! Ha!'

Bev's tone was casual, but when Amy stole another glance in her direction, she looked pained.

'Bev, of course you're my best friend. It wouldn't have occurred to me to say anything, but you are, for sure. I'd be lost without you. Like tonight, for example. I would have died of starvation, or gotten a second wind and tried to unpack boxes and then died of exhaustion. Or I would have gotten paranoid and barricaded the door with my one stick of furniture. Before you came over, I was feeling so unsafe here. Not for any good reason, but just because I felt alone. And now that you've been here, even when you go home, I won't feel that way. I feel safe now because someone knows where I am and gives a fuck.'

'And it won't change when you get a new boyfriend?'

'No. Will it change when you get a new boyfriend?'

'No, and anyway, it's impossible to imagine that happening.'

Amy shook the wine bottle, determined that there was still a little bit left, and divided it equally between their glasses. 'Well, we're still relatively young, you know? I'm sure all kinds of unimaginable things will happen.'

Emily Gould, *Friendship* (2014)

NELLIE STRETCHED HER legs out and said a perfect friendship was a fine thing. Had Caroline ever had a friend?

'I had plenty of friends, at school and in the church, everywhere. Dozens I suppose if you count them all.'

Nellie said earnestly that was not what she meant, 'You can't have dozens of friends. You can only have one, one true friend. Have you never had a true friend?'

'Oh, yes, when I was about eighteen I had one. We used to take long walks together. We were both interested in serious questions. She was lovely: so true.'

'And she was your true friend, pet?'

'We got on because we weren't too close and weren't alike. That's best. Our lives ran parallel and never met: no friction. And she's loyal and so am I.'

'Ah, no, your lives didn't run parallel; they met.'

'No, my life never met anyone's until I met Barry, my husband. He was more like a best friend. I was very happy. I knew the risk I was taking coming home.'

She paused and Nellie waited. Caroline continued, 'We live through everything. Sometimes I think life is a strange disease that attacks different people in different ways; and at different ages it attacks you differently.'

'Aye, but with a true friend you can fight off that disease; you can hold on to the true solution, the cure.'

'What's the cure?' Caroline laughed sadly.

'There are two, sweetheart: love, and death.'

'Oh, both those are diseases, too.'

'Ah, you're depressed, love. You see, you never understood what friendship is. The friendship at school and at church, that's good; but it's the loaf of bread; it's not the wine.'

Nellie went on in a sweet thin craven tone, asking if Caroline thought they could be friends.

'You're missing something if you haven't a friend.'

'But we are friends, aren't we? I know it's early.'

'It's early for an ordinary companionship, aye; but where there's a genuine basis, it ought to begin at once. It only needs an act of willing and knowing. Would you say we couldn't be friends now?'

Caroline looked at her, still puzzled.

Nellie went on in a dreamy coaxing tone, 'It's no good playing the ascetic, no; the thick armour of self-sufficiency which you have, pet, covers a wound, a scar is there. Self-knowledge must be struggled for. Confess what you know, confess what you don't know. You need a friend for that, to tell your inmost secrets to.'

'I'll tell you the truth,' said Caroline and paused.

'Ah, now, that's better: let's be frank.'

'I've written to Barry, but had no reply. He never caused me any pain. I feel quite sensible now. It was harmony with him, as you say. If he is free, I would go there now.'

She looked at Nellie as if she had told her the whole story.

Nellie said, 'Then there's no hope for us as friends?'

'Why not?'

Caroline looked at her eccentric face and topknot and the glasses standing before her sympathetically. She added, with warmth, 'You know, I think it is you who don't know about friendship. For a woman the best friend is a man. There's no deeper feeling.'

Nellie cried in a rage, 'That's a damn hypocritical superior attitude. I won't take it from you or anyone else. So women are second-class citizens. Like families in slums who need housing. Subjects for pity!'

Caroline sat up in angry astonishment.

Nellie cried, 'So that's it. Women are inferior, incapable of friendship. Of all the goddamn backward bourgeois attitudes. A woman's not the equal of a man. I resent it. You can't put that over on me. So we're second-class citizens to you.'

Caroline said indignantly, 'Well, if it seems that way to you.'

'You see what a bourgeois you are? The superiority feeling in everything! You're incapable of a decent human relation with another woman.'

Caroline did not reply.

Nellie began to lament, 'You see how contorted your attitudes are? You're formed by the middle-class marriage hunt; man first, last and always. Aren't you ashamed, a little ashamed? Ashamed to put your sisters on such a level?'

'I can't see what you mean. If Barry answers, he will be all to me.'

'That's a terrible confession.'

Caroline said, 'A confession?'

'A confession; a terrible confession.'

'Of what?'

'Of weakness, inferiority, of needing the superior conquering sex.'

Caroline began to laugh weakly, 'You make everything so unusual. I want to get married again; that's all. I'm glad to have some women friends.'

She felt she had hurt Nellie and added, 'We were brought up so differently.'

'Yes, we were. I was not brought up with pretty pictures
painted on me eyelids.'

'If you're my friend, shouldn't you try to understand me?'

Nellie said bitterly, 'I understand you very well . . .'.

Christina Stead, *Cotters' England* (1966)

EVERYTHING SHE HAD was mine, she said. I could wear
any of her clothes anytime, without asking first. I could
use her telephone whenever I liked – if the conversation was
private, I should just tell her and she'd go and wait in the
hall. I could use the stereo anytime, too, and play any of her
records I liked.

Whatever she owned, I could borrow. Whatever she had
was mine, too.

I did not touch her clothes, most of which would have been
too small for me anyway. I did not use her phone, and though
the records were too much temptation for me to resist, I
played them only when she wasn't there, and afterward was
careful to make it look as if nothing had been touched.

Her class schedule was taped to her desk. I learned by
heart the hours when she would be out. Other times, if
I didn't have class myself, I'd arrange to be elsewhere.
Evenings, after dinner, instead of going back to our room,
I would hang out in the room of some friends down the
hall or in one of the common rooms. There was a TV room
and a room called the Quiet Study, and both were usually
empty. I would spend hours there, neither watching TV nor

studying (I would do almost no studying that semester), but daydreaming (I was a champion daydreamer in those days) or reading magazines or writing letters to good old high school friends whom I missed and with whom, I could already tell – it was part of the abiding homesickness of that first year – I would soon lose touch. Or I would write in the journal I had started keeping that summer, which, when I read it years later, would be charged with the same sense of loss, itself like a letter to someone on the point of vanishing, my own adolescent self.

When, finally, I would go to our room, it was often late. And no matter how late it was, I would always find Ann awake, as if she had been waiting up for me. She was usually reading when I came in the door, and she would close her book and smile at me – shyly, but without trying to hide how glad she was to see me. She would put on some music, her beloved Simon and Garfunkel, or Billie Holiday or Bob Dylan, and we would get ready for bed. She would stand in front of her dresser mirror and set her hair. ('Oh, I *wish* I could wear an Afro!') And while she was setting her hair, we would talk. Or more precisely, she would talk, rattling on without stopping for breath, as if she had been waiting all day for this moment, for me to come home and hear every detail about her courses, her parents, and her period.

Once the lights were out, the talk would go on, even if it was well past midnight and we both had early morning classes. It might go on as long as an hour or two. It might go on till dawn. And it was not just us; all up and down those halls, roommates were awake far into the night. (*And somebody's eyes must meet the dawn* – Dylan.) And it was during these times that my guard slipped, my resistance cracked – I was tired, after all – and something about the lateness and the music and Ann's hushed voice – I would picture her thin, thin lips moving in the dark – cast a spell on me.

I say *spell* because in fact the more Ann talked, the more I wanted to hear her.

Sigrid Nunez, *The Last of Her Kind* (2006)

'DRAW UP,' SAID Mrs Briggs. 'I'll mash the tea. I always mash it myself, you know, because I can't trust them girls. The stuff they send in on a Sunday! You wouldn't believe.' She bustled happily with caddy and kettle, her cheeks faintly pink.

If Jane had expected afternoon-tea such as she read about in the fashion papers, she was not to experience it at Glenroyd. But it was more heartening to see luscious tinned peaches decorated with turrets of whipped cream, and plates of all kinds of bread: white, brown and currant bread; and all kinds of home made cakes: rock-buns, jumbles, parkin.

'I had a bit of a bake this morning,' explained Mrs Briggs. 'They don't like me being in the kitchen, but I was determined to give you a proper tea, because I don't suppose you get overmuch to eat where you are. Mrs Chadwick looks as if she'd skimp you a bit.'

A dish of sausages, accompanied by bread sauce, was here brought in, and Jane began on a meal such as she had not eaten for many a year.

'Now you must make a good tea,' said her hostess, creaking over to push one loaded plate after another towards Jane.

'Oh, I shall,' said Jane, her young teeth making a vigorous crescent in a piece of oven-bottom cake.

She was happy, warm and comfortable, and so was Mrs Briggs. As the meal progressed, they became communicative. Jane told Mrs Briggs all about herself, her dead parents, her stepmother, Alice and Eddy, how she came to Chadwick's, about Maggie and Wilfrid, and Mrs Briggs was just in the middle of her account of Albert, Willy and Lizzie and Peggy, and Michael and Baby, when the door opened. Mrs Briggs looked up and her face changed. All its comfort fell away.

'Oh, Albert . . .' she faltered. 'Have you come home? You're early, aren't you?'

Mr Briggs ignored her and stared at Jane. He did not remember his wife having anybody to tea before.

'You'd better introduce me, Martha,' he said, heavily gallant.

'It's Miss Carter, Albert. From Mr Chadwick's, the draper's.'

'How d'you do?' said Albert, nodding. A shop-girl. Funny how they managed to make themselves look like ladies nowadays.

He walked to the fire and watched them from the hearthrug.

Mrs Briggs and Jane made a pretence of going on with tea. Mrs Briggs moved things aimlessly about and nibbled at her bread-and-butter. Jane could not avoid a view of Mr Briggs from her place. His fingers were like pale sausages, she thought; and she thought he must suffer from what she had heard of, but never before seen: 'A dropped stomach,' she said to herself, getting through her piece of parkin under his eye. 'A dropped stomach, obviously. And no manners,' she added, beginning to blush.

She was moved to this criticism because he embarrassed her, and because she felt Mrs Briggs was afraid of him. Perhaps not afraid, but anxious and embarrassed, too, in his presence.

'You'll be wanting your tea, Albert,' said Mrs Briggs. 'I'll just get Lucy to see to it.'

'Ring the bell, then,' said Albert, testily. 'You've no need to go into the kitchen about it.'

'No,' said Mrs Briggs, ringing the bell obediently. 'It won't be long. I dare say it's laid ready in the dining-room. You see, I didn't expect you home yet,' she apologised.

Her face was wistful. Her little entertainment of her new friend was spoiled. She looked round in bewilderment. What could they do, now he had made a third?

'I must be going,' said Jane.

Mrs Briggs seemed to think it would be best.

'You must come again,' she whispered on the way upstairs. 'He isn't home as early as this not once in six months. It's a pity it just happened like that today. But I've enjoyed our chat,' she said, brightening. 'You will come again, won't you?'

She went to the front door with her guest, looking round with some anxiety in case Albert caught her usurping the office of the parlourmaid.

'Goodbye, love. That is a pretty hat. You look like – eh, I

don't know what! But just what I should've liked my girl to look like, if she'd lived. I've only Willy now, you know, and he's married and doing very well, so I don't see much of him. Goodbye, and you will come again, won't you?'

On a sudden impulse, Jane proffered her lips to Mrs Briggs. They kissed. They were, inexplicably, friends: warm friends.

Jane went down the drive, winking away a slight, and, she sternly judged, absurd mist of tears. Poor Mrs Briggs! The house was far too grand for her; the husband and the son, too grand. It was obvious Mrs Briggs did not take kindly to grandeur. She suffered in it.

Dorothy Whipple, *High Wages* (1930)

SHE SAT ON the floor – that was her first impression of Sally – she sat on the floor with her arms round her knees, smoking a cigarette. Where could it have been? The Mannings'? The Kinloch-Jones's? At some party (where, she could not be certain), for she had a distinct recollection of saying to the man she was with, 'Who is *that*?' And he had told her, and said that Sally's parents did not get on (how that shocked her – that one's parents should quarrel). But all that evening she could not take her eyes off Sally. It was an extraordinary beauty of the kind she most admired, dark, large-eyed, with that quality which, since she hadn't got it herself, she always envied – a sort of abandonment, as if she could say anything, do anything: a quality much commoner in foreigners than in Englishwomen. Sally always said she had French blood in her veins, an ancestor had been with Marie Antoinette, had his head cut off, left a ruby ring . . . They sat up till all hours of the night talking. Sally it was who made her feel, for the first time, how sheltered life at Bourton was. She knew nothing about sex – nothing about social problems. She had once seen an old man who had dropped dead in a field – she had seen cows just after their calves were born. But Aunt Helena never liked discussion of anything (when Sally gave her William Morris, it had to be wrapped in brown paper). There they sat, hour after hour, talking in her bedroom at the top of the house, talking about life, how they were to reform the world. They meant to found a society to abolish private property, and actually had a letter written, though not sent out. The ideas were Sally's, of course – but very soon she was just as excited – read Plato in bed before breakfast; read Morris; read Shelley by the hour.

Sally's power was amazing, her gift, her personality. There was her way with flowers, for instance. At Bourton they always had stiff little vases all the way down the table. Sally went out, picked hollyhocks, dahlias – all sorts of flowers that had never been seen together – cut their heads off, and made them swim on top of water in bowls. The effect was extraordinary – coming in to dinner in the sunset. (Of course Aunt Helena thought it wicked to treat flowers like that.) Then she forgot her sponge, and ran along the passage naked. That grim old housemaid, Ellen Atkins, went about grumbling – 'Suppose any of the gentlemen had seen?' Indeed she did shock people. She was untidy, Papa said.

The strange thing, looking back, was the purity, the

integrity, of her feeling for Sally. It was not like one's feeling for a man. It was completely disinterested, and besides, it had a quality which could only exist between women, between women just grown up. It was protective, on her side; sprang from a sense of being in league together, a presentiment of something that was bound to part them (they spoke of marriage always as a catastrophe), which led to this chivalry, this protective feeling which was much more on her side than Sally's. For in those days she was completely reckless; did the most idiotic things out of bravado; bicycled round the parapet on the terrace; smoked cigars. Absurd, she was – very absurd. But the charm was overpowering, to her at least, so that she could remember standing in her bedroom at the top of the house holding the hot-water can in her hands and saying out loud, 'She is beneath this roof . . . She is beneath this roof!'

Virginia Woolf, *Mrs Dalloway* (1925)

4

CONFESSIONS, CLOSENESS, CONTRASTING CHARACTERS

The two friends talked every night. Not for many years had the spare room walls heard such animation. Mary had received many confidences; it was part of her business in life. To impart, to confide herself was an unfamiliar delight.

F. M. Mayor, *The Rector's Daughter* (1924)

Elaine Dundy ∼ *Sarah Waters* ∼ *George Eliot* ∼ *Tessa Hadley*
Doris Lessing ∼ *George Gissing* ∼ *F. M. Mayor*
Winifred Holtby ∼ *Elizabeth von Arnim*

Our friends are mirrors, not mirror images: the more clearly we see them, the more clearly we see ourselves; we must accept them, faults and all, just as we must accept our own flaws and failings. Fun, I think, is quite often the result of being led astray, of accepting a certain kind of dare; encouragement comes in many guises. But all this – closeness – is complicated. As Susie Orbach and Luise Eichenbaum point out in their book about female friendships, *Bittersweet*, there is an inevitable tension between autonomy and connectedness. 'A woman knows herself and gathers her sense of self through her connection and sense of attachment to others,' they write. Independence, in the eyes of Orbach and Eichenbaum, isn't necessarily straightforward. On some very deep level, we may not believe it's possible to be a separate person, with our own thoughts and desires, and still receive the love and support of others.

Perhaps this idea is somewhat outmoded now. *Bittersweet* was published in 1987; even as so many feminist gains have been made, friendship has never been more central to our culture. But still, it seems to me that both intimacy and difference are essential to the deepest, most mutually beneficial relationships, and that the two must somehow be kept in balance. Disagreements have their place, but so does the whispering of secrets. When – if – important information is withheld, the friendship may ultimately be imperilled; a friend can often sense, even if they cannot quite see it, the gauze that is non-disclosure.

JUDY WAS SO different from me that it was really ludicrous. Whereas I was hell-bent for living, she was content, at least for the time being, to leave all that to others. Just as long as she could *hear* about it. She really was funny about this. Folded every which way on the floor, looking like Bambi – all eyes and legs and no chin – she would listen for ages and ages with rapt attention to absolutely any drivel that you happened to be talking. It was unbelievable.

'And *then* what did you do?' she would ask with real avidity at the end of a dreary, over-long and absolutely pointless anecdote.

Elaine Dundy, *The Dud Avocado* (1958)

HER EXPRESSION, NOW, was so stripped, so solemn, Helen reached and touched her arm. 'Viv,' she said. 'You look so awfully sad.'

Viv grew self-conscious again. She coloured, and laughed. 'Oh, don't mind me. I've been feeling a bit sorry for myself lately, that's all.'

'What's the matter? Aren't you happy?'

'Happy?' Viv blinked. 'I don't know. Is anybody happy? Really happy, I mean? People pretend they are.'

'I don't know either,' said Helen, after a moment. 'Happiness is such a fragile sort of thing these days. It's as though there's only so much to go around.'

'As if it's on the ration.'

Helen smiled. 'Yes, exactly! And so you know, when you've got some, that it's going to run out soon; and that keeps you from enjoying it, you're too busy wondering how you're going to feel when it's all gone. Or you start thinking about the person who's had to go without so that you can have your portion.'

Her own mood sank, as she thought this. She began picking at blisters of paint on the metal platform, exposing fibres of rust beneath. She went on quietly, 'Maybe it's right, after all, what the newspaper prophets say: that one gets paid back in the way one deserves. Maybe we've all forfeited our right to happiness, by doing bad things, or by letting bad things happen.'

She look at Viv. They'd never spoken to each other quite so freely before, and she realised, as if for the first time, just how fond she was of Viv, and how much she liked doing this – just this – sitting out here, talking, on this rusting metal platform. And she thought of something else. *Were you friends with Julia then?* Viv had asked lightly, before – as if it were the most natural thing in the world that Helen should have been; as if it were perfectly normal that Helen should have stayed in London, in a war, for a woman's sake . . .

Her heart began to beat faster. She wanted, suddenly, to be able to confide in Viv. She wanted to, desperately! She wanted to say, *Listen to me, Viv. I'm in love with Julia! It's a marvellous thing, but terrible, too. Sometimes it makes a sort of child of me. Sometimes it feels like it's almost killing me! It leaves me helpless. It makes me afraid! I can't control it! Can that be right? Is it like this with other people? Has it ever been like this, with you?*

She felt her breath rising, until it seemed trapped in her chest. Her heart was beating wildly now, in her cheeks and fingertips. 'Viv—' she started.

But Viv had turned away. She'd put her hands to the pockets of her cardigan and, 'Oh heck,' she said. 'I've left my cigs inside. I'll never get through the afternoon without one.' She started to rise, seizing hold of the rail of the platform and making the whole thing rock. She said, 'Will you give me a push-up?'

Helen got to her feet more quickly. 'I'm closer,' she said. 'I'll get them.'

'Are you sure?'

'Yes, of course. It'll only take a moment.'

Her breath still seemed to be crushed in her chest. She clambered awkwardly over the sill and landed with a thud beside the lavatory. There was still time, she thought, to say something. She wanted to more than ever now. And a cigarette would steady her nerves. She straightened her skirt. Viv called through the window: 'They're in my handbag!'

Sarah Waters, *The Night Watch* (2006)

'WHAT A BROWN patch I am by the side of you, Rosy! You are the most unbecoming companion.'

'Oh no! No one thinks of your appearance, you are so sensible and useful, Mary. Beauty is of very little consequence in reality,' said Rosamond, turning her head towards Mary, but with eyes swerving towards the new view of her neck in the glass.

'You mean *my* beauty,' said Mary, rather sardonically.

Rosamond thought, 'Poor Mary, she takes the kindest things ill.'

Aloud she said, 'What have you been doing lately?'

'I? Oh, minding the house – pouring out syrup – pretending to be amiable and contented – learning to have a bad opinion of everybody.'

'It is a wretched life for you.'

'No,' said Mary, curtly, with a little toss of her head. 'I think my life is pleasanter than your Miss Morgan's.'

'Yes; but Miss Morgan is so uninteresting, and not young.'

'She is interesting to herself, I suppose; and I am not at all sure that everything gets easier as one gets older.'

'No,' said Rosamond, reflectively; 'one wonders what such people do, without any prospect. To be sure, there is religion as a support. But,' she added, dimpling, 'it is very different with you, Mary. You may have an offer.'

'Has anyone told you he means to make me one?'

'Of course not. I mean, there is a gentleman who may fall in love with you, seeing you almost every day.'

A certain change in Mary's face was chiefly determined by the resolve not to show any change.

'Does that always make people fall in love?' she answered, carelessly; 'It seems to me quite as often a reason for detesting each other.'

'Not when they are interesting and agreeable. I hear that Mr Lydgate is both.'

'Oh, Mr Lydgate!' said Mary, with an unmistakable lapse

into indifference. 'You want to know something about him,' she added, not choosing to indulge Rosamond's indirectness.

'Merely, how you like him.'

'There is no question of liking at present. My liking always wants some little kindness to kindle it. I am not magnanimous enough to like people who speak to me without seeming to see me.'

'Is he so haughty?' said Rosamond, with heightened satisfaction. 'You know that he is of good family?'

'No; he did not give that as a reason.'

'Mary! You are the oddest girl. But what sort of looking man is he? Describe him to me.'

'How can one describe a man? I can give you an inventory: heavy eyebrows, dark eyes, a straight nose, thick dark hair, large solid white hands – and – let me see – oh, an exquisite cambric pocket handkerchief. But you will see him. You know this is about the time of his visits.'

Rosamond blushed a little, but said, meditatively, 'I rather like a haughty manner. I cannot endure a rattling young man.'

'I did not tell you that Mr Lydgate was haughty; but *il y en a pour tous les goûts*, as little Mamselle used to say, and if any girl can choose the particular sort of conceit she would like, I should think it is you, Rosy.'

'Haughtiness is not conceit; I call Fred conceited.'

'I wish no one said any worse of him. He should be more careful. Mrs. Waule has been telling uncle that Fred is very unsteady.' Mary spoke from a girlish impulse which got the better of her judgment. There was a vague uneasiness associated with the word 'unsteady' which she hoped Rosamond might say something to dissipate. But she purposely abstained from mentioning Mrs. Waule's more special insinuation.

'Oh, Fred is horrid!' said Rosamond. She would not have allowed herself so unsuitable a word to anyone but Mary.

'What do you mean by horrid?'

'He is so idle, and makes papa so angry, and says he will not take orders.'

'I think Fred is quite right.'

'How can you say he is quite right, Mary? I thought you had more sense of religion.'

'He is not fit to be a clergyman.'

'But he ought to be fit.'

'Well, then, he is not what he ought to be. I know some other people who are in the same case.'

'But no one approves of them. I should not like to marry a clergyman; but there must be clergymen.'

'It does not follow that Fred must be one.'

'But when papa has been at the expense of educating him for it! And only suppose, if he should have no fortune left him?'

'I can suppose that very well,' said Mary, dryly.

'Then I wonder you can defend Fred,' said Rosamond, inclined to push this point.

'I don't defend him,' said Mary, laughing; 'I would defend any parish from having him for a clergyman.'

'But of course if he were a clergyman, he must be different.'

'Yes, he would be a great hypocrite; and he is not that yet.'

'It is of no use saying anything to you, Mary. You always take Fred's part.'

'Why should I not take his part?' said Mary, lighting up. 'He would take mine. He is the only person who takes the least trouble to oblige me.'

'You make me feel very uncomfortable, Mary,' said Rosamond, with her gravest mildness; 'I would not tell mamma for the whole world.'

'Why would you not tell her?' said Mary, angrily.

'Pray do not go into a rage, Mary,' said Rosamond, mildly as ever.

'If your mamma is afraid that Fred will make me an offer, tell her that I would not marry him if he asked me. But he is not going to do so, that I am aware. He certainly has never asked me.'

'Mary, you are always so violent.'

'And you are always so exasperating.'

'I? What can you blame me for?'

'Oh, blameless people are always the most exasperating. There is the bell – I think we must go down.'

'I did not mean to quarrel,' said Rosamond, putting on her hat.

'Quarrel? Nonsense; we have not quarrelled. If one is not to get into a rage sometimes, what is the good of being friends?'

George Eliot, *Middlemarch* **(1871–72)**

THEY WERE DRINKING China tea with lemon, in Lydia's room; sitting cross-legged on her unmade bed, in a

THE VIRAGO BOOK OF FRIENDSHIP

crumpled scarlet silk kimono, her eyes painted with kohl, she waved a cigarette about between her fingertips in the affected way she had, puffing at it superficially. Lydia could make Christine feel very unworldly. She was unworldly in those days: tall and thin and oblivious, with a rope of light brown hair coiled round her head like a caricature of an old-fashioned lady scholar, though she was only twenty-two; she rode an old bicycle round everywhere, with her books in the front basket, kicking off with one foot from the pavement then sitting very upright on the saddle, almost comically upright, in dense London traffic. Christine had grown up in London, she was perfectly at ease in the city, yet she lived there somehow as if she was in exile from a more stately, slower world. There was something virginal about her, although she wasn't literally a virgin. Lydia envied her friend's calm self-possession: she couldn't ride a bike, couldn't imagine ever making her way so unprotected and trusting through the city traffic.

– So what's his wife like? Christine asked, concerned.

– One of those miniature doll-bodies, dyed black hair, parchment skin, nervous. I should think she was a child-bride. Juliet by name, Juliet by nature. Apparently she's an actress. Going out of her mind looking after the kid all day while Alex writes his poetry.

– Does he write poetry?

– He has a book of poems coming out. He's a genius of course.

Lydia never hesitated when she was pronouncing judgements in her flat, hard little girl's voice – though afterwards she would laugh at herself, at her own excesses. The friends had felt such relief at finding each other's irony when they first met at their girls' grammar school – each had feared she was the only unbeliever. Lydia doubted everything. It was almost a disappointment to Christine that Lydia had fallen heavily in love at last: it had always been the boys who pursued her, while she kept aloof. And Alex wasn't supposed to be Lydia's type – she had claimed that she hated intellectuals, so awkward and so self-important. Her boyfriends until now had been the pretty boys she met in clubs, or at the bar where she worked: lithe and skinny, with bleached hair or wearing eye make-up, hard and dangerous. When these boys took furtive calls on the house phone, monosyllabic or coaxing, Christine thought they might be dealing drugs. She had kept herself apart from this aspect of Lydia's life – not because she disapproved of it, but because she was shy, and afraid that the boys would despise her plummy accent, her good manners.

Lydia felt herself at some crisis, now they'd arrived at the end of their formal education. Dissent and scepticism had been easy while they were held tight inside its frame – now something more was called for, and she dreaded testing her reserves of imagination and energy, finding them empty. At first she had played at falling in love with Alex because it gave a shape to her days, and a motivation: then her obsession had swallowed up its original purpose. Her lack of him gnawed at her, making her incomplete; she thought fatalistically that if she had any talent it was probably for this, for a destructive passion. Lydia had the biggest room in the shared house, with the biggest bed – where she slept sprawling luxuriantly in dirty sheets, rarely getting up before midday. Her room was chaotically untidy, with clothes heaped on every piece of furniture, or dropped on the floor where she'd taken them off. She had a gift for finding treasures – old couture silks and satins, stiff net petticoats – among the dross in junk shops; everything smelled of mothballs, or of beer and cigarette smoke from the bar.

The whole house was a semi-ruin and they lived in it like children camping, playing at grown-up life. Christine's room on the ground floor was half the size of Lydia's and chilly, with a greenish light she loved: its French windows opened onto a ruined conservatory and overgrown garden. It was in this green-lit room that Christine pored over her books of poetry, making notes, working in the evenings in the light from her desk lamp, hearing the subdued frisson of rain on the leaves in the garden at her back. The male teachers at the university had tried to dissuade her, saying Rossetti's verse was too flimsy, wouldn't bear up to that level of sustained attention. She persevered, but not without self-doubt. If Lydia had a night off from bar-work, then Christine would take a tray of tea things up to her room at the end of the evening. Lydia would have been reading too: the whole house would seem charged with their separate concentration, their silence. But Lydia read so differently: always novels, not poetry, devouring them one after another, classics and contemporary fiction and thrillers muddled in together, opening up something new almost as soon as she'd finished reading the last words of the previous one. While she read she was utterly absorbed, then she closed the books mostly without comment, or with a snap judgement uttered with finality: *dull*, or *excellent*. Christine would pick up the book and puzzle into its pages, worrying over so many words.

– But *why* is it dull?

– The heroine had such a silly name.

As soon as she'd finished her last university exam, Lydia had stopped thinking about books in the critical language she'd had to learn for her degree; yet in her exams she'd done very well, almost as well as Christine. She spoke about that critical analysis as if it was a trick you could put on or off, for strategic purposes; this was bruising to Christine, who was betting her future on analysis. But then she was used to being bruised by Lydia, she didn't mind. Christine had had such a happy childhood, she'd been so encouraged, she had a lot to make up for. Lydia's family were perfectly all right too: her parents ran a pub. Only they were very interested in their daughter's cleverness, and wondered why she didn't get a proper job. When she won a free place at grammar school they'd supposed she might become a businesswoman, or a lawyer. Christine was in awe of Lydia's parents because in those days she romanticised the working classes, so they thought that Lydia's inseparable friend was stand-offish. And certainly didn't think of themselves as working class.

The friends had met in a long look of shared incredulity at their first school Founder's Commemoration Day, across so many submissive heads bowed in prayer, the muddy tide of voices obediently murmuring forms of words learned by rote. It wasn't that they were naughty: other girls who believed everything the school told them were far naughtier. Christine Drinkwater and Lydia Smith had the subversive earnestness of true dissenters. They pinned on the noticeboard newspaper articles denouncing the evils of private education, they boycotted the Form Charity – which was always for animals. Christine was drawn to Lydia's concentrated energy, which wasn't turned outward but was like something unrealised, burning with a slow heat inside her. Her daring negativity opened up possibilities, promised adventures.

Tessa Hadley, *Late in the Day* **(2019)**

'IT'S A PLEASURE,' said Anna. 'But do you know something? I discovered while you were away that for a lot of people you and I are practically interchangeable.'

'You've only just understood that?' said Molly, triumphant as always when Anna came up with – as far as she was concerned – facts that were self-evident.

In this relationship a balance had been struck early on: Molly was altogether more worldly-wise than Anna who, for her part, had a superiority of talent.

Anna held her own private views. Now she smiled, admitting that she had been very slow.

'When we're so different in every way,' said Molly, 'it's odd. I suppose because we both live the same kind of life – not getting married and so on. That's all they see.'

'Free women,' said Anna, wryly. She added, with an anger new to Molly, so that she earned another quick scrutinising glance from her friend: 'They still define us in terms of relationships with men, even the best of them.'

'Well, we do, don't we?' said Molly, rather tart. 'Well, it's awfully hard not to,' she amended, hastily, because of the look of surprise Anna now gave her. There was a short pause, during which the women did not look at each other but reflected that a year apart was a long time, even for an old friendship.

Molly said at last, sighing: 'Free. Do you know, when I was away, I was thinking about us, and I've decided that we're a completely new type of woman. We must be, surely?'

'There's nothing new under the sun,' said Anna, in an attempt at a German accent. Molly, irritated – she spoke half a dozen languages well – said: 'There's nothing new under the sun,' in a perfect reproduction of a shrewd old woman's voice, German accented.

Anna grimaced, acknowledging failure. She could not learn languages, and was too self-conscious ever to become somebody else: for a moment Molly had even looked like Mother Sugar, otherwise Mrs Marks, to whom both had gone for psycho-analysis. The reservations both had felt about the solemn and painful ritual were expressed by the pet name, 'Mother Sugar'; which, as time passed, became a name for much more than a person, and indicated a whole way of looking at life – traditional, rooted, conservative, in spite of its scandalous familiarity with everything amoral. *In spite of* – that was how Anna and Molly, discussing the ritual, had felt it; recently Anna had been feeling more and more it was *because of*; and this was one of the things she was looking forward to discussing with her friend.

Doris Lessing, ***The Golden Notebook*** **(1962)**

THE VISITORS TOOK their leave at about five o'clock.
'Poor things! Poor things!' sighed Miss Barfoot, when
she was alone with her friend. 'What can we possibly do for
the older ones?'

'They are excellent creatures,'* said Rhoda. 'Kind, innocent women; but useful for nothing except what they have
done all their lives. The eldest can't teach seriously, but she
can keep young children out of mischief and give them a nice
way of speaking. Her health is breaking down, you can see.'

'Poor woman! One of the saddest types.'

'Decidedly. Virginia isn't quite so depressing – but how
childish!'

'They all strike me as childish. Monica is a dear little girl;
it seemed a great absurdity to talk to her about business. Of
course she must find a husband.'

'I suppose so.'

Rhoda's tone of slighting condescension amused her
companion.

'My dear, after all we don't desire the end of the race.'

'No, I suppose not,' Rhoda admitted with a laugh.

'A word of caution. Your zeal is eating you up. At this
rate, you will hinder our purpose. We have no mission to
prevent girls from marrying suitably – only to see that those
who can't shall have a means of living with some satisfaction.'

---

* George Gissing's novel, *The Odd Women*, tells the story of five unmarried
women: Alice, Monica and Virginia Madden have been reduced to poverty by
the death of their father; Rhoda Nunn, a New Woman, and her older friend,
Mary Barfoot, who is independently wealthy, have vowed to devote their
lives to helping young women find independence. Here, Rhoda and Mary,
friends who have different temperaments, discuss the Madden sisters' future
prospects, about which they disagree.

'What chance is there that this girl will marry suitably?'

'Oh, who knows? At all events, there will be more likelihood of it if she comes into our sphere.'

'Really? Do you know any man that would dream of marrying her?'

'Perhaps not, at present.'

It was clear that Miss Barfoot stood in some danger of becoming subordinate to her more vehement friend. Her little body, for all its natural dignity, put her at a disadvantage in the presence of Rhoda, who towered above her with rather imperious stateliness. Her suavity was no match for Rhoda's vigorous abruptness. But the two were very fond of each other, and by this time thought themselves able safely to dispense with the forms at first imposed by their mutual relations.

George Gissing, *The Odd Women* (1893)

S HE, ON HER side, was delighted to revisit Dedmayne.
'Canon Jocelyn is not a day older,' said she. 'His voice was splendid in that beautiful sermon last night. I wish *you* looked better Mary. We must feed you up. I shall go and talk to cook.'

She always noticed the physical more than the mental, or she might have seen that what had changed most was Mary's expression. Her eyes had always been sad; they are perhaps sadder now, but they had gained that special something which often makes the eyes of the middle-aged more interesting, even more beautiful, than the eyes of youth.

Mary found there was a barrier between them – Mr Herbert's kiss. To open her heart freely had been a need of her warm nature from childhood – a need which had never been satisfied. She had, too, a conscientiousness of repulsion against concealment which was morbid, perhaps, a weakness, but a strength. When Dora said, with the delight in other people's virtues which was one of her characteristics, 'Mary, I *do* think you're the best person I've ever met,' Mary longed to tell her all, to be no longer under false pretences. And it was true. If Dora had known of Mr Herbert, Mary would have forfeited her high place for ever.

They had embarked on one of Dora's stories, long, certainly, and in this case, though not in most cases, painfully interesting. 'And one thought she seemed *so* respectable – dressed so quietly. When she told me there was going to be a baby, I said, "I cannot *think* how you could have done it, Annie," and she said, "He seemed so unhappy, and she did lead him a life." He was married, which made it so much worse. "It was all over in a rush, but I know it was wrong." She wants us to take her back, but we *couldn't*, could we?'

'No,' said Mary, 'I suppose you couldn't, but in a way I wish you would. I feel,' – her heart beat, she made a sudden resolution – 'I feel I understand it more now.'

'Understand what more now?'

'I know love isn't everything, not even the most important thing. I used to think it was, but doesn't Shakespeare say it's like madness? It makes one do the thing one hates most, and yet one would not, no, one would not have had it.'

'What *do* you mean, Mary?'

'Once I – there was a man – I would rather tell you, Dora –'

She became prey to the incoherence that exasperated Canon Jocelyn in her girlhood.

'Yes, I am not all you think me. It was before I was ill and came to Southsea. It really was the strain of that——'

In counting up her misfortunes Mary might have included that the narrow, uncomprehending Dora was her only intimate friend, if she had not already mentioned Dora's active sympathy in counting up her advantages. Had Dora not been Dora, she would now have told her all. But she saw Dora's gentle, innocent gaze, benevolent to almost all, particularly benevolent to her, turn to hardness. The resolution which had nerved her failed suddenly. If she had gone on talking all night, she could never have made Dora understand. She shrank into herself and said, 'Never mind, it was nothing, at least nothing I can talk about.'

The secret remained a barrier between them. Mary never felt for Dora what she had felt before. In the close friendship which lasted till death, Mary was never entirely at ease with her again. They sat silent. Dora felt her heart beating. She was convinced that Mary was going out of her mind, and the flushed face, burning eyes, and hurried, stuttering words gave grounds for uneasiness. She braced herself to speak in a few seconds, and said with peculiar gentle cheerfulness, which indicated exactly what was in her mind, 'Seeing Annie in the hospital brought back my old hospital days. You know I trained for some time, don't you, and then my ankles were too weak.' She talked on about hospital as a doctor entertains a patient when his mind is occupied with another case. After the right interval of distraction she said, 'Mary, dearest, you look a little tired, and so am I. What about early bed tonight?'

She did not go to bed herself, but listened long outside Mary's door, and heard her tossing, for Mary's night was broken with questioning of what she ought to have done.

At exactly the right hour for refreshment Dora brought Mary 'a little cup of Benger. I have just been making myself some, and it's so soothing. Let me arrange your bed for you, dear, and your *pillow*. I was wondering whether maltine would be a good thing in the middle of the morning. Gertrude found it splendid.'

She watched with a careful eye next day, but could see no further sign of the hallucination. She said to Mildred when she went home, 'I think the strain of Canon Jocelyn – he's wonderful, but it *is* a strain – is beginning to tell on dear Mary. She is getting a little neurotic –' She had picked up that favourite nurse's word in hospital. 'I shall go there as often as I can.'

F. M. Mayor, *The Rector's Daughter* (1924)

SHE HEARD THAT Delia was ill in bed, and went along the passage to her room. She found her propped up by pillows dictating letters to an obviously intimidated but competent secretary.

'Oh, Muriel – wait a minute. Yes, yes, Miss Beach? Where were we? "The demonstration proposed to take place on July 15th in the Kingsway Hall will be postponed in order that an answer from the Home Secretary may first be received. As the deputation has been fixed for July 30th, we hope to hold the Kingsway Hall meeting on August 1st, which will just avoid Bank Holiday. I hope that the altered date will not affect your kind promise to speak for us – Yours truly . . ." That's all, I think. Well, Muriel? Arrived? Found a flat for us yet? I've got an internal chill or something and can't get up, as you see.'

Muriel, who had caught the early train, forgotten to eat her lunch, and found her own way to Morrison House with much fear but with considerable self-congratulation, felt that this was a cold reception.

'You'll have to do it yourself,' continued Delia. 'Get a furnished one. I'll give you the addresses of some agents in Bloomsbury. Miss Beach, have you a directory there? You might go round this afternoon, Muriel. The sooner the better.'

But, after Miss Beach had left the room, she had turned to Muriel with her rare swift smile.

'My dear child, you are in for a dreadful time. I've got my hands full of work. I'm feeling perfectly rotten – which means bad tempered and you'll have to do everything your-self. Can you face it?'

'Do you want me?'

Delia glanced comically round the room. A cup half full of boiled milk that stood on a pile of papers on the dressing-table had grown cold; the washstand paraphernalia had been swept aside to make room for a typewriter; ink pads, stamps, directories and ledgers strewed the chairs and floor; and in the middle of the litter Delia lay on the disordered bed with a coat buttoned over her blue striped pyjamas.

'Now, doesn't it rather look as though I wanted you?' she said.

That was enough for Muriel.

House agents scared her, but furniture shops offered her unalloyed delight. Her instincts of economy refused to allow her to take a furnished flat. She braved motor-buses and tubes, she faced landladies, caretakers and decorators. When Delia, nearly convalescent but still shockingly unfit for work, departed northwards on a speaking tour, Muriel worked almost day and night to prepare a home for them both. She spent part of her own dress allowance on blue curtains and hand-painted lamp-shades and the most luxurious of soft arm-chairs for Delia's weary body. Here at last Delia, who had missed the softer things of life, should find a home.

On the afternoon of her expected return, Muriel could hardly keep still. Twenty times she went to the window, twenty times she looked back with satisfaction on the restful charm of the sitting-room. Roses in rough blue vases; dark bookshelves ranged against the plain buff walls, space, space everywhere and a complete absence of irritating decoration – surely the room meant the materialization of her dreams?

'She must like it, she must like it,' she told herself, and for the first time in her life was confident that she had done well.

The electric bell pierced the silence with deafening shrillness. She ran to the door. Delia's figure stood in the passage. Delia, tall, dynamic, ruthless, swept in.

'Muriel, oh, thank goodness you're here! What did you do with Hansard for May 21st last year? That wretched Cutherlick man has threatened to denounce me for misstatements in my Lincoln speech. We shall have a libel action some time. I've got to fly down to South Cross by the 5.40 if I can catch it to answer him to-night at this meeting.'

'What meeting? What speech? Oh, Delia, you can't; you're worn out. You must—'

But Delia brushed past her into the lovely little room. She never saw the blue vases nor the lamp-shade nor the cushions. She was down on her knees flinging books from the shelves on to the beautiful new carpet.

'Where in the name of fortune did you put the Hansards? I'll never catch that train. Why couldn't you put the things where I'd find them? Have you a kettle boiling? Can't I have some tea before I go?'

But, when Delia had found the Hansards and the notes of her Lincoln speech and had telephoned to Lady Ballimore-Fenton, no time was left to drink the tea that Muriel had prepared. She rushed away to catch her train, leaving the overturned dispatch case on the floor, the bookshelves in a chaos and her bedroom littered with the disorder of her haste.

It was then that Muriel realized the disadvantages of trying to please people possessed by an idea. For nearly two hours alone in the flat, she forced back a desire to run away – could she face this continual possibility of Delia's displeasure? Could she continue to please somebody who never acknowledged her efforts?

'I'm being just as unselfish as she is,' Muriel told herself indignantly. 'This is my flat as much as hers. I've spent far more money on it. I've had all the trouble of making it nice. She ought just to have said – it doesn't take a minute to say "how pretty".'

But Muriel's resentment passed when Delia, almost blind with fatigue, stumbled into the flat just after midnight.

'It's all right,' she said, and that was all. But she allowed Muriel to take her hot tweed coat, to pull the hair-pins out of her heavy hair, to bring her soup in a blue and yellow bowl, and a fish *soufflé* made as only Rachel Hammond's daughter could have made it. For half an hour she accepted passively. She ate, drank, and allowed Muriel to prop the cushions behind her in the new arm-chair and put the bowl of yellow roses on the table by her elbow and light her cigarette. Then she lay back, smiled, and looked round the room.

'Well, Muriel,' she said, 'I always knew that you had discrimination, but this amounts to genius. One day your husband will be grateful to me for giving you a little training in the wifely habit.'

'But I'm not going to marry,' protested Muriel.

Delia flicked the ash off her cigarette. 'You must learn never to argue with tired people,' she said sternly, then smiled and fell fast asleep there in the big arm-chair without even waiting to be taken to her pretty bedroom.

After Delia's return, Muriel's life in London fell into its new routine. She spent her mornings in the office of the Twentieth Century Reform League, entering figures in big ledgers and reviving her acquaintance with double entry and other mysterious systems. She found that her old love of figures returned to her. Method was pure joy. She reduced to order the chaos of the office slowly and peacefully, taking each day a new section at which to work.

She organized the little household in 53a Maple Street, keeping a stern eye on the 'daily help', the housekeeping books and Delia's appetite. She filled her days entirely with small trifles, seeing at first no farther than her ledgers and Delia's hollow cheeks, which surely began to fill out a little under her vigorous treatment of stout and milk and new-laid eggs. Yet somehow she did not feel completely safe. Such obvious things as there were to do she did and did quite competently, but always she felt that one day some problem would present itself or some crisis arise and that she would be lost again.

Delia seemed to be both pleased and fattened by her ministrations, but that did not make her entirely contented with Muriel's companionship. One night she came in irritated and disturbed. A newspaper article had questioned her sincerity. She pretended to ignore such criticisms, and could not. They rankled while she laughed at them. She stalked up and down the flat, hurt and sore, and uncertain what to do.

'I'm awfully sorry. I wish I could do something,' sighed Muriel helplessly for the fifth time.

'Do. Do? Oh, you never do anything except the things I tell you. You're always wringing your hands and looking sorry, but I always have to think of the things to do.'

This statement Muriel felt to be true rather than kind, but she accepted it with chastened fortitude.

Winifred Holtby, *The Crowded Street* (1924)

THEY PASSED ALONG another flat bit of path, with a black shape like a high wall towering above them on their right, and then the path went up again under trellises, and trailing sprays of scented things caught at them and shook raindrops on them, and the light of the lantern flickered over lilies, and then came a flight of ancient steps worn with centuries, and then another iron gate, and then they were inside, though still climbing a twisting flight of stone steps with old walls on either side like the walls of dungeons, and with a vaulted roof.

At the top was a wrought-iron door, and through it shone a flood of electric light.

'Ecco,' said Domenico, lithely running up the last few steps ahead and pushing the door open.

And there they were, arrived; and it was San Salvatore; and their suit-cases were waiting for them; and they had not been murdered.

They looked at each other's white faces and blinking eyes very solemnly.

It was a great, a wonderful moment. Here they were, in their mediaeval castle at last. Their feet touched its stones.

Mrs Wilkins put her arm round Mrs Arbuthnot's neck and kissed her.

'The first thing to happen in this house,' she said softly, solemnly, 'shall be a kiss.'

'Dear Lotty,' said Mrs Arbuthnot.

'Dear Rose,' said Mrs Wilkins, her eyes brimming with gladness.

Domenico was delighted. He liked to see beautiful ladies kiss. He made them a most appreciative speech of welcome, and they stood arm in arm, holding each other up, for they were very tired, blinking smilingly at him, and not understanding a word.

Elizabeth von Arnim, *The Enchanted April* **(1922)**

5

SOLIDARITY

For there is no friend like a sister
In calm or stormy weather;
To cheer one on the tedious way,
To fetch one if one goes astray,
To lift one if one totters down,
To strengthen whilst one stands.

Christina Rossetti, *Goblin Market* (1862)

William Shakespeare ⌢ *Constance Maud* ⌢ *Elizabeth Taylor*
Helen Fielding ⌢ *Elizabeth Jenkins* ⌢ *Rona Jaffe* ⌢ *Michèle Roberts*
Marilyn French ⌢ *Toni Morrison* ⌢ *Thomas Hardy* ⌢ *Joan Wyndham*
Bernardine Evaristo ⌢ *Shirley Conran*

Solidarity is a wonderful thing: a sword, a shield, and the source of the best jokes going. I first knew it at college, when I joined a women's group and began going on marches in my long coat and fingerless gloves; in middle age, I have it once again in the form of a WhatsApp group to which I and six colleagues belong (rare is the day when we don't message one another, our outrage and our one-liners typed at lightning speed whatever the hour, and wherever we happen to be in the world).

In this chapter are suffragettes, trying their hardest to keep up one another's spirits, and second-wave feminists, funny and furious in their strange, new consciousness-raising groups. But solidarity takes many forms, and I use the word here in its widest sense. A bully makes sisters of us all. We may listen to, and sympathise with, the friend who has been betrayed by a lover, our indignation rising hotly on her behalf. Or perhaps we find ourselves accompanying her to an abortion clinic, knowing she would do exactly the same for us were things the other way round. New mothers make natural allies, as do those who find themselves far from home (especially during wartime, as in Joan Wyndham's high-spirited memoir, *Love is Blue*). A bad boss, the swapping of secrets, a shared bottle of wine: all of these may engender not only the fortifying embrace of unity, but the kind of writing which is in itself a form of solidarity, consolatory and confiding.

*C*ELIA. O MY poor Rosalind, whither wilt thou go?
    Wilt thou change fathers? I will give thee mine.
I charge thee, be not thou more grieved than I am.
Rosalind. I have more cause.
Celia. Thou has not, cousin.
Prithee, be cheerful; knows thou not the Duke
Hath banished me, his daughter?
Rosalind. That he hath not.
Celia. No, hath not? Rosalind lacks then the love
Which teacheth thee that thou and I am one.
Shall we be sundered? Shall we part, sweet girl?
No, let my father seek another heir.
Therefore devise with me how we may fly,
Whither to go, and what to bear with us,
And do not seek to take your change upon you,
To bear your griefs yourself and leave me out;
For, by this heaven, now at our sorrows pale,
Say what thou canst, I'll go along with thee.
Rosalind. Why, whither shall we go?
Celia. To seek my uncle in the Forest of Arden.
Rosalind. Alas, what danger will it be to us,
Maids as we are, to travel forth so far?
Beauty provoketh thieves sooner than gold.
Celia. I'll put myself in poor and mean attire
And with a kind of umber smirch my face.
The like do you; so shall we pass along
And never stir assailants.
Rosalind. Were it not better,

Because that I am more than common tall,
That I did suit me all points like a man?
A gallant curtle-axe upon my thigh,
A boar-spear in my hand, and in my heart
Lie there what hidden woman's fear there will
We'll have a swashing and a martial outside,
As many other mannish cowards have
That do outface it with their semblances.
Celia. What shall I call thee when thou art a man?
Rosalind. I'll have no worse a name than Jove's own page,
And therefore look you call me 'Ganymede'.
But what will you be called?
Celia. Something that hath a reference to my state:
No longer 'Celia', but 'Aliena'.

William Shakespeare, *As You Like It* (1599?)

THE MOVEMENT WAS growing and spreading its branches out far and wide. Every variety of bird began to find home and shelter beneath these branches – this was the living Tree of Life for which those in the desert, parched and thirsty, had been longing, towards which they had been half unconsciously journeying. In vain the Powers-that-Be, 'dressed in their little brief authority, played such fantastic tricks' with the laws of equity as 'made the angels weep'. The Tree had life, an appalling amount of life, they conceded with dismay. The roots struck downwards so deep into the very heart of humanity, that lopping away the branches and mutilating the leaves and blossoms had no effect, except that of causing new shoots to spring forth with renewed vigour.

Jenny Clegg, Mrs Toppin, and Mary O'Neil, together with fifteen other women, had been arrested and sentenced, some to six, some eight weeks, in the second division, for holding a protest meeting outside the grim walls of a Midland county jail, where some of their companions were, they considered, undergoing a most unjust sentence. The public at this meeting had shown the authorities how dangerously sympathy with the Women's Cause was increasing. Again they had recourse to hacking away at the branches, and again with the result of strengthening the roots of the tree they desired to destroy.

It was six o'clock on a chill November morning. During the night it had frozen hard, and now the snow was falling, though as yet it was too early for the prisoners inside their dark cells to get a glimmer of anything outside.

The wardress had been on her rounds and lit the feeble gas-jet which gave barely sufficient light to enable Jenny to get up and put on her clothes. With bones aching and teeth chattering, she did her best to wash with the small tin of icy water and scrap of a cloth which, for one week, had to do duty as the only towel.

But Jenny's calm cheerfulness was in no way affected by her depressing surroundings. She gave a whimsical look as she put on the heavy clumping shoes, and spoke aloud. To hear a pleasant, friendly voice, though her own, took off the feeling of loneliness. 'Now for my Cinderella slippers. It seems a pity they can't make them so as not to wear such holes in your feet. It's so hard on those poor old dames in the exercise yard.'

She sighed thoughtfully as she put on her dress and apron stamped with the universal broad arrow: 'It has become a symbol – this broad arrow – almost like the cross to some of us,' she said softly.

Before putting on the prison cap she held it up critically:

'The French girl, Charlotte Corday, wore such a cap. Well, of course, it wasn't so ugly – but somehow I never put this on without thinking of her, and what Father Peter said about her. What a wonderful spirit she had! Without a thought of herself – just giving her life for her country. Makes one feel very small to think of her. Fancy what she must have gone through, a sweet, gentle lady like her, before she made up her mind for such a deed and such a death as she knew must follow!'

Having finished her toilet, Jenny proceeded to make her bed; rolling up the bed-clothes on the shelf, and fastening the bed up sideways against the wall. She had hardly finished this when from the adjoining cell came a faint sound, like the notes of a call.

Jenny darted to the corner from where the sound came. Kneeling on the floor she put her ear where the hot-water pipe passed through the wall. Again came the notes of a call, the prison greeting of the Suffragettes:

'No sur-ren-der,' to the chimes of Big Ben.

Jenny gave the answering chimes:

'No sur-ren-der! Good morning. How are you, dear Miss O'Neil?'

'Splendid – only longing for a breath of fresh air, aren't you?' came the voice of Mary O'Neil.

'We must all go at the Governor again to-day,' sang out Jenny. 'Three days without air for speaking a few words at exercise isn't what political offenders ought to put up with – we've got to protest.'

'You're right, Jenny – we must protest. If he refuses to listen we must break our windows to-day, I suppose?'

'Yes,' said Jenny firmly. 'You fix the time with the others on your side – the wardresses dinner-hour, you know – I'll pass it on to Mrs Toppin.'

'All right,' said Mary. 'The signal "No surrender".'

'Yes – then all together with a crash. It's the only way to show we're in earnest,' said Jenny.

'Deeds not words,' replied the voice through the wall. 'Hope I'll see you at the pump, Jenny.'

'Hope so,' answered Jenny – 'it's the only thing to cheer one for the day now chapel and exercise are stopped.'

She got up and knelt down at the wall opposite:

'Mrs Toppin! No sur-ren-der!'

'Top o' the mornin' to yo', Jenny Clegg,' answered the vigorous tones of Keziah Toppin. 'No surrender, not whilst I've got a kick left.'

'Be ready to break your window, then – I'll pass you the signal at the dinner-hour.'

'My little shoe's ready,' answered the breezy voice.

'We need to let in a bit of air and light,' said Jenny, as she got up and returned to her morning duties.

Constance Maud, *No Surrender* (1911)

[L ILIAN] BEGAN TO cry softly. She had not slept for two nights, contemplating her first, dreaded act of violence. Caroline's look of compassion and encouragement across that dingy room steadied and emboldened her.* It was a look which went from one to the other many times in the years which followed: years during which history gave in. They wondered sometimes if their courage had been wasted; if time would not despite them have floated down to them casually what they had almost drowned in struggling to reach. Soon feminism became a weird abnormality; laughter was easily evoked at the strange figures of suffragettes with their umbrellas raised, their faces contorted and, one supposed, their voices made shrill with fury and frustration.

Elizabeth Taylor, *A Game of Hide and Seek* (1951)

E VENTUALLY, THE THREE of us worked out a strategy for Jude. She must stop beating herself over the head with *Women Who Love Too Much* and instead think more towards *Men Are from Mars, Women Are from Venus*, which will help her to see Richard's behaviour less as a sign she is co-dependent and loving too much and more in the light of him being like a Martian rubber band which needs to stretch away in order to come back.

---

* As young women, Lilian and Caroline were suffragettes, and together had once been hustled by policemen up the steps of a police station, having smashed some shop windows.

'Yes, but does that mean I should call him or not?' said Jude.

'No,' said Sharon, just as I was saying, 'Yes.'

After Jude had gone – because she has to get up at 5.45 and go to the gym and see her personal shopper before work starts at 8.30 (mad) – Sharon and I were suddenly filled with remorse and self-loathing for not advising Jude simply to get rid of Vile Richard because he is vile. But then, as Sharon pointed out, last time we did that they got back together and she told him everything we'd said in a fit of reconciliatory confession and now it is cripplingly embarrassing every time we see him and he thinks we are the Bitch Queens from Hell – which, as Jude points out, is a misapprehension because, although we have discovered our Inner Bitches, we have not yet unlocked them.

*

An unbelievable amount of food and wine was consumed since the generous girls, as well as bringing a bottle of wine each, had all brought a little extra something from M&S. Therefore, in addition to the three-course meal and two bottles of wine (1 fizzy, 1 white) I had already bought from M&S (I mean prepared by entire day's slaving over hot stove) we had:

   1 tub hummus & pkt mini-pittas

   12 smoked salmon and cream cheese pinwheels

   12 mini-pizzas

   1 raspberry pavlova

   1 tiramisu (party size)

   2 Swiss Mountain Bars

Sharon was on top form. 'Bastards!' she was already

yelling by 8.35, pouring three-quarters of a glass of Kir Royale straight down her throat. 'Stupid, smug, arrogant, manipulative, self-indulgent bastards. They exist in a total Culture of Entitlement. Pass me one of those mini-pizzas, will you?'

Jude was depressed because Vile Richard, with whom she is currently split up, keeps ringing her, dropping little verbal baits suggesting he wants to get back together to make sure he keeps her interested, but protecting himself by saying he just wants to be 'friends' (fraudulent, poisoned concept). Then last night he made an incredibly assumptive, patronising phone call, asking her if she was going to a mutual friend's party.

'Ah well, in that case I won't come,' he said. 'No. It really wouldn't be fair on you. You see, I was going to bring this, sort of, date with me. I mean, it's nothing. It's just some girl who's stupid enough to let me shag her for a couple of weeks.'

'What?' exploded Sharon, beginning to turn pink. 'That's the most repulsive thing I've ever heard anyone say about a woman. Arrogant little *prat*! How dare he give himself licence to treat you any way he likes under the name of friendship, then make himself feel clever by trying to upset you with his stupid new date. If he really minded about not hurting your feelings he'd just shut up and come to the party on his own instead of waving his stupid date under your nose.'

'"Friends?" Pah! The Enemy more like!' I shouted happily, tucking into another Silk Cut and a couple of salmon pinwheels. 'Bastard!'

By 11.30 Sharon was in full and splendid auto-rant.

'Ten years ago people who cared about the environment were laughed at as sandal-wearing beardy-weirdies and now look at the power of the green consumer,' she was shouting, sticking her fingers into the tiramisu and transferring it straight into her mouth.

'In years ahead the same will come to pass with feminism. There won't be any men leaving their families and postmenopausal wives for young mistresses, or trying to chat women up by showing off in a patronising way about all the other women throwing themselves at them, or trying to have sex with women without any niceness or commitment, because the young mistresses and women will just turn round and tell them to sod off and men won't get any sex or any women unless they learn how to behave properly instead of cluttering up the sea-bed of women with their SHITTY, SMUG, SELF-INDULGENT, BEHAVIOUR!'

'Bastards!' yelled Jude, slurping her Pinot Grigio.

'Bastards!' I yelled through a mouthful of raspberry pavlova mixed with tiramisu.

'Bloody bastards!' shouted Jude, lighting a Silk Cut with the butt end of the last one.

Just then the doorbell rang.

'I bet that's Daniel, the bloody bastard,' I said. 'What is it?' I yelled into the entry phone.

'Oh, hello, darling,' said Daniel in his gentlest, politest voice.

Helen Fielding, *Bridget Jones's Diary* **(1996)**

THE VIRAGO BOOK OF FRIENDSHIP

I MOGEN NOW LOOKED forward eagerly to a visit from Cecil,* who was to come for the first week-end in October, arriving on a Saturday morning in time for lunch. As the time approached, Evelyn produced an invitation from Blanche Silcox for them all to dine with her on the Saturday evening. Whatever might have been Imogen's feelings in other circumstances, she was glad of this. She longed for Cecil to see Blanche again, and in Evelyn's company, so that she herself might have the benefit of Cecil's observation. That Imogen should want this assistance was, on the face of it, surprising. She had had a good deal of experience with men and had been married for twelve years or more. Though Cecil's professional contacts were chiefly with men, she had no experience of men in an amorous or even an intimate relationship. Imogen was well fitted to learn a thing by the feel of it, as the saying is, and she had had plenty of opportunity in emotional relationships of perfecting this skill. Merely to be in the same room with a man and another woman would usually tell her more about their relations with each other than their friends could learn over weeks. Cecil on the other hand had none of this apparatus of intuitive perception, but the thing she had, she possessed to an unusual degree. She had very acute vision combined with the power of holding the mirror quite still so that the reflection did not waver. Her face, calm-eyed and close-lipped, never suggested that her powers, whatever they were, made up into happiness; Imogen's expression, pensive and even wistful as it often was, had that dawning luminosity that is on the verge of delight.

---

* Cecil is a woman, and Evelyn is Imogen's husband.

Nevertheless, on her arrival, Cecil looked better than she had ever looked in her life, tranquil rather than repressed, and beautifully dressed in tweeds the colour of tow and ashes, with rows of smoked pearls round her neck. Imogen was delighted by her appearance but Cecil was unable to return the compliment. In the spare room, Imogen kissed her and for a moment clung to her, trembling and sobbing in a way that all but unnerved Cecil, who was not easily dismayed. The next minute Imogen released her, laughed and wiped her eyes. Like many women who cry easily, she was not much disfigured by tears. When they went downstairs, she was only flushed; Cecil was some degrees paler than before.

*

They were in a taxi now, speeding down Fleet Street, to reach Piccadilly and Bond Street. Imogen squeezed Cecil's hand.

'What sort of dress must you have?' she asked eagerly.

'For sherry parties, dining out. Not a long skirt. Black, I think –' Cecil showed herself in one of her very rare moments of uncertainty and confusion. A black dress would be the best from many points of view but she did not know if she really wanted a black one. Imogen however would know how to choose. She luxuriated in the rare sensation of being able to leave a decision to somebody who was more capable of making it than she was. Two hours later, the frock had been bought, conforming to the requirements Cecil had laid down but presenting a romantic variation on them; for the skirt was not long, but it was spreading, and the colour was dark, but a dark greenish blue sprinkled with small gold stars. Imogen's own parcels were now collected, and arranged round her in a carriage at Waterloo. She and

Cecil had arranged that the latter would come to Chalk the weekend after next.

'You'll have all about the Leepers' party to tell by that time.' Imogen looked surprised, as if she had forgotten this impending event. 'So I shall,' she said. A guard now motioned Cecil off the carriage step and she retreated some paces. From this distance, she saw Imogen seated in the far corner, turned away from her to answer some question from a man opposite about the carriage window. Imogen looked very elegant and graceful, prosperous, poised. She would have looked almost unapproachable had it not been for the gentleness and simplicity that formed such a charming feature of her appearance. But then Imogen turned to look through the window for the last of Cecil. Her face might have belonged to a different person; it was troubled, searching, and looked on the verge of tears. Cecil evaded the guard and pressed forward again, waving. Imogen's eyes lighted up and she kissed her hand with an eager, affectionate gesture, as the train started.

Cecil walked slowly out of the great station, now filling with the crowds who used it at this time every evening. She took a taxi to the Post Office in the neighbourhood of Long Acre which her business experience had taught her stayed open late, and here she was able to consult an up-to-date edition of the London Telephone Directory. In it, she saw that Blanche Silcox had an address in Halkin Street.

Elizabeth Jenkins, *The Tortoise and the Hare* (1954)

THE ONLY PERSON April had told besides Dexter was Caroline. She had never expected the feeling of warmth she could get from a friend's honest concern, and Caroline's devotion was the only thing in this whole situation that comforted her. There was no panic in Caroline. 'What can I do?' Caroline asked. And when April told her that Dexter had arranged for the abortion Caroline had seemed to sense immediately how April felt about all men at this moment.

'Have him drive you up to my house in Port Blair for the weekend,' Caroline said. 'You mustn't be alone in your apartment after an operation. You can stay with me and we'll take care of you. You'll rest and eat well and I'll keep you company. Dexter can stay too, or he can pick you up on Sunday night if you prefer.'

'Do you think he'll be insulted if I tell him I want to stay with you alone?' April asked.

'Insulted?' Caroline's voice shook with emotion. 'Insulted? What right has *he* to be insulted about anything?'

'It's funny,' April said, 'I love him but I just can't face being with him afterward. I know I'll say the wrong thing, or he will. I feel so strange.'

'I know it sounds stupid to tell you everything will be all right, knowing the way you feel,' Caroline said, 'but, believe me, it *will* be all right. All your friends love you. I love you. We all care very much what happens to you. If there's anything friends can do for you now, we'll do it.'

'I know,' April said softly. 'Thank you.' For the first time in her life, she felt as if she had crossed over a bridge which had no way to return. She was twenty-one years old but she was no longer a young girl in any way and she could not turn to her family or any friends of the family for help, but only to her own contemporaries. Without her friends she would be alone. And her friends understood how she felt and were not shocked, only indignant that she had to suffer pain and near-disaster instead of having the husband and child she wanted more than anything in the world. Instinctively April knew that if she were to tell Barbara, Barbara would feel the same way Caroline did.

'I'll come back with you after work on Friday and stay with you until Dexter comes,' Caroline said. 'We'll have a drink or two and I'll help you pack for the country.'

'I'll feel scared facing your family,' April said. 'Your father's a doctor. Do you think he'll be able to tell from looking at me that something just happened?'

Caroline laughed. 'Do you think doctors have X-ray eyes? My father will take one look at your young fresh face and leave us scrupulously alone so we can giggle together about our boy friends.'

'Yes . . .,' April said. 'So would mine . . . Thank God. My poor father . . .'

On Friday April was almost unable to do any work. She tried harder than ever to concentrate on her typing, but all the time she was thinking how silly it was to be so careful not to make mistakes because Monday morning Miss Farrow would probably have to ask for a new secretary. These letters, this work she was doing in the office, suddenly took on a great importance, as if she had already died and was looking at them from a poignant, untouchable distance, like Emily in *Our Town* after she had died. She wanted to make a mark somewhere, leave something; and on an impulse she took her initialed handkerchief out of her purse and tucked it under the edge of her blotter. They could find it on Monday. But when five o'clock came and it was time to make the mad rush out of the office for the elevators April reached the door of the bullpen and then came back and took the handkerchief out of the blotter and put it back into her purse. She didn't want anything of her own to remain alone and unprotected if she was not there to own it, not even a handkerchief with her name on it.

It was only a short walk from the office to April's apartment, but Caroline insisted on taking her there in a taxi and paying for it. Upstairs April sat on her chair and looked at the furniture in her room, hardly seeing it. Caroline was briskly removing underthings and a nightgown from the bureau drawer and looking for April's suitcase. She had brought a pint bottle of gin.

'You'll never get high enough on Scotch,' Caroline said. 'Where do you keep the orange juice, or haven't you any?'

'I don't know.'

'I'll go downstairs and get some. You stay here. Don't move.'

'Where would I go?' April asked hopelessly.

Caroline returned in a few minutes with a paper container of orange juice from the grocery store. 'This is the special Harvard Weekend punch,' she said cheerfully, mixing it in a pot she had found on the stove. 'You don't even taste the gin, and then – boom!'

April smiled weakly.

'More innocent girls have been seduced as a result of this punch than you could imagine,' Caroline went on. 'You won't even want an anesthetic.'

'They're not going to give me one!'

'Well, I'm giving you one. Old Caroline is here. Drink this, my dear innocent girl.'

April sipped at the drink, forcing the sweetness past the obstruction that seemed to have lodged in her throat. Even at that moment, knowing everything was settled and almost finished, the thought came to her that orange juice was good for pregnant women. She wondered whether someone who was about to be put into the electric chair and was being given his last dinner would refrain from eating dessert because he was on a diet. I would, she thought. But then, I'm a fool.

The doorbell rang and April jumped. Caroline walked to the door and opened it. 'Hello, Dexter,' she said sweetly, as if he had come to pick up April to take her to the movies.

How proper Dexter was, how polite. He smiled and asked Caroline how she was feeling. April wondered whether he was resenting the fact that Caroline was there. Caroline was telling him how to get to Port Blair from the Merritt Parkway and he was nodding studiously.

'We may be a little late,' he said. 'I know it will be long after dinner.'

The cocktail party, April thought bitterly, may last longer than we expect.

Rona Jaffe, *The Best of Everything* **(1958)**

FEMINISM COULD BE carnivalesque and amusing. It could also disturb. Consciousness raising, for example, let women meet together in small groups to talk confidentially about any subject we chose. During those hours our allegiance was to each other as women, not to our husbands and lovers. Pamphlets and articles written at this time describe how we put hitherto unexpressed feelings into words. Within the safety of the group we told each other our secrets. We trusted each other not to report back to our men. This meant you could take the lid off your life and have a good look at it. You could try to, anyway. But how did you find the words to express your searches and your discoveries? They did not yet exist. That realisation pushed me towards writing, because the private act of writing allowed me to take all the time I needed to discover what I really thought. Other women, speaking at meetings, often seemed so much more articulate than I. Then later I would discover that they felt exactly the same: that I was very articulate in public. It's true. I was. But my articulateness sometimes felt like glibness to me: opinions rather than true explorations.

Michèle Roberts, *Paper Houses* (2007)

V ALERIE, OF COURSE, snorted when she heard this. We were sitting around in Val's place one night, Iso and Ava, Clarissa, Kyla and me, and Mira told us about her experience of childbirth. It was in the late fall of 1968, and we didn't know each other well as a group. We were still skirting around the edges of politeness, not yet sure enough of each other to let it go completely, but getting there.

Although we weren't aware of this then, we had been brought together by our dislike of the same things – values and behavior we saw all around us at Harvard. Our dislike was of a specific kind: all the first-year graduate students were unhappy there. But we were not so much unhappy as outraged, and our dislike, as we would come to realize, was the expression of a profound and positive sense of the way things *ought* to be. On this evening, however, we were still feeling each other out.

We were complimenting Val on the beauty of her apartment. She had little money, but she'd painted it, filled it with plants, and strewn it with odds and ends collected in her travels. It was a delightful place.

And Mira said – in that gushing suburban way she had – how wonderful women were, look at Val's beautiful apartment, no man would have been willing to do it or would have had the imagination, especially with so little money. And Kyla, who had also beautifully fixed up her and Harley's apartment, jumped to agree. Then Mira said she'd suddenly seen how great women were after giving birth to Normie, and she described the experience. And Val snorted.

'You bought it! You bought the whole damned bag!'

Mira blinked.

'How convenient to have a whole class of people who give up their lives for other people! How nice, while you're out doing things that serve your ego, to have somebody home washing the bathroom floor and picking up your dirty underwear! And never, never cooking Brussels sprouts because you don't like them.'

Everybody burst in at once.

'It's true, it's true!!' Kyla crowed.

'How come you don't do that for me?' Isolde grinned at Ava.

Clarissa, serious-faced, tried to get a word in – 'I don't think . . .'

But Val was not to be stopped. 'I mean, Mira, don't you hear what you're saying? "Women's greatness lies in their selflessness." You might as well say women's place is in the home.'

'Nonsense!' Mira began to turn a little pink. 'I'm not prescribing. I'm describing. The constrictions exist. No matter what you say about the way things ought to be, they are the way they are. And if the world changed tomorrow, it would be too late for those women . . .'

'Is it too late for you?' Kyla shot in.

Mira leaned back, half laughing. 'Look, all I'm saying is that women are great because they get so little and give so much . . .'

'Exactly!' Val stormed.

Isolde giggled. 'She'll never be allowed to get it out.'

'They have so little room,' Mira went on doggedly, 'but they don't get bitter and mean, they try to make that little room graceful and harmonious.'

'Tell it to the women in the schizophrenic wards. Or the ones who sit in their kitchens drinking themselves to death. Or the ones covered with bruises from the husbands who got drunk last night. Or the ones who burn their children's hands.'

'I'm not saying all women . . .'

'Okay,' Clarissa began authoritatively, and the room

THE VIRAGO BOOK OF FRIENDSHIP

quietened a bit, 'but not all these things spring from the same root. Men have constrictions too.'

'I'm not worried about men,' Val exclaimed. 'Let them worry about themselves. They've taken pretty good care of themselves for the past four thousand years. And women's problems *do* all spring from the same root: that they're women. Everything Mira's told us about her life shows it to be one long training in humiliation, an education in suppressing self.'

'That's as if you're saying women have no individual identity,' Isolde demurred.

'They don't. Not when you talk about women's greatness or women's constrictions: as soon as you say that, you're admitting an identity among all women, which implies lack of individuality. Kyla asked if Mira had been destroyed by her constrictions, and the answer is yes, or nearly so. Look!' she plunked her glass down on the table, 'My real point is that to tell women they're great because they've given themselves up is to tell them to go on doing it.'

Mira held her hand up like a traffic cop ordering *Stop*. 'Wait,' she ordered. 'I want you to keep quiet a minute, Val, because I want to answer you, but I have to figure out what I want to say.'

Val laughed and got up. 'Okay. Who wants more wine?'

When she returned, Mira said, 'Okay,' in that thoughtful way we had all picked up from Clarissa, whose mind clicked points off like a clock measuring precise moments, each one preceded by 'Okay'. 'Yes, I want them to go on doing it.'

Howls.

'I mean it. What will happen to the world if they don't

do it? It would be unbearable. Who else would do it? The men go to work to make life possible and the women work to make it bearable.'

'Why are you in graduate school, then?' Kyla was nearly leaping out of her chair. 'Why are you living in – pardon me – that sterile grungy drab apartment of yours? Why aren't you making a nice cozy home for your boys and your husband?'

'I was! I would be!'

'And you loved it.'

'I hated it.'

They all laughed, and Mira too grinned wryly, then began to laugh.

'Okay. You're not saying – tell me if I'm wrong, Mira – but you're not saying that creating felicity is all women should do. You're saying it's part of what they should do. Am I right?' Kyla still perched forward, as if Mira's answer were the most important thing in the world to her.

'No. I'm saying it's what they do do, and it's beautiful.'

'Okay.' It was Clarissa this time. 'But if they want to and can do other things as well, so much the better, right?'

Mira nodded, and everyone leaned back. A kind of peace fell among them.

Marilyn French, *The Women's Room* (1977)

THEY MOVED TOWARD the ice cream parlor like tight-rope walkers, as thrilled by the possibility of a slip as by the maintenance of tension and balance. The least sideways glance, the merest toe stub could pitch them into those creamy haunches spread wide with welcome. Somewhere beneath all of that daintiness, chambered in all that neatness, lay the thing that clotted their dreams.

Which was only fitting, for it was in dreams that the two girls had first met. Long before Edna Finch's Mellow House opened, even before they marched through the chocolate halls of Garfield Primary School out onto the playground and stood facing each other through the ropes of the one vacant swing ('Go on.' 'No, You go.') they had already made each other's acquaintance in the delirium of their noon dreams. They were solitary little girls whose loneliness was so profound it intoxicated them and sent them stumbling into Technicolored visions that always included a presence, a someone, who, quite like the dreamer, shared the delight of the dream. When Nel, an only child, sat on the steps of her back porch surrounded by the high silence of her mother's incredibly orderly house, feeling the neatness pointing at her back, she studied the poplars and fell easily into a picture of herself lying on a flowered bed, tangled in her own hair, waiting for some fiery prince. He approached but never quite arrived. But always, watching the dream along with her, were some smiling sympathetic eyes. Someone as interested as she herself in the flow of her imagined hair, the thickness of the mattress of flowers, the voile sleeves that closed below her elbows in gold-threaded cuffs.

Similarly, Sula, also an only child, but wedged into a household of throbbing disorder constantly awry with things, people, voices and the slamming of doors, spent hours in the attic behind a roll of linoleum galloping through her own mind on a gray-and-white horse tasting sugar and smelling roses in full view of someone who shared both the taste and the speed.

So when they met, first in those chocolate halls and next through the ropes of the swing, they felt the ease and comfort of old friends. Because each had discovered years before that they were neither white nor male, and that all freedom and triumph was forbidden to them, they had set about creating something else to be. Their meeting was fortunate, for it let them use each other to grow on. Daughters of distant mothers and incomprehensible fathers (Sula's because he was dead; Nel's because he wasn't), they found in each other's eyes the intimacy they were looking for.

Nel Wright and Sula Peace were both twelve in 1922, wishbone thin and easy-assed. Nel was the color of wet sandpaper – just dark enough to escape the blows of the pitch-black true bloods and the contempt of old women who worried about such things as bad blood mixtures and knew that the origins of a mule and a mulatto were one and the same. Had she been any lighter-skinned she would have needed either her mother's protection on the way to school or a streak of mean to defend herself. Sula was a heavy brown with large quiet eyes, one of which featured a birthmark that spread from the middle of the lid toward the eyebrow, shaped something like a stemmed rose. It gave her otherwise plain face a broken excitement and blue-blade threat like the keloid scar of the razored man who sometimes played checkers with her grandmother. The birthmark was to grow darker as the years passed, but now it was the same shade as her gold-flecked eyes, which, to the end, were as steady and clean as rain.

Their friendship was as intense as it was sudden. They found relief in each other's personality. Although both were unshaped, formless things, Nel seemed stronger and more consistent than Sula, who could hardly be counted on to sustain any emotion for more than three minutes. Yet there was one time when that was not true, when she held on to a mood for weeks, but even that was in defense of Nel.

Four white boys in their early teens, sons of some newly arrived Irish people, occasionally entertained themselves in the afternoon by harassing black schoolchildren. With shoes that pinched and woolen knickers that made red rings on their calves, they had come to this valley with their parents believing as they did that it was a promised land – green and shimmering with welcome. What they found was a strange accent, a pervasive fear of their religion and firm resistance to their attempts to find work. With one exception the older residents of Medallion scorned them. The one exception was the black community. Although some of the Negroes had been in Medallion before the Civil War (the town didn't even have a name then), if they had any hatred for these newcomers it didn't matter because it didn't show. As a matter of fact, baiting them was the one activity that the white Protestant residents concurred in. In part their place in this world was secured only when they echoed the old residents' attitude toward blacks.

These particular boys caught Nel once, and pushed her from hand to hand until they grew tired of the frightened helpless face. Because of that incident, Nel's route home from school became elaborate. She, and then Sula, managed to duck them for weeks until a chilly day in November when Sula said, 'Let's us go on home the shortest way.'

Nel blinked, but acquiesced. They walked up the street until they got to the bend of Carpenter's Road where the boys lounged on a disused well. Spotting their prey, the boys sauntered forward as though there was nothing in the world on their minds but the gray sky. Hardly able to control their grins, they stood like a gate blocking the path. When the girls were three feet in front of the boys, Sula reached into her coat pocket and pulled out Eva's paring knife. The boys stopped short, exchanged looks and dropped all pretense of innocence. This was going to be better than they thought. They were going to try and fight back, and with a knife. Maybe they could get an arm around one of their waists, or tear . . .

Sula squatted down in the dirt road and put everything down on the ground: her lunchpail, her reader, her mittens, her slate. Holding the knife in her right hand, she pulled the slate toward her and pressed her left forefinger down hard on its edge. Her aim was determined but inaccurate. She slashed off only the tip of her finger. The four boys stared open-mouthed at the wound and the scrap of flesh, like a button mushroom curling in the cherry blood that ran into the corners of the slate.

Sula raised her eyes to them. Her voice was quiet. 'If I can do that to myself, what you suppose I'll do to you?'

The shifting dirt was the only way Nel knew that they were moving away; she was looking at Sula's face, which seemed miles and miles away.

But toughness was not their quality – adventuresomeness was – and a mean determination to explore everything that interested them, from one-eyed chickens high-stepping in their penned yards to Mr Buckland Reed's gold teeth, from the sound of sheets flapping in the wind to the labels on Tar Baby's wine bottles. And they had no priorities. They could be distracted from watching a fight with mean razors by the glorious smell of hot tar being poured by roadmen two hundred yards away.

In the safe harbor of each other's company they could afford to abandon the ways of other people and concentrate on their own perceptions of things. When Mrs Wright reminded Nel to pull her nose, she would do it enthusiastically but without the least hope in the world.

'While you're sittin' there, honey, go ahead and pull your nose.'

'It hurts, Mamma.'

'Don't you want a nice nose when you grow up?'

After she met Sula, Nel slid the clothespin under the blanket as soon as she got in the bed. And although there was still the hateful hot comb to suffer through each Saturday evening, its consequences – smooth hair – no longer interested her.

Joined in mutual admiration they watched each day as though it were a movie arranged for their amusement. The new theme they were now discovering was men. So they met regularly, without even planning it, to walk down the road to Edna Finch's Mellow House, even though it was too cool for ice cream.

Toni Morrison, *Sula* (1973)

WHEN TWO O'CLOCK arrived the professional reed-drawers tossed off the last half-pint in their flagon, put down their hooks, tied their last sheaves, and went away. Marian and Izz would have done likewise, but on hearing that Tess meant to stay, to make up by longer hours for her lack of skill, they would not leave her. Looking out at the snow, which still fell, Marian exclaimed, 'Now, we've got it all to ourselves.' And so at last the conversation turned to their old experiences at the dairy; and, of course, the incidents of their affection for Angel Clare.

'Izz and Marian,' said Mrs Angel Clare, with a dignity which was extremely touching, seeing how very little of a wife she was: 'I can't join in talk with you now, as I used to do, about Mr Clare; you will see that I cannot; because, although he is gone away from me for the present, he is my husband.'

Izz was by nature the sauciest and most caustic of all the four girls who had loved Clare. 'He was a very splendid lover, no doubt,' she said; 'but I don't think he is a too fond husband to go away from you so soon.'

'He had to go – he was obliged to go, to see about the land over there!' pleaded Tess.

'He might have tided 'ee over the winter.'

'Ah – that's owing to an accident – a misunderstanding; and we won't argue it,' Tess answered, with tearfulness in her words. 'Perhaps there's a good deal to be said for him! He did not go away, like some husbands, without telling me; and I can always find out where he is.'

After this they continued for some long time in a reverie, as they went on seizing the ears of corn, drawing out the straw, gathering it under their arms, and cutting off the ears with their bill-hooks, nothing sounding in the barn but the swish of the straw and the crunch of the hook. Then Tess suddenly flagged, and sank down upon the heap of wheat-ears at her feet.

'I knew you wouldn't be able to stand it!' cried Marian. 'It wants harder flesh than yours for this work.'

Just then the farmer entered. 'Oh, that's how you get on when I am away,' he said to her.

'But it is my own loss,' she pleaded. 'Not yours.'

'I want it finished,' he said doggedly, as he crossed the barn and went out at the other door.

'Don't 'ee mind him, there's a dear,' said Marian. 'I've worked before. Now you go and lie down there, and Izz and I will make up your number.'

'I don't like to let you do that. I'm taller than you, too.'

However, she was so overcome that she consented to lie down awhile, and reclined on a heap of pull-tails – the refuse after the straight straw had been drawn – thrown up at the further side of the barn. Her succumbing had been as largely owing to agitation at re-opening the subject of her separation from her husband as to the hard work. She lay in a state of percipience without volition, and the rustle of the straw and the cutting of the ears by the others had the weight of bodily touches.

She could hear from her corner, in addition to these noises, the murmur of their voices. She felt certain that they were continuing the subject already broached, but their voices were so low that she could not catch the words. At last Tess grew more and more anxious to know what they were saying, and, persuading herself that she felt better, she got up and resumed work.

Then Izz Herbert broke down. She had walked more than a dozen miles the previous evening, had gone to bed at midnight, and had risen again at five o'clock. Marian alone, thanks to her bottle of liquor and stoutness of build, stood the strain upon back and arms without suffering. Tess urged Izz to leave off, agreeing, as she felt better, to finish the day without her, and make equal division of the number of sheaves.

Izz accepted the offer gratefully, and disappeared through the great door into the snowy track to her lodging. Marian, as was the case every afternoon at this time on account of the bottle, began to feel in romantic vein.

'I should not have thought it of him – never!' she said in a dreamy tone. 'And I loved him so! I didn't mind his having *you*. But this about Izz is too bad!'

Tess, in her start at the words, narrowly missed cutting off a finger with the bill-hook.

'Is it about my husband?' she stammered.

'Well, yes. Izz said, "Don't 'ee tell her"; but I am sure I can't help it! It was what he wanted Izz to do. He wanted her to go off to Brazil with him.'

Tess's face faded as white as the scene without, and its curves straightened. 'And did Izz refuse to go?' she asked.

'I don't know. Anyhow he changed his mind.'

'Pooh – then he didn't mean it! 'Twas just a man's jest!'

'Yes he did; for he drove her a good-ways towards the station.'

'He didn't take her!'

They pulled on in silence till Tess, without any premonitory symptoms, burst out crying.

'There!' said Marian. 'Now I wish I hadn't told 'ee!'

Thomas Hardy, *Tess of the D'Urbervilles* (1891)

Sunday, 6th April 1941
The long, harrowing weeks of training are over and we are now fully-fledged Filter Room Plotters, reading to keep track of anything that flies from a wild goose to a Heinkel.

Up at the crack of dawn, we packed our duffel bags – (Hitler invades Greece, announced somebody's wireless) – and set off gloomily for our new home, Preston, apparently the worst posting you can get apart from Stornoway! Luckily I'm going with my three best pals, Gussy, Pandora and Oscarine.

Our first view from the train windows didn't exactly cheer us up – grey lines of brick houses, cobbled streets, a pall of smoke from factory chimneys and a thundery sky. It was early evening and already it was growing dark.

As we lugged our duffel bags across to the truck we were aware of a strong reek of fish and chips. Leering old women with lank grey hair were tottering along in clogs and shawls over the damp, greasy cobbles, and most of the younger women seemed to be in the family way. Some of the children had pink-eye, or rickets, or were going bald, and we saw a lot of men who were crippled. We began to feel more and more apprehensive.

About five miles outside of Preston the truck stopped

before what appeared to be the half-finished skeleton of a house. Surely this couldn't be it? It was. Gussy, Pandora, Oscarine and self staggered out, lugging our kit bags, and sat wearily down on the bare metal bedsteads. Through cracks in the plaster an icy wind whistled around a large, bare room containing twenty beds, with metal lockers beside them.

'Oh, where we are is Hell, and where Hell is, there must we ever be!' quoted Oscarine, always the scholar – she is mad about Marlowe.

Gussy's fair curls were hanging down in wisps around her miserable little face; even the queenly Pandora, usually endowed with British phlegm, seemed a little dismayed.

None of the rooms seemed to have any doors nor the lavatories any paper nor the lavatory doors any locks, and the mattresses were bags stuffed with straw – great ears of corn sticking out right and left.

Gussy and I went gloomily up to the bathroom to wash, and a WAAF tore in, sat herself down on the WC and began to pee.

'What's this place like?' we asked.

'Lousy as hell,' she replied, wiping herself with a large sheet of newspaper. 'Just you wait and see!'

Hardly had she left when a peroxide blonde, nude except for a pair of soiled blue satin drawers, lurched in and began to retch into the basin.

'My God, I'm bloody drunk!' she said, rather unnecessarily.

Gussy and I took one look and fled.

Downstairs our sergeant was dishing out mugs of watery cocoa and spam sandwiches. Apparently it was too late for us to march up to the mess hall for supper, so we sat on the edge of our beds and clasped freezing hands around our mugs. In spite of our despair we felt happy that at least we were still together. Oscarine was my best friend at training camp. She was called Oscarine because her mother started having her during a matinée of *The Importance of Being Earnest*, but we usually call her Oscar. I think she is one of the prettiest girls I have ever seen. Soft dark hair falling forward over her cheeks, blue smudges under her almond eyes, and small wire spectacles which she wears on the end of her nose for reading, which she does all the time – mainly very highbrow things like Thomas Mann and Jung. I passionately admire her thin, keen, rather lesbian appearance, so unlike my own squashy femininity.

Gussy is gorgeous in quite a different way, a sort of blonde nymphomaniac with totally round, blue-grey eyes which make her look rather innocent. She walks in a very sexy way, leaning back from the hips as if offering herself to some invisible lover. She once told Oscar that her whole body was one vast erogenous zone. We looked this up, and are very jealous.

Pandora is one of those tall beautiful repressed girls who come from a good Catholic family – her mama is Lady Wynn-Waterlow. She has rather a handsome face, like a thoroughbred horse – high cheekbones, slightly reddened, and piercing grey eyes. I think being in the WAAFs is doing her a power of good, loosening her up and making her more human.

That night it was freezing cold and we all slept in our underclothes – except, that is, for Pandora, who changed into her oyster-grey silk pyjamas. She kept her pearls on too, because she says real pearls die if you take them off for too long.

I lay shivering in bed, thinking of my lost studio in Chelsea, so warm and cheery with the oil stove, and Rupert playing his guitar. I must remember to buy a hot water bottle tomorrow.

Joan Wyndham, *Love is Blue: A Wartime Diary*
(1986)

YAZZ DECIDED THAT although Courtney was quite igno-
rant of other cultures, she'd shown strength of character and chutzpah, a precondition for joining the Unfuckwithables where they all tended to speak their minds and you had to fight back and not run off crying to the toilet like a wimp
  she liked Courtney
  and if she liked her
  she was in the squad
  one Monday morning a few months later, Yazz informed her, as they queued for the toilet after the Race, Class and Gender class, that she was in effect now an honorary sistah with an *h*, a term that originated with black women which was now being appropriated (typical!) by those who weren't
  however, Courtney could never be a fully-fledged sistah, only honorarily so
  she explained that being a sistah was a response to how we're seen as much as who we are, which actually defies

simplistic reductionism, and that who we are is partly a response to how we're seen, babe

Yazz found herself calling people she liked 'babe' these days, it wasn't forced or pretentious, it just happened naturally

it's a conundrum, Yazz continued the conversation over lunch of bean soup for her (protein for the brain) and meat, mash and mushy peas for Courtney

people won't see you as just another woman any more, but as a white woman who hangs with the brownies, and you'll lose a bit of your privilege, you should still check it, though, have you heard the expression, check your privilege, babe?

Courtney replied that seeing as Yazz is the daughter of a professor and a very well-known theatre director, she's hardly underprivileged herself, whereas she, Courtney, comes from a really poor community where it's normal to be working in a factory at sixteen and have your first child as a single mother at seventeen, and that her father's farm is effectively owned by the bank

yes, but I'm black, Courts, which makes me more oppressed than anyone who isn't, except Waris who is the most oppressed of all of them (although don't tell her that)

in five categories: black, Muslim, female, poor, hijabbed

she's the only one Yazz can't tell to check her privilege

Courtney replied that Roxane Gay warned against the idea of playing 'privilege Olympics' and wrote in *Bad Feminist* that privilege is relative and contextual, and I agree, Yazz, I mean, where does it all end? is Obama less privileged than a white hillbilly growing up in a trailer park with a junkie single mother and a jailbird father? is a severely disabled

person more privileged than a Syrian asylum-seeker who's
been tortured? Roxane argues that we have to find a new
discourse for discussing inequality

Yazz doesn't know what to say, when did Court read
Roxane Gay – who's amaaaazing?

was this a student outwitting the master moment?
#whitegirltrumpsblackgirl

Bernadine Evaristo, *Girl, Woman, Other* (2019)

K ATE GASPED.
'Jesus!' said Judy.

'Wrong again,' said Kate, who could never resist a
one-liner. Astonished, she stood in the doorway, trying to
decide what this was all about. Judy and Pagan were sitting
on a couple of apricot velvet couches placed at right angles
to each other; at either end of the couches, huge vases of
madonna lilies and imported apple blossoms stood on low
smoked-glass tables and beyond, to the right, in a beige velvet
armchair, sat Maxine.

'What's this, a surprise reunion?' asked Kate.

Pagan fingered the delicate little green malachite butter-
fly that hung around her neck on a fine gold Cartier chain.
Maxine said in a fast, low voice, 'We'd better be careful
what we say.'

The atmosphere was tense. Kate did not have time to
move over to the other women before the double doors at the
far end of the room were flung open and in walked a small,

gold-skinned young woman, wearing a white silk gown draped like an ancient Greek tunic.

Star quality radiated from Lili. A cloud of black, soft hair hung to her shoulders, swept back from an oval face with high, slanting cheekbones. Her small nose had a faintly predatory hook, her full lower lip was slightly too large, but when you looked at her you only noticed her eyes. They were huge shining chestnut eyes, thickly lashed, that glistened as if a crystal tear were about to fall from each one.

Tonight, however, Lili's eyes did not glisten. They glared. They projected rage and fury. For a moment the star stood silent as she surveyed the four older women: Kate in her Mulberry suit by the door; Pagan in pink, sprawled across apricot cushions; Maxine poised, porcelain cup in one hand, the saucer held on her blue silk lap; Judy in brown velvet, on the edge of the sofa with shoulders hunched, hands under her chin, elbows on her knees, scowling right back at Lili.

Then Lili spoke.

'All right,' she said, 'which one of you bitches is my mother?'

Shirley Conran, *Lace* (1982)

6
LONELINESS AND LONGING

'I have no friends at all,' said Mary. 'I never had.
My Ayah didn't like me and I never played with
anyone.'

Frances Hodgson Burnett,
The Secret Garden (1911)

Stevie Smith $\sim$ Marjorie Hillis $\sim$ Lorna Sage $\sim$ Katherine Philips
Anthony Quinn $\sim$ Henry Handel Richardson $\sim$ Stella Gibbons
Elizabeth Gaskell $\sim$ Anita Brookner

'We really have no absent friends,' writes Elizabeth Bowen, in *The Death of the Heart*. When a friend leaves us, Bowen insists, we turn them into a kind of traitor, however sad or unwilling they may have been at the departure themselves.

Perhaps there's some truth to this: betrayals aside, time is a great healer, restoring even the sorest and most jagged heart. But the prospect of renewed loneliness is painful nonetheless. The seventeenth-century poet Katherine Philips puts it best when she writes: '. . . neither Chance nor Compliment/Did element our Love;/'Twas sacred Sympathy was lent/Up from the quire above/ That Friendship Fortune did create . . .'. Lightning, in other words, doesn't strike twice. Good friends are rare, even miraculous. They cannot easily be replaced.

Loneliness comes in many shades. It may be born of shyness or ineptitude; to feel oneself a misfit is often to experience a circular prophecy. It can also be the result of circumstance: a new job or city, widowhood, a divorce or separation. In this chapter, I've included a section of Marjorie Hillis's spirited guide to the single life, *How to Live Alone and Like It*, a book that was first published in 1936 and is in some senses just a charming period piece now: impossible to imagine any twenty-first century agony aunt recommending a board game as a means of making friends. But what's striking, and a little sad, is that the problems it addresses haven't gone away either – or at any rate, loneliness hasn't. Looking through some small ads in early 2024, I found a notice in the smart magazine best known as a place where well-off families find their au pairs. 'Intelligent, single female, early 60s, seeking some nice lady friends, straight, solvent, for friendship,' it said. But it was the second sentence that made the heart ache: 'Previous responses must have got lost in Christmas mail.'

The Persian

The gas fire
Seemed quite a friend
Such a funny little humming noise it made
And it had a name, too, carved on it you know,
'The Persian'. The Persian!
Ha ha ha; ha ha.

Now Agnes, pull yourself together.
You and your friends.

Stevie Smith, 'The Persian', *Collected Poems and*
Drawings **(2018)**

As we have already suggested, one of the great secrets of living alone successfully is not to live alone too constantly. A reasonably large circle of friends and enemies whom you can see when you want to, and will often see when you don't want to, is an important asset. Anybody can acquire it, but it takes a little doing.

Perhaps you have them already – but just wait till you're established in your one-woman apartment, and see how rapidly they fade out of the picture unless you do what is known as Keeping Up Your End.

This keeping-up requires far more planning in a small establishment than in a large one. In most big families, somebody is always asking somebody else to a meal, and parties are a matter of spontaneous combustion. Also, you are apt to be included in invitations to other members of your family – all of which makes gay life comparatively effortless.

But, in your own solitary ménage, parties won't happen unless you plan them, and there won't be many guests unless you invite them. Moreover, you won't be a guest yourself unless you are also a hostess. Why should you be?

The most popular woman in the world might be invited to Mrs Smith's house two – or even three – times without a return engagement. But it's a safe bet that, unless she does something for Mrs Smith, she won't be invited a fourth time. If she were, she wouldn't go. The old-fashioned notion that single women are objects of social charity was killed in the War.

Nor is the invitation to Mrs Smith enough. You've got to give her – to say nothing of Mr Smith – a good time when she gets there.

This is really a simple matter. The best parties (we are not referring to Beaux Arts Balls or liquor marathons, but to parties of four to perhaps eight) are not tricky affairs. They consist chiefly of guests and food that mix well and drinks that are well mixed.

Don't think that your establishment is too simple even for this. You can get over any embarrassment you may feel in this respect by entertaining, first, guests who are in the same fix as you – or worse. Preferably worse. Perhaps you do *not* live in an eight-room apartment with a large and handsome dining-room and two maids. A four-room apartment with a foyer that does double duty as a dining room, and one maid, may be just as chic as the larger one – if you know how to make it so. Or perhaps, instead of the four-room apartment, yours is a two-room affair. Many a clever woman is a charming hostess at a refectory table set in the window of her living-room, with a maid who comes in for company occasions. Or perhaps you live in a one-room apartment, and your kitchen is a hole in the wall. You can still feel like a grande dame if you entertain a lady living in a single bedroom with no kitchen whatsoever. In fact, with ingenuity and the things that now come out of cans, you can give her a Park Avenue dinner.

The point is to get her, and her sisters (not to mention her brothers), to come and to like it. Singly, if that's easier, but often. She'll have to ask you back. And so, with a little persistency, begins a series of activities that may lead to anything, but will certainly put an end to loneliness.

Of course, it is not parties, but companionship that is essential to happiness. Every woman needs to have friends who drop in for tea or cocktails or supper, and who ask her to drop in. She needs friends with whom to share expeditions, friends to whom she can pour out her enthusiasm and troubles and show off her new hats and her old beaux.

If you live where you've always lived, you already have a circle of friends – or ought to have. Then, it's largely a matter of rearranging them. In the first place, if your solitary state is recent, don't expect to see as much of the married ones as you used to. And don't be so hurt by the new state of affairs that you spoil the party when they do include you.

Remember, you're a lot of trouble to them anyway. And you probably wouldn't have enjoyed being a fifth wheel – or a seventh, or any other number that is disturbing to bridge games, dinner-tables, tête-à-têtes, or dancing. Above all, don't get to be one of those tiresome women who drop in on their relatives' parties and expect to be cut into a game, while some invited guest sits by and watches.

It's a good idea to collect Odd Numbers like yourself, the way Mr Frick collected paintings. You can build up quite a coterie if you take enough trouble, mix your friends intelligently, and show a little shrewdness as to when to invite them, and what for. Include as few relatives as possible in one group, on the principle that it's infinitely better for a Lone Female to offend her relatives by not inviting them enough, than to bore her relations by inviting them too often. In other words, it's better to be a snob than a hanger-on.

If you have recently come to a new town, your difficulties are greater, but by no means hopeless. And this is true whether your contacts are through the Junior League, or the sales-girls in a department store. If you haven't any contacts, put your hat right on and go out and start making them. You probably have, at least, a fourth cousin to look up or a few letters to present. If not, there are always business women's organizations, dancing classes, literary courses, political clubs, churches, YWCAs, poetry groups, bridge lessons, musical circles, skating clubs, riding classes, college-extension courses, and what-not. Be a Communist, a stamp collector, or a Ladies' Aid worker if you must, but for heaven's sake, be something.

When you are something, do something about it. Pick out

your logical prey, and pounce. This process is called 'going half-way' and often means going two-thirds of the way or more. (It does not, however, mean going too far.)

A good beginning is to find out what the other person likes to do. You then intimate that you like to do it, too, and after some parleying eventually reach, 'Let's do it together.'

Games are among the best get-together aids yet invented. Tennis, golf, bridge, backgammon. You might even polish up your croquet and take on Mr Woollcott. It makes very little difference what you play, but it's a good idea to play it really well. If you find yourself marooned in Woodbine, Iowa, and the favorite game there is Parchesi, don't be above giving a little serious attention to Parchesi. There may be only a comparatively few smart games, but there are innumerable good games, and an ability to play them is insurance against boredom.

Food is, of course, the Great Uniter. While only a very rare party can survive dull refreshments, people are almost always friendly if you feed them well enough – well enough meaning, not quantity, but quality, as applied to the standards of the guests. There is probably no field with a greater range between provincialism and sophistication than that of the dinner-table. You can be as funny serving caviar in the sticks as serving candlestick salad on Park Avenue. But over a really delicious, well-planned meal, friendships can blossom like the dandelion, while a reputation for good cuisine is an almost certain step towards popularity.

A course in cooking may do more than a course in conversation, since the perfect hostess is, after all, not so much the one who is good at talking as the one who is good at making guests talk. Nor does good cooking mean elaborate cooking, even in the most sophisticated of circles – what with Lady Mendl serving corned-beef hash to Nobility, and scrambled eggs and sausages being favorite dishes at the smartest débutante parties. As with so many things, it's a matter of being in the know.

We have left the real crux of the problem till the last, feeling that it's a delicate matter. For the truth is that if you're interesting, you'll have plenty of friends; and if you're not, you won't – unless you're very, very rich. Fortunately, the first is easily accomplished, and we hope to tell you how in a later chapter.

*

Case XIII: Miss B. – Two years ago, Miss B.'s position made it necessary for her to move from Buffalo to Chicago, where she had no friends whatever. She soon found a pleasant one-room-and-bath-dressing-room apartment, but the matter of getting to know people proved more of a problem. Miss B., however, though neither beautiful nor dashing and having a very limited salary, is a friendly young lady with resources.

After a few rather drab weeks, she took herself firmly in hand. She joined a Tuesday-night gymnasium class at the YWCA and a Thursday-night class in Interior Decoration, and she budgeted her expenses so that she could go to a play or a good movie on Saturday nights. To back up her study of decoration, she spent at least half of her lunch hours visiting exhibitions, fine furniture shops, rooms arranged in the larger department stores, textile exhibits, and the Art Institute. In addition, she mapped out a course in reading the books she'd always meant to read – and pursued it on free evenings.

Miss B. is beginning her third year in Chicago, but she knows more people than many natives and has so few free evenings that when she wants to read she makes a date with herself and goes to bed with her book. The nucleus of her circle of friends were met in her work and the two classes, and the rest are friends of the nucleus, or friends of the friends. She still, however, goes to class once a week. This year, it's tap-dancing.

Marjorie Hillis, *How to Live Alone and Like It* **(1936)**

⁓

Try as i might to lose myself in the landscape, however, I was still only an apprentice misfit and self-conscious in the part. Other kids who hung about at all hours turned out to have errands – big brothers or sisters to fetch, a message to carry to someone working down the fields, or to Dad in the pub. You loiter with a lot more conviction if you've even the shadow of a purpose to neglect and that I lacked. And the truth was that often no amount of trudging would get me to the state of dreamy abstraction I craved. Then I was simply lonely. I wanted friends desperately and, as it happened, the move to The Arowry held out hope, for it gave me a second chance with two girls from school who'd had nothing to do with me when I'd lived in the vicarage – Janet Yates and Valerie Edge, who were now neighbours. Valerie, brown, rosy, curly-haired and tall for eight, lived at the first council house to be finished, which already had a proper garden with dahlias in the borders. Janet – slighter than me, but unlike me, neat and tidy – came from a smallholding down the lane, with a bush of pungent, grey 'Old Man' at the gate and a path made of red-and-blue bricks. Gates and gardens figured large in our friendship because we spent a lot of our time together leaning or swinging on one or other of our gates. With Valerie and Janet you didn't wander off, not because they weren't allowed to, exactly, but because they were too grown-up, they saw no point in it.

They were busy being big girls, practising for real life, which meant not so much mothering dolls or playing house or dressing up (although we must have done all these things), as whispering in a huddle, sharing secrets, giggling behind our hands and linking arms around each other's waists. It was like a dance, a dance of belonging with no private space in it, all inside-out intimacy, and I found it euphoric, intoxicating. And then we would quarrel, for the magic number three is a formula for dissension: two against one, two whispering together, turning away and giggling, the third shamed and outcast. It's obvious now that this was the real point of the whole elaborate dance, its climactic figure, but back then, of course, each quarrel seemed a disaster and I'd run home, tears streaming, and howl on my own back doorstep for hours. My mother, dismayed in the first place by my obsession with such ordinary (if not common) little girls and even more put out by the intensity of my grief when they turned their backs on me, would say, 'It's not the end of the world'. But she unwittingly provided me with exactly the right words. That's what it was, the end of the world, every time.

I cast myself as the odd one out, but in truth it wasn't

always so at all. The real shame that sticks to this memory comes when I recall the pang of pleasure I felt when Valerie and I shut out Janet. Our emotional triangle was a very good rehearsal for the world, the mimic anticipation of group psychology was perfect, even down to the fact that Valerie was never excluded. She was more sure of herself to start with and she remained innocent of the needy jealousy the other two of us suffered, so became ever more blithely, unconsciously cruel, our unmoved mover.

Lorna Sage, *Bad Blood* (2000)

To Mrs M. A. at Parting

I have examin'd and do find,
Of all that favour me,
There's none I grieve to leave behind
But only, only thee.
To part with thee I needs must die,
Could parting separate thee and I.

But neither Chance nor Compliment
Did element our Love;
'Twas sacred Sympathy was lent
Up from the quire above.
That Friendship Fortune did create,
Still fears a wound from Time or Fate.

Our chang'd and mingled souls are grown
To such acquaintance now,
That if each would resume their own,
Alas! we know not how.
We have each other so engross,
That each is in the union lost.

And thus we can no Absence know,
Nor shall we be confin'd;
Our active souls will daily go
To learn each other's mind.
Nay, should we never meet to Sense,
Our souls would hold Intelligence.

Inspired with a flame divine,
I scorn to court a stay;
For from that noble soul of thine
I ne'er can be away.
But I shall weep when thou dost grieve;
Nor can I die whilst thou dost live.

By my own temper I shall guess
At thy felicity,
And only like my happiness
Because it pleaseth thee.
Our hearts at any time will tell,
If thou, or I, be sick, or well.

All Honour sure I must pretend,
All that is good or Great;

She that would be Rosania's Friend,
Must be at least complete.
If I have any bravery,
'Tis cause I have so much of thee.

Thy linger soul in me shall lie,
And all thy thoughts reveal;
Then back again with mine shall fly
And thence to me shall steal.
Thus still to one another tend;
Such is the sacred Name of Friend.

Thus our twin-souls in one shall grow,
And teach the World new love,
Redeem the age and sex, and show
A flame Fate dares not move:
And courting Death to be our friend,
Our lives together too shall end.

A dew shall dwell upon our Tomb
Of such a quality,
That fighting armies, thither come,
Shall reconcilèd be.
We'll ask no Epitaph, but say
ORINDA and ROSANIA.

**Katherine Philips (1632–64), 'To Mrs M. A. at
Parting'**

'I've burnt my boats, I'm afraid. I saw the college prin-cipal this morning and,' – Freya kept her tone light, she couldn't bear to be self-pitying – 'and they've sent me down.'

Nancy's face seemed to crumple in stages. She just managed to get out 'Oh, Freya, *no*,' before her voice broke and tears sprang to her eyes. She was so distraught that Freya instinctively put her arms around her, and whispered fragments of consolation in her ear. If she had ever required proof of Nancy's enduring tenderness, here it was.

As she felt the flood of distress start to clear, Freya said, 'Shouldn't I be the one in tears?' She felt another convulsion in Nancy's shoulders that was somewhere between a sob and a laugh. She raised her smudged face to Freya's and said: 'Can't you appeal against it – surely you've got someone there who'd defend you?'

Freya shook her head. 'Bedders was kind. She said I'd shown enough promise to be given a second chance. But the others didn't think so – and once they'd handed down my sentence I realised I didn't really *want* a reprieve.'

Nancy turned her head away, swallowing hard. After a moment she said, 'I can't bear the thought of my life without you in it.'

Stunned by the simple avowal, Freya said hesitantly, 'Even after what I did? How I hurt you?'

'Yes, you did hurt me. But you're still my dearest friend.' She said it almost as a matter of fact. Then her expression stiffened slightly. 'I suppose you've told Robert.'

Freya's laugh was abrupt and unhappy. 'You haven't heard then? I saw him last night at a party. He was with someone else, a pretty girl called Cressida. So maybe I've got what I deserved.'

"That's not what I think,' said Nancy.

'I know. You're kind – altogether too kind.' She felt her own eyes reluctantly moisten. A tear rolled down her cheek and she impatiently brushed it away. 'I don't know what I'd have done if you hadn't—'

'He's not worth crying over, Freya.'

Freya shook her head. 'It's not just Robert. I ran into Jean Markham this morning, someone else I seem to have mortally offended. The look she gave me . . . Honestly, Nance, I know I've behaved badly, but – I'm not *such* a bloody cow, am I?'

Nancy smiled, and took hold of her hand. 'If I said something like that you'd tell me to stop being a ninny. Now drink this tea before it gets cold.'

Freya sank into an armchair, and drank the cooling tea. The light through Nancy's windows was pearly from the rain. As they looked at each other through tear-stung eyes she felt a kind of exhilarated sadness. She didn't care about being sent down – the shame of it didn't weigh a feather for her – but she feared what would happen now to her and Nancy. Oxford wasn't far from London, of course, they would only be a train journey away from one another. Only she knew that she had no staying power when it came to friendship; before Nancy she had made and shed friends as steadily as a tree its leaves. It had been her proud conviction that she was nobody's fool. But she had wondered, in moments of alarm, if she was nobody's friend, either.

Anthony Quinn, *Freya* (2016)

IN ALL THE three years Laura had been at school, she had not got beyond a surface friendliness with any of her fellows. Even those who had been her 'chums' had wandered like shades through the groves of her affection . . . to none of them had she been drawn by any deeper sense of affinity. And though she had come to believe, in the course of the last, more peaceful year, that she had grown used to being what you would call an unpopular girl – one, that is, with whom no one ever shared a confidence – yet seldom was there a child who longed more ardently to be liked, or suffered more acutely under dislike. Apart however from the brusque manner she had contracted, in her search after truth, it must be admitted that Laura had but a small talent for friendship; she did not grasp the constant give-and-take intimacy implies; the liking of others had to be brought to her, unsought, she, on the other hand, being free to stand back and consider whether or no the feeling was worth returning. And friends are not made in this fashion.

Henry Handel Richardson,
The Getting of Wisdom (1910)

Mrs steggles's jealous and irritable temperament made her unconsciously desire the friendship and affection which it kept at bay, and occasionally loneliness drove her to make violent friendships with women she hardly knew, whose acquaintance she had made in a teashop or a queue. At first all would go well and no praise could be too high for the new friend, but soon her nature would assert itself, and she would begin to find fault and give unwanted advice, and the friendship would rapidly cool until it was extinct. Each failure added to her bitterness, for it never occurred to her that it might be her fault, and she accused everybody of being jealous and spiteful and two-faced.

Stella Gibbons, *Westwood* (1946)

Mrs mason was a widow, and had to struggle for the sake of the six or seven children left dependent on her exertions; thus there was some reason, and great excuse, for the pinching economy which regulated her household affairs. On Sundays she chose to conclude that all her apprentices had friends who would be glad to see them to dinner, and give them a welcome reception for the remainder of the day; while she, and those of her children who were not at school, went to spend the day at her father's house, several miles out of the town. Accordingly, no dinner was cooked on Sundays for the young workwomen; no fires were lighted in any rooms to which they had access.

On this morning they breakfasted in Mrs Mason's own parlour, after which the room was closed against them through the day by some understood, though unspoken prohibition.

What became of such as Ruth, who had no home and no friends in that large, populous, desolate town? She had hitherto commissioned the servant, who went to market on Saturdays for the family, to buy her a bun or biscuit, whereon she made her fasting dinner in the deserted workroom, sitting in her walking-dress to keep off the cold, which clung to her in spite of shawl and bonnet. Then she would sit at the window, looking out on the dreary prospect till her eyes were often blinded by tears; and, partly to shake off thoughts and recollections, the indulgence in which she felt to be productive of no good, and partly to have some ideas to dwell upon during the coming week beyond those suggested by the constant view of the same room, she would carry her Bible, and place herself in the window-seat on the wide landing, which commanded the street in front of the house. From thence she could see the irregular grandeur of the place; she caught a view of the grey church-tower, rising hoary and massive into mid-air; she saw one or two figures loiter along on the sunny side of the street, in all the enjoyment of their fine clothes and Sunday leisure; and she imagined histories for them, and tried to picture to herself their homes and their daily doings.

Elizabeth Gaskell, *Ruth* (1853)

IT WAS AT moments like these that she would speak to me of letting the spare room, preferably to myself. The idea was overwhelmingly attractive to me. A move from Maida Vale would be symbolic; it would signify a complete break with the old sad way of life. I could walk out on the zig-zag rugs and the creaking hide chairs and the china and glass birds with as little sense of remorse as if I had never seen them before; they would be left to the next tenant and in that way I would not feel a pang of sorrow at seeing my parents' flat dismantled. Nancy could be dispatched to her sister in Cork, which would be appropriate, for I must admit that I did not look forward to her inevitable decline. She had been there at the beginning of my life; I did not want to witness the end of hers. I need bring nothing away with me. And there would be company at the Frasers'. If I moved in with them I would be delivered from the silence of Sundays, and all those terrible public holidays – Christmas, Easter – when I could never, ever find an adequate means of using up all the available time.

I find, however, that this particular dilemma, which I will call Public Holiday Syndrome and which I would rank next to Two-Star Hotel Bedroom Syndrome as an affliction to which I am particularly prone, is not to be talked about, even as a joke. It is generally felt that complaints about loneliness are unseemly and should be turned over to professional Samaritans. My own friendships have always been strong, but they no longer satisfy me. I do not seek friends so that they will offer consolation: I have a horror of that. I am an extremely good listener, and thus pretty well in demand, although recently I suppose I have been lazy. I have been aware of a boredom, a restlessness, that no ordinary friendship can satisfy: only an extraordinary one. I have grown tired of my lot, I suppose, and have wanted strenuously to change it. So I write, and I take a lot of long walks, and I ferment my ideas, and if I am lucky they come out as vivid as I should like real life to be. That may indeed be the purpose of the exercise. It just tends to break down at times like Good Friday or in places like dim foreign hotels. Then, the lure of company, any company, is enormous, and I feel it might be more sensible to prepare myself for contingencies like these by accepting the sort of offer that Alix was now making.

Anita Brookner, *Look at Me* **(1983)**

7

FRENEMIES AND FALLING OUT

Heigh-ho! sing, heigh-ho! unto the green holly:
Most friendship is feigning, most loving mere folly

William Shakespeare, *As You Like It* (1599?)

Katherine Mansfield ⌒ Ida Baker ⌒ Terry Castle ⌒ Sheila Heti

Jean Lucey Pratt ⌒ Zoë Heller ⌒ Charlotte Brontë ⌒ Margaret Atwood

Katie Roiphe ⌒ Ottessa Moshfegh ⌒ Meg Wolitzer ⌒ Dolly Alderton

Nora Ephron ⌒ Jane Austen

On 10 August 1784, the novelist Fanny Burney wrote to her friend Mrs Piozzi. Her letter was an apology (of sorts) for the fact that Mrs Piozzi felt Burney had not sent 'cordial congratulations' on her recent marriage, a union of which Burney openly disapproved. Three days later, Mrs Piozzi replied. She told her 'sweetest Burney' not to worry: she was far too happy herself to want to make a friend feel otherwise. 'Quiet your kind heart immediately,' she wrote. To this, Burney responded swiftly, with warmth and affection. But she would receive no reply. In fact, she would never hear from Mrs Piozzi again. The two women's correspondence of six years was at an end. The editor of Burney's letters, her niece Charlotte Barrett, tells us that her aunt could only conjecture that perhaps Mr Piozzi was behind 'the cessation'.

This may be one of the first recorded examples of what we now call ghosting: a person breaking off a relationship suddenly and without explanation, disappearing almost without trace. In the eighteenth century, it must have been a relatively easy strategy to pull off, communications and transport being as they were (also, one's servant could answer the door if necessary). In the twenty-first century, it's both more difficult, more public and more painful: a matter of unfriending, unfollowing and blocking on social media and mobile phones. The blue ticks of WhatsApp are, for the abandoned left shouting into a void, an instrument of torture. Is there a good way of ending a friendship? This is one for the problem pages. Most of us favour the approach – kinder and easier, if more cowardly – that is technically known as 'drifting apart'.

Why do friendships end? Boredom, envy, irritation, frustration, betrayal: all of these may play a part (and politics, too, if you're that way inclined). Some friends are false, toxic from the start, like horrible Barbara in Zoë Heller's *Notes on a Scandal*. Others, like Emma Woodhouse in *Emma*, are interfering (this chapter ends with Austen's heroine doing her best to ruin the happiness of poor Harriet Smith). A very few friendships seem to thrive on conflict: they come with an element that may only be described as sadomasochistic. This section begins with a series of letters in which the writer Katherine Mansfield complains about – and to – Ida Baker, better known as LM, one of her oldest friends. Baker met Mansfield at school in 1903, and their relationship continued, almost unbroken, until Katherine's death in 1923. Baker was not literary, and Mansfield excluded her from those circles. But she relied on her to provide emotional support and to carry out menial tasks; Baker kept house for her, and occasionally gave her money. Sometimes, Mansfield was grateful for all this. At others, Baker's attitude of supplication drove her mad. Baker must have been shocked and upset when Mansfield's diaries and letters were published after her death, and the world was able to read what her dearest friend had really thought of her. But she stayed silent for a long time. Not until 1971 did she attempt to set the record straight by publishing a book of her own, *Katherine Mansfield: The Memories of LM*.

LM HAS MADE me perfectly *sick* today. She's skittish. 'Dearie, I'm very proud. I remembered the word for candle – *bougie*. That's right, isn't it? I'm not really very stupid, you know. It's only when I am with you, because you are so many million miles ahead of all the rest of mankind—' and so on. I *squirm*, try and hold my tongue, and then – bang! and again I shoot her dead, and up she comes again . . .

Katherine Mansfield, Letter to John Middleton Murry, 2 March, 1918

IT'S A VERY dull day here with wild ragged clouds and a cold halting miserable wind. My black fit is on me – not caused by the day altogether. Christ! to *hate* like I do. It's upon me today. You don't know what hatred is because I know you have never hated anyone – not as you have loved – equally. That's what I do. My deadly enemy has got me today and I'm simply a blind force of hatred. Hate is the *other* passion. It has all the opposite effects of Love. It fills you with death and corruption, it makes you feel hideous, degraded and old, it makes you long to DESTROY. Just as the other is light, so this is darkness. I hate like that – a million times multiplied. It's like being under a curse. When LM goes, I don't know what I shall do. I can only think of breathing – lying quite still and breathing. Her great fat arms, her tiny blind breasts, her baby mouth, the underlip always wet and a crumb or two or a chocolate

stain at the corners – her eyes fixed on me – fixed – waiting
for what I may do that she may copy it. Think what you
would feel if you had consumption and lived with such a
deadly enemy! That's one thing I shall begrudge Virginia*
all her days – that she and Leonard were together. We can't
be; we've got to wait our six months, but when they are up,
I WILL not have LM near. I shall rather commit suicide.
That is dead earnest. In fact, I have made up my mind that I
shall commit suicide if I don't tear her up by the roots then.
It would be kinder for us both – for you and me, of course
I mean. We'd have no love otherwise. You'd only grow to
think I was first wicked and then mad. You'd be quite right.
I'm both with her – mad, really mad, like Lawrence was,
only worse. I leaned over the gate today and dreamed she'd
died of heart-failure and I heard myself cry out 'Oh, what
heaven! what heaven!'

Katherine Mansfield, Letter to John Middleton Murry, 20 November, 1919

PERHAPS JACK† IS right; I am a tyrant. But . . . look here
a) Will you please either date your letters or put the
day at the top b) Do you mind cutting out the descriptions
as much as you can? That kind of yearning sentimental
writing about a virginia creeper and the small haigh voices
of tainy children is more than I can stick. It makes me hang

---

*   Virginia Woolf.
†   Mansfield's husband, John Middleton Murry.

my head; it makes Jack play the mouth organ whenever we meet it in females. But I shall say no more. This is where the tyrant comes in. It's so much worse when the spelling is wrong, too.

Katherine Mansfield, Letter to Ida Baker, 29 August, 1921

WE CANNOT LIVE together in any sense until we – I – are am stronger. It seems to me it is my job, my fault, and not yours. I am simply unworthy of friendship, as I am. I take advantage of you, demand perfection of you, crush you. And the devil of it is that even though that is true as I write it I want to laugh. A deeper self looks at you and a deeper self in you looks back and we laugh and say 'what nonsense'. It's very queer, Jones, isn't it? Can you believe it – that looking back upon our times in Italy and Garavan – even the afternoon when you were raking the garden and I was proving our purely evil effect on each other I keep on remembering that it was a lovely day or that the button daisies were ducks. How nice – how very nice it would be to bowl along in one of those open cabs with the wind ruffling off the sea and a smell of roasting coffee and fresh lemons from the land. Oh dear! Oh dear! And do you remember standing at your window in your kimono one morning at five o'clock while I sat up in bed behind the mosquito curtains and talked of decomposition? No, we can't simply live apart for all our lives from now on. We shall have to visit at least. How can we live? What is the best plan? The future is so wrapt in mystery. Until I am well, it's foolishness for us to be together . . .

Katherine Mansfield, Letter to Ida Baker, 15 March, 1922

THERE IS ONE thing which I must try to explain. So often people have passed judgement on the way Katherine behaved to me, saying 'She made use of you.' But if she did make use of me, it was because I saw to it that she did. 'She must have been terribly difficult to live with', they have also said. Katherine believed that one should try to live perfectly, down to the smallest detail. No human being could always maintain that standard, and though I entirely approved of it and attempted to do so, I fell below it often, even in the simplest things. Katherine failed too, as she often acknowledged, but through all the difficult later years of her life she held bravely to her faith and succeeded far better than it is possible to relate. If she asked much of others she asked more of herself, and felt strongly that, if you wished to be a fine artist, you must discipline yourself and learn to live finely.

Ida Baker, *The Memories of LM* (1971)

NO DOUBT HUNDREDS (thousands?) of people knew Susan Sontag better than I did. For ten years ours was an on-again, off-again semi-friendship, constricted by role-playing and shot through in the end by mutual irritation. Over the years I labored to hide my growing disillusion, especially during my last ill-fated trip to New York, where she regaled me – for the umpteenth time – about the siege of Sarajevo, the falling bombs, and how the pitiful Joan Baez had been too terrified to come out of her hotel room. Sontag flapped her arms and shook her big mannish hair – inevitably described in the press as a 'mane' – contemptuously. *That woman is a fake! She tried to fly to California the next day! I was there for months. Through all of the bombardment, of course, Terry.* Then she ruminated. Had I ever met Baez? Was she a secret lesbian? I confessed that I'd once waited in line behind the folk singer at my cash machine (Baez lives near Stanford) and had taken the opportunity to inspect the hairs on the back of her neck. Sontag, who sensed a rival, considered this non-event for a moment, but after further inquiries, was reassured that I, her forty-something slave girl from San Francisco, still preferred her to Ms Diamonds and Rust.

At its best, our relationship was rather like the one between Dame Edna and her feeble sidekick Madge, or possibly Stalin and Malenkov. Sontag was the Supremo and I the obsequious gofer. When she came to San Francisco, usually once or twice a year, I instantly became her female aide-de-camp: a one-woman posse, ready to drop anything at a phone call (including the classes I was supposed to be teaching at Stanford) and drive her around to various Tower Records stores and dim sum restaurants. Most important, I became adept at clucking sympathetically at her constant kvetching: about the stupidity and philistinism of whatever local sap was paying for her lecture trip, how no one had yet appreciated the true worth of her novel *The Volcano Lover*, how you couldn't find a decent dry cleaner in down-town San Francisco, etc., etc.

True: from my point of view, it had all begun extraordinarily well. Even now I have to confess that, early on, Sontag gave me a couple of the sweetest (not to mention most amusing) moments of my adult life. The first came one gray magical morning at Stanford in 1996, when after several hours of slogging away on student papers, I opened a strange manila envelope that had come for me, with a New York return address. The contents, a brief fan letter about a piece I'd written on Charlotte Brontë and a flamboyantly inscribed paperback copy of her play, *Alice in Bed* ('from Susan') made me dizzy with ecstasy. Having idolized Sontag literally for decades – I'd first read *Notes on Camp* as an exceedingly arch nine-year old – I felt as if Pallas Athena herself had suddenly materialized and offered me a cup of ambrosia. (O Great Susan! Most august Goddess of Female Intellect!) I zoomed around, showing the note to various pals. To this day, when I replay it in my mind, I still get a weird toxic jolt of adolescent joy, like taking a big hit of Krazy Glue vapors out of a paper bag.

Things proceeded swiftly in our honeymoon phase. Sontag, it turned out, was coming to Stanford for a writer-in-residence stint that spring and the first morning after her arrival abruptly summoned me to take her out for breakfast. The alacrity with which I drove the 40 miles down from San Francisco – trying not to get flustered but panting a bit at the wheel nonetheless – set the pattern for our days. We made the first of several madcap car trips around Palo Alto and the Stanford foothills. While I drove, often somewhat erratically, she would alternate between loud complaints about her faculty club accommodation, the bad food at the Humanities Centre, the 'dreariness' of my Stanford colleagues (*Terry, don't you loathe academics as much as I do? How can you abide it?*) – and her Considered Views on Everything (*Yes, Terry, I* do *know all the lesser-known Handel operas. I told Andrew Porter he was right – they are the greatest of musical masterpieces*). I was rapt, like a hysterical spinster on her first visit to Bayreuth. *Schwärmerei* time for T-Ball.

The Sarajevo obsession revealed itself early on: in fact, inspired the great comic episode in this brief golden period. We were walking down University Avenue, Palo Alto's twee, boutique-crammed main drag, on our way to a bookshop. Sontag was wearing her trademark intellectual-diva outfit: voluminous black top and black silky slacks, accessorized with a number of exotic, billowy scarves. These she constantly adjusted or flung back imperiously over one shoulder, stopping now and then to puff on a cigarette or expel a series of phlegmy coughs. (The famous Sontag 'look' always put me in mind of the stage direction in *Blithe Spirit*: 'Enter Madame Arcati, wearing barbaric jewellery.') Somewhat incongruously, she had completed her ensemble with a pair of pristine, startlingly white tennis shoes. These made her feet seem comically huge, like Bugs Bunny's. I half expected her to bounce several feet up and down in the air whenever she took a step, like one of those people who have shoes made of Flubber in the old Fred McMurray movie.

She'd been telling me about the siege and how a Yugoslav woman she had taken shelter with had asked her for her autograph, even as bombs fell all around them. She relished the woman's obvious intelligence (*Of course, Terry, she'd read* The Volcano Lover, *and like all Europeans, admired it tremendously*) and her own sangfroid. Then she stopped abruptly, and asked, grim-faced, if I'd ever had to evade sniper fire. I said, no, unfortunately not. Lickety-split she was off, dashing in a feverish crouch from one boutique doorway to the next, white tennis shoes a blur, all the way down the street to Restoration Hardware and the Baskin-Robbins store. Five or six perplexed Palo Altans stopped to watch as she bobbed zanily in and out, ducking her head, pointing at imaginary gunmen on rooftops and gesticulating wildly at me to follow. No one, clearly, knew who she was, though several of them looked as though they thought they should know who she was.

In those days, I felt like an intellectual autodidact facing the greatest challenge of her career: the Autodidact of all Autodidacts. The quizzing was relentless. Had I read Robert Walker (*Ooooh errg blush, ahem, little cough, um: No, I'm ashamed to say* . . .) Had I read Thomas Bernhard? (*Yes! Yes, I have!* Wittgenstein's Nephew! *Yay! Yippee! Wow! Phew! Dodged the bullet that time!*) It seemed, for a while at least, that I had yet to be contaminated by the shocking intellectual mediocrity surrounding me at Stanford U. This exemption from idiocy was due mainly, I think, to the fact that I could hold my own with her in the music-appreciation department. Trading CDs and recommendations – in a peculiar, masculine, train-spotting fashion – later became part of our fragile bond. I scored a coup one time with some obscure Busoni arrangements she'd not heard of (though she assured me that *she had, of course, known the pianist* – the late Paul Jacobs – *very well*); but I almost came a cropper when I confessed I had never listened to Janáček's *The Excursions of Mr Brouček*. She gave me a surprised look, then explained, somewhat loftily, that I owed it to myself, as a 'cultivated person', to become acquainted with it. (*I adore Janáček's sound world*, she opined.) A recording of the opera appeared soon after in the mail, so I knew I'd been forgiven, but after listening to it once I couldn't really get anywhere with it. (It *does* tend to go on a bit, in the same somewhat exhausting Central European way I now associate with Sontag herself.) The discs are still on my shelf. Given their exalted provenance I can't bear to unload them at the used CD shop in my neighborhood.

And she also flirted, in a coquettish, discombobulating, yet unmistakable fashion. She told me she had read my book, *The Apparitional Lesbian*, and 'agreed with me entirely' about Henry James and *The Bostonians*. She made me describe at length how I'd met my then girlfriend. (*She wrote you a letter! And you answered? Terry, but I would never answer one! Of course, Terry, I'm stunned!*)

Though I was far too cowed to ask her directly about her own love life, she would reveal the occasional titbit from her legendary past, then give me a playful, almost girlish look. (*Of course, Terry, everyone said Jeanne Moreau and I were lovers, but you know, we were just good friends.*) My apotheosis as tease-target came the night of her big speech in Kresge Auditorium. She had begun by reprimanding those in the audience who failed to consider her one of the 'essential' modern novelists, then read a seemingly interminable section of what was to become *In America*. (Has any other major literary figure written such an excruciatingly turgid book?) At the end, as the audience gave way to enormous, relieved clapping – thank God that's over – she made a beeline towards me. Sideswiping the smiling president of Stanford and an eager throng of autograph-seekers, she elbowed her way towards me, enveloped me rakishly in her arms, and said very loudly, 'Terry, we've got to stop meeting like this.' She seemed to think the line hilarious and chortled heartily. I felt at once exalted, dopey, and mortified, like a plump teenage boy getting a hard-on in front of everybody.

Terry Castle, 'Desperately Seeking Susan',
***The Professor and Other Writings* (2010)**

A WEEK BACK IN Toronto, Sheila receives an email from Margaux . . .

1   i know i can be intense sometimes, and i know
    you have a lot going on, and this is not that big of a
    deal, but i wanted to say that it really startled me in
    miami when you bought the same yellow dress that i
    was buying.

2   after we looked at a thousand dresses for you – and
    the yellow dress being the first dress i was consider-
    ing – i really was surprised when you said you were
    getting it too.

3 i suggested you try it on when i thought there was
   only one size, but when you said you were also
   getting it, i didn't know what to say or think.

4 i think it's pretty standard that you don't buy the
   dress your friend is buying, but i was trying to convince myself that maybe it was okay to buy the same
   dress your friend is buying. you know, trying to
   think about it positively, hence the 'we'll wear them
   in our music video' statement from me.

5 when you said that you'd only wear it out of town
   and never in toronto, it sort of seemed reasonable.

6 but not really, since of course we only exist in
   pictures.

7 i should have been clearer in the store about how
   it made me uncomfortable, or i just shouldn't have
   bought the dress.

8 i really do need some of my own identity, and this is
   pretty simple and good for the head.

9 i'm going to get rid of the dress now, cause it makes
   me a little sad to look at it.

10 you don't have to reply to this email.
   Hurt and shocked, I did not.

Sheila Heti, *How Should a Person Be?* (2012)

I WANT NOCKIE'S SYMPATHY, approval, help and encouragement, of course I do, and I get them in large measure,
and yet in the next breath she will have got her claws into

a dream and will have rent it asunder. She cannot let well alone. As I lay in bed last night and when I woke this morning I felt bruised.

She cannot bear to think that I might at any time find a greater happiness than she has done. Or that I should do any work which she herself could not do too and excel in.

When she comes to analysing my doings she draws from her own experience – and the yardstick of her own ego is brought out. She wants me to be happy, to have a happy love affair or marriage. But to her own standards. She will never wholly approve of any man I fall for. Because I have now fallen for a business type, she suggests a tall American who'd call you 'honey'. Because she is in love with an American, I must fall in love with an American too. Because she is not really happy in her job and despises the people (civil servants) she works with, she thinks that I must not like my job and companions either. If I followed her pattern, if I were like her, she knows she could beat me and be 'top'.

*

Dear N. is now to be called Nicola instead of Nockie, a name F. has made for her and suits her well. She is I think my dearest enemy. She sat on my bed yesterday after she was up about 7 a.m. and lectured me with greatest kindness and affection about A. I'm never at my best at that hour and her thoughts are always freshest and most forceful then. She had to tell me what she'd been thinking. Swept at me like the Charge of the Light Brigade and left me crawling after my dead and wounded. As many women do, as she did for nearly 10 years with her American T., she says I am clinging to a corner I won't spring clean. I am wasting myself on A., he is worthless. A man like that, who can behave as he does will NEVER etc. etc. She is *never* wrong about a man, the situation could never be a happy one . . .

Jean Lucey Pratt, 'March 26, 1947', *A Notable Woman: The Romantic Journals of Jean Lucey Pratt* ed. Simon Garfield (2015)

B Y SUMMER, MY connection to Sheba was well-established. Hardly a week went by when we didn't see each other outside of school hours. Sue Hodge had not yet been utterly vanquished: she was still hanging in there, waddling with us to lunches at La Traviata. But her days were definitely numbered. Now, on afternoons when it rained, it was I – not Sue – who heaved Sheba's bicycle into the back of my car and drove her home . . . Sue had fought a valiant battle but, in the end, she simply wasn't able to put the sort of work into Sheba that I was. She had her impending Sue-Spawn, her ghastly little love nest with Ted, to worry about. Try as she might, she couldn't keep her eye on the ball.

Shortly after Sue caught on to the fact that I had leap-frogged her in Sheba's affections, it became apparent that she was saying things about Sheba and me to other members of staff. Sheba and I were a bit *too* fond of one another, she told people; a bit *too* close. The implication was that Sheba and I were engaged in some sort of Sapphic love affair. I was not distressed on my account. I have been on the receiving end of this sort of malicious gossip more than once in my career and I am quite accustomed to it by now. Vulgar speculation about sexual proclivity would seem to be an occupational hazard for a single woman like myself, particularly one who insists on maintaining a certain discretion about her private life. I know who I am. If people wish to make up lurid stories about me, that is their affair. I could not be sure, however, that Sheba would be capable of matching my indifference. I feared that she would be offended, or enraged, or else horribly embarrassed. After considering the matter carefully, I decided it was best not to tell her about the rumours.

It wasn't easy keeping quiet. It was immensely irritating, in fact, not to be able to expose Sue's rank hypocrisy. Sheba was always so generous to Sue. She would allow her to sit there, sucking up to her for hours, and never let on for a second that she was bored. She wouldn't even tolerate me making jokes at Sue's expense. Once, when Sue left our table at La Traviata to go to the toilet, I made the mistake of calling her a 'fat fool'. Sheba just frowned at me and said quietly, 'What energy you spend on hating people!'

Sheba was always very up front that way – never afraid to express her disapproval when she thought I was being bitchy. Once or twice, when we were on the phone together, she actually slammed the receiver down in protest at me being 'too negative'. The first time it happened, I was in mid-sentence and it was a few moments before I realised that I was alone on the line. I called back, assuming that we'd been cut off but, no, she told me, she'd simply grown tired of hearing me drone on.

It was a new experience, being told off like that. In my

other friendships over the years, I have tended to dominate. I've never made any conscious bid for power; it has always come about quite naturally that I should be the one to lead. But I can see now that my imposing personality has caused problems. It has created inequality and that inequality has bred resentment. Jennifer always *seemed* perfectly happy for me to be in charge. She never uttered a critical word against me until the very end. (And then, of course, criticism was the *only* thing that came out of her mouth.) But after we had parted ways, I came to understand that there had been something subtly aggressive in all her meek compliance. There is, I see now, such a thing as the tyranny of the humble person – the person who nods and watches quietly while you babble and show off and shout too loudly and generally make a fool of yourself. How much healthier to have a friend who isn't afraid to take you on, to tell you what's what! It is never pleasant to be upbraided. There were many times, I don't mind saying, when I badly wanted to give Sheba a shove. Yet, even in my anger, I always knew that her forthrightness was an asset for our relationship – something that could only strengthen our bond.

And certainly, I felt, there was some strengthening to be done. Loving and attentive as Sheba was when I was with her, I did not yet have the sense that I could truly count on her. She had a strong tendency to scattiness. She was often elusive. There were times when she did not return my calls all weekend; times when having made arrangements for an outing with me, she would forget having made them. I tried not to take these slights personally. Sheba had a family, I told myself. She had little Ben to look after. And her time management skills were not all they might have been. But even after I had made such allowances, it was hard not to conclude that I occupied a very low place on Sheba's list of priorities.

Zoë Heller, *Notes on a Scandal* (2003)

'WHAT DO YOU mean by not coming to see me this afternoon, as you promised?' was her address to Caroline as she entered the room.

'I was not in the humour,' replied Miss Helstone, very truly.

Shirley had already fixed on her a penetrating eye.

'No,' she said; 'I see you are not in the humour for loving me: you are in one of your sunless, inclement moods, when one feels a fellow-creature's presence is not welcome to you. You have such moods: are you aware of it?'

'Do you mean to stay long Shirley?'

'Yes: I am come to have my tea, and must have it before I go. I shall take the liberty then of removing my bonnet, without being asked.'

And this she did, and then stood on the rug with her hands behind her.

'A pretty expression you have in your countenance,' she went on, still gazing keenly, though not inimically, rather indeed pityingly at Caroline. 'Wonderfully self-supported you look, you solitude-seeking, wounded deer. Are you afraid Shirley will worry you, if she discovers that you are hurt, and that you bleed?'

'I never do fear Shirley.'

'But sometimes you dislike her: often you avoid her. Shirley can feel when she is slighted and shunned. If you had not walked home in the company you did last night, you would have been a different girl today. What time did you reach the Rectory?'

'By ten.'

'Humph! You took three-quarters of an hour to walk a mile. Was it you, or Moore, who lingered so?'

'Shirley, you talk nonsense.'

'*He* talked nonsense – that I doubt not; or he looked it, which is a thousand times worse: I see the reflection of his eyes on your forehead at this moment. I feel disposed to call him out, if I could only get a trustworthy second: I feel desperately irritated: I felt so last night, and have felt it all day.

'You don't ask me why,' she proceeded, after a pause, 'you little, silent, over-modest thing; and you don't deserve that I should pour out my secrets into your lap without an invitation. Upon my word, I could have found it in my heart to have dogged Moore yesterday evening with dire intent: I have pistols, and can use them.'

'Stuff, Shirley! Which would you have shot – me or Robert?'

'Neither, perhaps – perhaps myself – more likely a bat or a tree-bough. He is a puppy – your cousin: a quiet, serious, sensible, judicious, ambitious puppy. I see him standing before me, talking his half-stern, half-gentle talk, bearing me down (as I am very conscious he does) with his fixity of purpose, etc.; and then – I have no patience with him!'

Miss Keeldar started off on a rapid walk through the room, repeating energetically that she had no patience with men in general, and with her tenant in particular.

'You are mistaken,' urged Caroline, in some anxiety: 'Robert is no puppy or male flirt; I can vouch for that.'

'*You* vouch for it! Do you think I'll take your word on the subject? There is no one's testimony I would not credit sooner than yours. To advance Moore's fortune, you would cut off your right hand.'

'But not tell lies; and if I speak the truth, I must assure you that he was just civil to me last night – that was all.'

'I never asked what he was – I can guess. I saw him from the window take your hand in his long fingers, just as he went out at my gate.'

'That is nothing. I am not a stranger, you know. I am an old acquaintance, and his cousin.'

'I feel indignant; and that is the long and short of the matter,' responded Miss Keeldar. 'All my comfort,' she added presently, 'is broken up by his manoeuvres. He keeps intruding between you and me: without him we should be good friends; but that six feet of puppyhood makes a perpetually recurring eclipse of our friendship. Again and again he crosses and obscures the disk I want always to see clear: ever and anon he renders me to you a mere bore and nuisance.'

'No, Shirley; no.'

'He does. You did not want my society this afternoon, and I feel it hard: you are naturally somewhat reserved, but I am a social personage, who cannot live alone. If we were but left unmolested, I have that regard for you that I could bear you in my presence for ever, and not for the fraction of a second do I ever wish to be rid of you. You cannot say as much respecting me.'

'Shirley, I can say anything you wish: Shirley I like you.'

'You will wish me at Jericho tomorrow, Lina.'

'I shall not. I am every day growing more accustomed to – fonder of you. You know I am too English to get up a vehement friendship all at once; but you are so much better than common – you are so different to everyday young ladies – I esteem you – I value you: you are never a burden to me – never. Do you believe what I say?'

'Partly,' replied Miss Keeldar, smiling rather incredulously; 'but you are a peculiar personage: quiet as you look, there is both a force and a depth somewhere within, not easily reached or appreciated: then you certainly are not happy.'

'And unhappy people are rarely good – is that what you mean?'

'Not at all. I mean rather that unhappy people are often pre-occupied, and not in the mood for discoursing with companions of my nature. Moreover there is a sort of unhappiness which not only depresses, but corrodes – and that, I fear, is your portion. Will pity do you any good, Lina? If it will, take some from Shirley: she offers largely, and warrants the genuine article.'

'Shirley, I never had a sister – you never had a sister; but it flashes on me at this moment how sisters feel towards each other. Affection twined with their life, which no shocks of feeling can uproot, which little quarrels only trample an instant that it may spring more freshly when the pressure is removed; affection that no passion can ultimately outrival, with which even love itself cannot do more than compete in force and truth. Love hurts us so, Shirley: it is so tormenting, so racking, and it burns away our strength with its flame; in affection is no pain and no fire, only sustenance and balm. I am supported and soothed when you – that is, *you only* – are near, Shirley. Do you believe me now?'

'I am always easy of belief when the creed pleases me. We really are friends, then, Lina, in spite of the black eclipse?'

'We really are,' returned the other, drawing Shirley towards her, and making her sit down, 'chance what may.'

Charlotte Brontë, *Shirley* (1849)

I'M STANDING OUTSIDE the closed door of Cordelia's room. Cordelia, Grace, and Carol are inside. They're having a meeting. The meeting is about me. I am just not measuring up, although they are giving me every chance. I will have to do better. But better at what?

Perdie and Mirrie come up the stairs, along the hall, in their armor of being older. I long to be as old as they are. They're the only people who have any real power over Cordelia, that I can see. I think of them as my allies; or I think they would be my allies if they only knew. Knew what? Even to myself I am mute.

'Hello, Elaine,' they say. Now they say, 'What's the little game today? Hide and seek?'

'I can't tell,' I answer. They smile at me, condescending and kind, and head towards their room, to do their toenails and talk about older things.

I lean against the wall. From behind the door comes the indistinct murmur of voices, of laughter, exclusive and luxurious. Cordelia's Mummie drifts by, humming to herself. She's wearing her painting smock. There's a smudge of apple-green on her cheek. She smiles at me, the smile of an angel, benign but remote. 'Hello, dear,' she says. 'You tell Cordelia there's a cookie for you girls, in the tin.'

'You can come in now,' says the voice of Cordelia from inside the room. I look at the closed door, at the doorknob, at my own hand moving up, as if it's no longer a part of me.

Margaret Atwood, *Cat's Eye* (1988)

I SUPPOSE, IN ACCORDANCE with the general and damaging abstraction of those years, I was fulfilling some misplaced idea of myself. I was finally someone who took things lightly. I thought a lot about "lightness" then. Even though I wasn't someone who took things lightly at all, I liked, that year, to think of myself as someone who did – all of which raises another question in my mind. Was at least part of the whole miserable escapade the fault of the Milan Kundera book everyone was reading, *The Unbearable Lightness of Being*? That sublime adolescent ode to emotional carelessness, that ubiquitous paperback expanding an obscure eastern European profundity in moral lapses? The more I think about it, the more I think it's fair to apportion a tiny bit of the blame to Mr Kundera. (Here Stella would raise her eyebrows. "A book forced you to do it? How literary of you, how well read you must be…")

I suppose, also, in some corner of my fevered and cowardly brain I must have thought we could get away with it. I must have thought we would sleep together once and get it out of our systems. It turned out, however, that the boy believed in "honesty," an approach I would not have chosen on my own. He called Stella at the soonest possible second and told her. It was not hard to imagine the frantic look in Stella's eyes when he told her. Stella looked frantic when she had to pour cornflakes in a bowl. I hated him for telling her. I couldn't bear the idea of her knowing. Strangely enough, I felt protective of her, as if I could somehow protect her from the threat of myself.

I don't think I grasped right away the magnitude of what I had done. It felt like waking up in the middle of a René Magritte painting and finding tiny men with bowler hats suddenly falling from the sky. It didn't make sense, even to me, and I was startled, in a way, to find that it was real. To have the boy in my house the next morning, wanting coffee, and to have his soft blue-and-green flannel shirt spread out on the floor, was for some reason extremely startling. Cause and effect were sufficiently severed in my mind that I had not apprehended the enormity of the betrayal. In the light of day, it seemed a little unfair that I couldn't take it back.

Katie Roiphe, 'Beautiful Boy, Warm Night', *In Praise of Messy Lives* (2012)

I LOVED REVA, BUT I didn't like her anymore. We'd been friends since college, long enough that all we had left in common was our history together, a complex circuit of resentment, memory, jealousy, denial, and a few dresses I'd let Reva borrow, which she'd promised to dry clean and return but never did. She worked as an executive assistant for an insurance brokerage firm in Midtown. She was an only child, a gym rat, had a blotchy red birthmark on her neck in the shape of Florida, a gum-chewing habit that gave her TMJ and breath that reeked of cinnamon and green apple candy. She liked to come over to my place, clear a space for herself on the armchair, comment on the state of the apartment, say I looked like I'd lost more weight, and complain about work, all while refilling her wine glass after every sip.

*

Jealousy was one thing Reva didn't seem to feel the need to hide from me. Ever since we'd formed a friendship, if I told her that something good happened, she'd whine 'No fair' often enough that it became a kind of catchphrase that she would toss off casually, her voice flat. It was an automatic response to my good grade, a new shade of lipstick, the last popsicle, my expensive haircut. 'No fair.' I'd make my fingers like a cross and hold them out between us, as though to protect me from her envy and wrath. I once asked her whether her jealousy had anything to do with her being Jewish, if she thought things came easier to me because I was a WASP.

'It's not because I'm Jewish,' I remember her saying. This was right around graduation, when I'd made the dean's list despite having skipped more than half my classes senior year, and Reva had bombed the GRE. 'It's because I'm fat.' She really wasn't. She was very pretty, in fact.

*

'There, there,' I said, sucking down the coffee. I was intensely bored of Reva already. This would be the end of our friendship, I felt. Sometime soon, my cruelty would go too far, and now that her mother was dead, Reva's head would start to clear of its superficial nonsense. She'd probably go back to therapy. She'd realize that we had no good reason to be friends, and that she would never get what she needed from me. She'd send me a long letter explaining her resentments, her mistakes, explaining how she had to let me go in order to move on in her life. I could already imagine her phrasing. 'I've come to realize that our friendship is no longer serving me' – that was language her therapist would have taught her – 'which is not a criticism of you.' But of course it was about me: I was the friend in the friendship she was describing.

As we drove through Farmingdale, I wrote my reply to her would-be 'Dear John' letter in my head. 'I got your note,' I would begin. 'You have confirmed what I've known about you since college.' I tried to think of the worst thing I could say about a person. What was the cruelest, most cutting, truest thing? Was it worth saying? Reva was harmless. She wasn't a bad person. She'd done nothing to hurt me. I was the one sitting there full of disgust, wearing her dead mother's shoes. 'Good-bye.'

**Ottessa Moshfegh, *My Year of Rest and Relaxation*
(2018)**

Greer took in a ragged breath and then stood up in front of Zee as if about to do a little presentation. 'I wasn't going to say this, ever,' she said, 'but now I guess I am. Now I guess I have to.' She closed her eyes, then opened them again. 'I never gave Faith the letter.'

'What are you talking about? What letter?'

Greer looked down at the floor and her mouth twisted up strangely, in the stroke face of the about-to-cry. '*Your* letter,' Greer said, and then she stopped there, as though it would be so obvious what she meant.

'What?'

'Your *letter*,' Greer tried again with agitation now, and a little sob. Then she thrust out her hands, as if that would clarify it. 'The one you gave me like four years ago to give to Faith, when you wanted a job there, too. I still have it. I haven't opened it or anything. But I have it. I never gave it to her.'

Zee just kept looking at her. She let the silence expand, trying to work out what this actually meant. 'I'm confused,' Zee said. 'Because you told me you gave it to her, back then, and that she said there were no jobs.'

'I know, Zee, I lied to you.'

Zee let this moment bloom its shitty little bloom. Whenever she found out something shocking or even disappointing about someone she cared about, she was taken by surprise. She thought about her clients, and how surprised they always were by behaviors in the people they loved, which, from the outside, might not have seemed surprising.

A depressed husband took his own life. A grandmother collapsed. A daughter who had been agitated had a psychotic episode. Zee's clients were more than surprised by all of this; they were shocked to the point of trauma.

Today, Greer had come to Chicago in her own kind of shock. She had been an acolyte of Faith's, but had been startled by Faith's betrayal. It hadn't ever been even between Greer and Faith, and never could be.

But maybe it wasn't entirely even between Greer and Zee either. Greer had made it uneven, and now they too needed a correction. What was astonishing was that Greer and Zee, unlike Greer and Faith, had had an actual friendship. It had been real, but look at that, Greer had secretly fucked Zee over anyway.

Zee might actually have had a chance to work for Faith back in the beginning, to help push the foundation forward. It was possible that Faith would've said yes after reading her letter. 'I know it was horrible,' Greer was saying. 'I mean, I'm sure it doesn't make it better to say that you wouldn't even have *liked* working there, but it's true. In the beginning it was good, but then you know it got so impersonal, and I stopped getting to meet the women whose lives we were trying to help. It was like we were just pouring money into a speakers' bureau and that was it. And I literally had the thought, several times: Zee would hate this. In your work you're actually there on the ground. And we're just at arm's length too much of the time. I remind myself of this sometimes, as though it somehow makes it better that I did what I did to you. But I know it doesn't make it better. It was horrible of me,' she repeated.

'Yeah, it was,' said Zee in a quiet, contained little voice. Maybe Greer was right, and she would have hated it there. But what did it matter? The thing that mattered was that Greer had kept her from being there, which was so peculiar, so hurtful, and made everything between them appear strange and different now. 'But why would you do that?' Zee asked. 'I was the one to talk to you about her. I was the one who basically led you into everything. You had barely even heard of Faith Frank.'

'It was . . . about my parents, I think,' Greer said. 'About wanting someone to see something in me.'

'I saw something in you. And Cory did too.'

'I know. This was different.' Greer looked down; she couldn't even seem to make eye contact with Zee, and maybe that was just as well. They needed a rest from looking so hard at each other. All Zee did all day was look hard at people. Her eyes were tired from all that looking, studying, empathizing with, scrutinizing; all that helping, helping, helping.

Now Greer was ashamed, so let her be ashamed, Zee thought. Greer had actually done a thing to her, a real thing.

Zee had gotten over her disappointment four years earlier and gone on to have a life that Faith would approve of; she was sure of that. Working one-on-one with people, instead of with roomfuls of them. She did emergency work that mattered, often involving issues that concerned women. But as the truth of what Greer had done became familiar information now, Zee felt as if the long affection that she had felt for Greer since college was made thin and wan. She felt exhausted, and was sorry that she'd invited Greer here for the weekend. Were they going to discuss the letter, and what Greer had done to Zee, again and again?

Greer came forward on the couch and took Zee's wrists like a desperate suitor. 'Zee,' she said. 'I'm the worst person, I know I am.' Zee stayed furiously silent. 'Apparently I never knew that I'm one of those women who hates women, like you always say. I confessed to Faith about your letter back in the beginning. She reacted like it wasn't a big deal! But yesterday when I quit my job, she was hurt and angry, and out of the blue she brought it up in front of everyone. She *busted* me. Said I was a bad friend. A bad feminist. A bad woman. And I guess she's right. I didn't want to share her, I didn't want to let you in. I am the *cuntiest* woman, Zee. I am a *cunt*,' Greer said fiercely. 'I seriously am.'

Meg Wolitzer, *The Female Persuasion* (2018)

*D*ear Dolly:
       I need help breaking up with a friend. 'Emma' and I have been friends since we were children and we're now in our mid-twenties and have been living together for about a year. We've got a little longer left on our contract, but when that's over I think I want to both physically and mentally distance myself from her. We've had no serious bust-up, it's been a slow and uncomfortable series of arguments, snide remarks and passive-aggressive WhatsApp messages that have led us here. Though she has always supported me through break-ups, work issues and money trouble, I feel like my life would be calmer and simpler without this friendship. Do I owe her an explanation, though I can't fathom exactly what's gone wrong between us myself? Would it be wrong to simply ghost her?

I have been in the handing-out-unwarranted-advice game since I acquired language, and the agony-aunting game for just over four months now. Every week my editor sends me a selection of letters from which to choose, and I file them all into a document. There are the very specific questions ('Should I send my ex something I made in my pottery class?'), there are some that do not require a page's worth of rumination ('Should I get a fringe cut?') and then there are the same problems that appear in different guises every single week. Without fail there is always a woman worrying about how to break up with a close friend.

I say this to reassure you – it is one of the most common relationship anxieties, and yet is so mired in guilt. I think we worry that a finished friendship always means failure, when actually it can mean freedom. If a friendship can't evolve as its two participants mature and change, it's likely that they'll grow out of it. This doesn't mean that it hasn't enriched you and it doesn't make your memories null and void. Your relationship and shared story is an achievement (childhood to mid-twenties – that's longer than the median length of a marriage!). It just may not serve you any longer.

But before you work out an exit strategy, I think you need to do some forensics on the friendship. You say that you don't know why you've drifted apart but the timeline suggests that the problems began when you moved in together. The issues you mentioned – arguments, passive-aggressive WhatsApp messages – reek of domestic quarrelling. (I lived with housemates for seven years and I am more than familiar with the 'Hey just went to get my Marmite out of the cupboard and noticed a recent knife mark in it that I don't recognise??? Would be great if someone could clear this up???' texts.) It could be that you're describing an incompatible flatmate rather than an incompatible friend. If so, you may find that not living together returns your relationship to a relaxed and respectful place without confrontation. Some friendships simply can't withstand flat-shares – there are many people in my life who I adore, but there aren't enough jars of Marmite in Christendom to get me to live with them.

If you absolutely know that the friendship has naturally come to an end, I would still avoid a big goodbye speech. Those conversations, which are basically one person telling the other one all the things that are wrong with them, can be traumatic. Anyone who has had a friend explain exactly why they don't want to be friends any more can attest that the reasons never quite leave you (thanks, ********** ***** in Year 9 during that lunch break). The fact that you don't know exactly why you've become distant means it's probably more mutual than you think – those dynamics of long-term relationships rarely change without both parties being aware of it.

Which doesn't mean you should ghost her. That is both cruel and cowardly. What I suggest instead is a slow and subtle cooling-off period, which often happens after two people move out of a shared home anyway.

If she is hurt and asks for answers, then you should be honest with her. Do this kindly – describe the change you've noticed in your friendship, rather than the flaws you see in her. Tell her that you cherish everything she has given you, but that you think the friendship might have run its course. If she doesn't agree, there's an opportunity for a conversation in which you both share your feelings and find a way to communicate clearly again.

And while I don't think you should retain a friendship with someone who makes you unhappy, I do encourage you to be open to adaptation rather than a break-up. Friendships can change to become healthy without ending entirely. It might be that you share less with each other, she might become someone you see twice a year on respective birthdays. History alone can't hold a friendship together, but it does become something you value more and more as you get older. One day, to your surprise, you may find she's the only person you want to call. And you might not be best friends, but you'll be happy to hear each other's voice.

Dolly Alderton, *Dear Dolly: On Love, Life and Friendship* (2022)

WHEN MY FRIEND Brenda slept with my first husband, Charlie, I made that mistake – I blamed Brenda. It seemed quite unsurprising that Charlie would betray me – he, after all, was a man, and men had been betraying me since the first grade. *But she was my friend!* She had been my friend since the day we'd met, when we were both five years old and standing in line for books in kindergarten; and I have never forgotten that moment because she turned around and I looked at her and decided she was the most beautiful thing I'd ever seen. Her flaxen hair came to her waist, her eyes were deep green, her skin was white as snow, just like a stupid fairy tale. I always hoped that Brenda would eventually lose her looks – my theory being that I would grow up and gain mine, she would lose hers, and we'd end up more or less even – but she never did. What made this worse when we were young was that every summer we went to camp together and performed as an act in the camp talent show, and she always got to be the girl and I always had to be the boy. I had been deeply and smolderingly resentful of Brenda for years simply because I so wanted to be the girl and never got to be, and the truth is that I was secretly pleased when she slept with Charlie because I was exonerated from the guilt of all those years of feeling jealous of her and was plunged suddenly into a warm bath of innocent victimization.

Nora Ephron, *Heartburn* (1983)

THE VERY DAY of Mr Elton's going to London produced a fresh occasion for Emma's services towards her friend. Harriet had been at Hartfield, as usual, soon after breakfast; and, after a time, had gone home to return again to dinner: she returned, and sooner than had been talked of, and with an agitated, hurried look, announcing something extraordinary to have happened which she was longing to tell. Half a minute brought it all out. She had heard, as soon as she got back to Mrs Goddard's, that Mr Martin had been there an hour before, and finding she was not at home, nor particularly expected, had left a little parcel for her from one of his sisters, and gone away; and on opening this parcel, she had actually found, besides the two songs which she had lent Elizabeth to copy, a letter to herself; and this letter was from him, from Mr Martin, and contained a direct proposal of marriage. 'Who could have thought it? She was so surprised she did not know what to do. Yes, quite a proposal of marriage; and a very good letter, at least she thought so. And he wrote as if he really loved her very much – but she did not know – and so, she was come as fast as she could to ask Miss Woodhouse what she should do. –' Emma was half-ashamed of her friend for seeming so pleased and so doubtful.

'Upon my word,' she cried, 'the young man is determined not to lose any thing for want of asking. He will connect himself well if he can.'

'Will you read the letter?' cried Harriet. 'Pray do. I'd rather you would.'

Emma was not sorry to be pressed. She read, and was surprised. The style of the letter was much above her expectation. There were not merely no grammatical errors, but as a composition it would not have disgraced a gentleman; the language, though plain, was strong and unaffected, and the sentiments it conveyed very much to the credit of the writer. It was short, but expressed good sense, warm attachment, liberality, propriety, even delicacy of feeling. She paused over it, while Harriet stood anxiously watching for her opinion, with a 'Well, well', and was at last forced to add, 'Is it a good letter? or is it too short?'

'Yes, indeed, a very good letter,' replied Emma rather slowly – 'so good a letter, Harriet, that every thing considered, I think one of his sisters must have helped him. I can hardly imagine the young man whom I saw talking with you the other day could express himself so well, if left quite to his own powers, and yet it is not the style of a woman; no, certainly, it is too strong and concise; not diffuse enough for a woman. No doubt he is a sensible man, and I suppose may have a natural talent for – thinks strongly and clearly – and when he takes a pen in hand, his thoughts naturally find proper words. It is so with some men. Yes, I understand the sort of mind. Vigorous, decided, with sentiments to a certain point, not coarse. A better written letter, Harriet (returning it,) than I had expected.'

'Well,' said the still waiting Harriet; – 'well – and – and what shall I do?'

'What shall you do! In what respect? Do you mean with regard to this letter?'

'Yes.'

'But what are you in doubt of? You must answer it of course – and speedily.'

'Yes. But what shall I say? Dear Miss Woodhouse, do advise me.'

'Oh no, no! the letter had much better be all your own. You will express yourself very properly, I am sure. There is no danger of your not being intelligible, which is the first thing. Your meaning must be unequivocal; no doubts or demurs: and such expressions of gratitude and concern for the pain you are inflicting as propriety requires, will present themselves unbidden to your mind, I am persuaded. You need not be prompted to write with the appearance of sorrow for his disappointment.'

'You think I ought to refuse him then,' said Harriet, looking down.

'Ought to refuse him! My dear Harriet, what do you

mean? Are you in any doubt as to that? I thought – but I beg your pardon, perhaps I have been under a mistake. I certainly have been misunderstanding you, if you feel in doubt as to the purport of your answer. I had imagined you were consulting me only as to the wording of it.'

Harriet was silent. With a little reserve of manner, Emma continued:

'You mean to return a favourable answer, I collect.'

'No, I do not; that is, I do not mean – What shall I do? What would you advise me to do? Pray, dear Miss Woodhouse, tell me what I ought to do.'

'I shall not give you any advice, Harriet. I will have nothing to do with it. This is a point which you must settle with your feelings.'

'I had no notion that he liked me so very much,' said Harriet, contemplating the letter. For a little while Emma persevered in her silence; but beginning to apprehend the bewitching flattery of that letter might be too powerful, she thought it best to say,

'I lay it down as a general rule, Harriet, that if a woman doubts as to whether she should accept a man or not, she certainly ought to refuse him. If she can hesitate as to "Yes", she ought to say "No" directly. It is not a state to be safely entered into with doubtful feelings, with half a heart. I thought it my duty as a friend, and older than yourself, to say thus much to you. But do not imagine that I want to influence you.'

'Oh! no, I am sure you are a great deal too kind to – but if you would just advise me what I had best do – No, no, I do not mean that – As you say, one's mind ought to be quite made up – One should not be hesitating – It is a very serious thing. – It will be safer to say "No", perhaps. – Do you think I had better say "No"?'

'Not for the world,' said Emma, smiling graciously, 'would I advise you either way. You must be the best judge of your own happiness. If you prefer Mr Martin to every other person; if you think him the most agreeable man you have ever been in company with, why should you hesitate? You blush, Harriet. – Does any body else occur to you at this moment under such a definition? Harriet, Harriet, do not deceive yourself; do not be run away with by gratitude and compassion. At this moment whom are you thinking of?'

The symptoms were favourable. – Instead of answering, Harriet turned away confused, and stood thoughtfully by the fire; and though the letter was still in her hand, it was now mechanically twisted about without regard. Emma waited the result with impatience, but not without strong hopes. At last, with some hesitation, Harriet said –

'Miss Woodhouse, as you will not give me your opinion, I must do as well as I can by myself; and I have now quite determined, and really almost made up my mind – to refuse Mr Martin. Do you think I am right?'

'Perfectly, perfectly right, my dearest Harriet; you are doing just what you ought. While you were at all in suspense I kept my feelings to myself, but now that you are so completely decided I have no hesitation in approving. Dear Harriet, I give myself joy of this. It would have grieved me to lose your acquaintance, which must have been the consequence of your marrying Mr Martin. While you were in the smallest degree wavering, I said nothing about it, because I would not influence; but it would have been the loss of a friend to me. I could not have visited Mrs Robert Martin, of Abbey-Mill Farm. Now I am secure of you for ever.'

Harriet had not surmised her own danger, but the idea of it struck her forcibly.

'You could not have visited me!' she cried, looking aghast. 'No, to be sure you could not; but I never thought of that before. That would have been too dreadful! – What an escape! – Dear Miss Woodhouse, I would not give up the pleasure and honour of being intimate with you for any thing in the world.'

'Indeed, Harriet, it would have been a severe pang to lose you; but it must have been. You would have thrown yourself out of all good society. I must have given you up.'

'Dear me! – How should I ever have borne it! It would have killed me never to come to Hartfield any more!'

'Dear affectionate creature! – You banished to Abbey-Mill Farm! – You confined to the society of the illiterate and vulgar all your life! I wonder how the young man could have the assurance to ask it. He must have a pretty good opinion of himself.'

'I do not think he is conceited either, in general,' said Harriet, her conscience opposing such censure; 'at least, he is very good natured, and I shall always feel much obliged to him, and have a great regard for – but that is quite a different thing from – and you know, though he may like me, it does not follow that I should – and certainly I must confess that since my visiting here I have seen people – and if one comes to compare them, person and manners, there is no comparison at all, one is so very handsome and agreeable. However, I do really think Mr Martin a very amiable young man, and have a great opinion of him; and his being so much attached to me – and his writing such a letter – but as to leaving you, it is what I would not do upon any consideration.'

'Thank you, thank you, my own sweet little friend. We will not be parted. A woman is not to marry a man merely because she is asked, or because he is attached to her, and can write a tolerable letter.'

'Oh no; – and it is but a short letter too.'

Emma felt the bad taste of her friend, but let it pass with a 'very true; and it would be a small consolation to her, for the clownish manner which might be offending her every hour of the day, to know that her husband could write a good letter.'

'Oh! yes, very. Nobody cares for a letter; the thing is, to be always happy with pleasant companions. I am quite determined to refuse him. But how shall I do? What shall I say?'

Emma assured her there would be no difficulty in the answer, and advised its being written directly, which was agreed to, in the hope of her assistance; and though Emma continued to protest against any assistance being wanted, it was in fact given in the formation of every sentence. The looking over his letter again, in replying to it, had such a softening tendency, that it was particularly necessary to brace her up with a few decisive expressions; and she was so very much concerned at the idea of making him unhappy, and thought so much of what his mother and sisters would think and say, and was so anxious that they should not fancy her ungrateful, that Emma believed if the young man had come in her way at that moment, he would have been accepted after all.

This letter, however, was written, and sealed, and sent. The business was finished, and Harriet safe. She was rather low all the evening, but Emma could allow for her amiable regrets, and sometimes relieved them by speaking of her own affection, sometimes by bringing forward the idea of Mr Elton.

'I shall never be invited to Abbey-Mill again,' was said in rather a sorrowful tone.

'Nor, if you were, could I ever bear to part with you, my Harriet. You are a great deal too necessary at Hartfield to be spared to Abbey-Mill.'

'And I am sure I should never want to go there; for I am never happy but at Hartfield.'

Some time afterwards it was, 'I think Mrs Goddard would be very much surprized if she knew what had happened. I am sure Miss Nash would – for Miss Nash thinks her own sister very well married, and it is only a linen-draper.'

'One should be sorry to see greater pride or refinement in the teacher of a school, Harriet. I dare say Miss Nash would envy you such an opportunity as this of being married. Even this conquest would appear valuable in her eyes. As to any thing superior for you, I suppose she is quite in the dark. The attentions of a certain person can hardly be among the tittle-tattle of Highbury yet. Hitherto I fancy you and I are the only people to whom his looks and manners have explained themselves.'

Harriet blushed and smiled, and said something about wondering that people should like her so much. The idea of Mr Elton was certainly cheering; but still, after a time, she was tender-hearted again towards the rejected Mr Martin.

'Now he has got my letter,' said she softly. 'I wonder what they are all doing – whether his sisters know – if he is unhappy, they will be unhappy too. I hope he will not mind it so very much.'

'Let us think of those among our absent friends who are more cheerfully employed,' cried Emma. 'At this moment, perhaps, Mr Elton is shewing your picture to his mother and sisters, telling how much more beautiful is the original, and after being asked for it five or six times, allowing them to hear your name, your own dear name.'

'My picture! – But he has left my picture in Bond-street.'

'Has he so! – Then I know nothing of Mr Elton. No, my dear little modest Harriet, depend upon it the picture will not be in Bond-street till just before he mounts his horse to-morrow. It is his companion all this evening, his solace, his delight. It opens his designs to his family, it introduces you among them, it diffuses through the party those pleas-antest feelings of our nature, eager curiosity and warm prepossession. How cheerful, how animated, how suspi-cious, how busy their imaginations all are!'

Harriet smiled again, and her smiles grew stronger.

Jane Austen, *Emma* (1815)

8

SHIFTING SANDS

It's hard when you don't like someone a friend
marries. First of all, it means you pretty much
have to confine your friendship to lunch, and I
hate lunch.

Nora Ephron, *Heartburn* (1983)

Virginia Woolf ∽ *Stella Gibbons* ∽ *Lizzie Stewart* ∽ *Henry James*
Rose Tremain ∽ *Jami Attenberg* ∽ *Nella Larsen* ∽ *Jane Austen* ∽ *Lore Segal*
Beatrice Webb ∽ *Lorrie Moore* ∽ *Vera Brittain* ∽ *Winifred Holtby*

All relationships change over time, and friendship is no exception. If one friend is more successful than another, or if she develops sudden new airs and graces, difficult times will almost certainly lie ahead. What happens when a friend falls in love (or lust)? When they set up home with someone, or get married? And what about children? Will the new mother have any time for her child-free friends, and will they, in turn, have even the remotest interest in her new baby? Friends may be very close, and then very much less close, with all the pain that attends such a drift; or they may find one another again after a long time apart, and remember in that moment why they liked one another so much in the first place.

I begin this chapter with quite a number of long extracts from Virginia Woolf's diaries, in which she describes over a period of three years her friendship with her fellow writer, Katherine Mansfield. Woolf's friendships were fascinatingly complex, and she often wrote about them in her journal: fondness giving way, over time, to exasperation, and back again (sometimes). Her friendship with an older woman – the composer, Ethel Smyth – is particularly interesting for its mixture of high regard and frustrated pity. But it is her relationship with Mansfield, the only writer of whom she was truly envious, on which I've chosen to focus here. Mansfield had an uncommon ability to get under Woolf's skin. She never knew quite where she stood with her; they were in many ways very different. But when they were together, and in the mood to get along (sometimes, a little ice had first to thaw), they were frankly intimate, able to talk to each other as with no one else about their work, and how much it mattered, and what a struggle it was to produce it.

The chapter ends with a series of letters between those two very great friends, Vera Brittain and Winifred Holtby, in which they worry away at their relationship. Brittain is newly married, and for them both this marks a huge change: how will it affect their (intensely close) relationship? It is interesting that Brittain is no less anxious about this than her single friend – and when Brittain then goes away to Africa for a while, it is her turn to worry. What has she missed? How has Holtby done without her? Might it be her, now, who has changed the most? These letters are marked by both women's honesty and, in the case of Holtby, immense generosity. Reassurance is her forte.

Woolf's diary entry following Mansfield's death in 1923, at the age of just thirty-four, is included in Chapter 10: 'Goodbyes'.

Tuesday, 18 February 1919

I<small>T IS AT</small> this point extremely doubtful whether I have the right to class her among my friends. Quite possibly I shall never see her again. Upstairs I have letters in which she speaks of finding the thought of me a joy, dwelling upon my writing with excitement; I have letters making appointments, pressing for visits, adding postscripts of thanks & affection to visits already paid. But the last is dated December, & it is now February. The question interests, amuses, & also slightly, no, very, decidedly pains me. If it were not that I suspect her of wishing to produce precisely these emotions, save that of amusement, I should be still more put out. As it is – well I should need to write a long description of her before I arrived at my queer balance of interest, amusement, & annoyance. The truth is, I suppose, that one of the conditions unexpressed but understood of our friendship has been precisely that it was almost entirely founded on quicksands. It has been marked by curious slides & arrests; for months I've heard nothing of her; then we have met again upon what has the appearance of solid ground. We have been intimate, intense perhaps rather than open; but to me at any rate our intercourse has always been interesting & mingled with quite enough of the agreeable personal element to make one fond – if that is the word – as well as curious. I was at pains to go up to Hampstead every week since mid October or November, I suppose. And then what happened? I go away for Christmas, & we send small bright presents, carefully timed to arrive on Christmas day. I add to mine one if not two long & affectionate letters; I propose to come as soon as I get back. My time in bed prevented this.

But meanwhile, for no reason given or to be guessed at with any certainty, she falls silent; I get no thanks, no answers, no enquiries. So suspecting but willing to make every test before coming to conclusions, I asked Murry whether she would like a visit; to which he replied cordially & without the shadow of hesitation. I proposed to go yesterday. About eleven she, or rather the female who keeps house, rang up & put me off, saying that K.M. was too unwell for my visit; but making no suggestion of another time, nor have I any word from her or K. this morning.

Saturday March 22, 1919

Further we have decided to take 2 cottages at Tregerthen [near St Ives, Cornwall] if we can get them; & this brings me to Katherine Murry from whom I heard of them. The inscrutable woman remains inscrutable I'm glad to say; no apologies, or sense of apologies due. At once she flung down her pen & plunged, as if we'd been parted for 10 minutes, into the question of Dorothy Richardson; & so on with the greatest freedom & animation on both sides until I had to catch my train. Perhaps its I who live in the suburbs & think it necessary to answer letters; that would be a proper retort to my jest of the underworld. But something – something dark & catastrophic possibly to do with Murry – has taken place since we met. So much she hinted; but said she wished now to forget it – something that had absorbed her, apparently. But this was a momentary revelation as I left. Otherwise, as I say, we chattered about the Athenaeum mostly, & I was much complimented to hear how much they wish for my writing, in proof of which I have a book this morning from Murry. And again, as usual, I find with Katherine what I

don't find with the other clever women a sense of ease &
interest, which is, I suppose, due to her caring so genuinely
if so differently from the way I care, about our precious art.
Though Katherine is now in the very heart of the professional
world – 4 books on her table to review – she is, & will always
be, I fancy, not the least of a hack. I don't feel as I feel with
Molly Hamilton [writer, journalist, civil servant and, later,
Labour MP for Blackburn], that is to say, ashamed of the
ink pot.

Monday May 31, 1920

I had my interview with K.M. on Friday. A steady discom-
posing formality & coldness at first. Enquiries about house &
so on. No pleasure or excitement at seeing me. It struck me
that she is of the cat kind: alien, composed, always solitary
& observant. And then we talked about solitude, & I found
her expressing my feelings, as I never heard them expressed.
Whereupon we fell into step, & as usual, talked as easily as
though 8 months were minutes – till Murry came in with a
pair of blue and pink Dresden candle pieces: 'How *very* nice,'
she said. 'But do fetch the candles.' 'Virginia, how *awful* what
am I to say? He has spent £5 on them,' she said, as he left the
room. I see that they're often hostile . . . A queer effect she
produces of someone apart, entirely self-centred; altogether
concentrated upon her 'art': almost fierce to me about it, I
pretending I couldn't write. 'What else is there to do? We
have got to do it. Life –' then how she tells herself stories
at night about all the lives in a town. 'Its a spring night. I
go down to the docks – I hear the travellers say –' acting it
in her usual way, & improvising. Then asked me to write
stories for the A. 'But I don't know that I can write stories,'

I said, honestly enough, thinking that in her view, after her review of me, anyhow, those were her secret sentiments. Whereupon she turned on me, & said no one else could write stories except me – Kew [Gardens] the right 'gesture'; a turning point – Well but Night & Day? I said, though I hadn't meant to speak of it.

'An amazing achievement,' she said. Why we've not had such a thing since I don't know when –,

But I thought you didn't like it?

Then she said she could pass an examination on it. Would I come & talk about it – lunch – so I'm going to lunch; but what does her reviewing mean then? – or is she emotional with me? Anyhow, once more as keenly as ever I feel a common certain understanding between us – a queer sense of being 'like' – not only about literature – & I think it's independent of gratified vanity. I can talk straight out to her.

Saturday June 5, 1920

I've gone back into winter clothes; its bitter windy; & the sun sparks & glints instead of burning. It burnt on Derby Day though [Wednesday 2 June] – the day I lunched with K.M. & had 2 hours priceless in the sense that to no one else can I talk in the same disembodied way about writing; without altering my thought more than I alter it in writing here. (I except L. from this). We talked about books, writing of course: my own. N&D. a first rate novel, she said. The suppression in it puzzling, but accounted for by circumstances. Then I said 'You've changed. Got through something;' indeed there's a sort of self command about her as if having mastered something subterfuges were no longer so necessary . . . She is nervous about her book coming out; fearing lest she hasn't done enough. What she feels exactly for fame & criticism, I don't know; but then in our perhaps too exalted talk, this is not very exactly told. Anyhow, I enjoyed myself; & this fragmentary intermittent intercourse of mine seems more fundamental than many better established ones.

Wednesday August 25, 1920

For the third time this summer, though no other summer, I went to London [on] Monday paid 5/- for a plate of ham, & said goodbye to Katherine. I had my euphemism at parting; about coming again before she goes; but it is useless to extend these farewell visits. They have something crowded & unnaturally calm too about them, & after all, visits can't do away with the fact that she goes for two years, is ill, & heaven knows when we shall meet again. These partings make one pinch oneself as if to make sure of feeling. Do I feel this as much as I ought? Am I heartless? Will she mind my going either? And then, after noting my own callousness, of a sudden comes the blankness of not having her to talk to. So on my side the feeling is genuine. A woman caring as I care for writing is rare enough I suppose to give me the queerest sense of echo coming back to me from her mind the second after I've spoken. Then, too, there's something in what she says of our being the only women, at this moment (I must modestly limit this to our circle) with gift enough to make talk of writing interesting. How much I dictate to other people! How often too I'm silent, judging it useless to speak. I said how my own character seemed to cut out a shape like a shadow in front of me. This she understood (I give it as an example of her understanding) & proved it by telling me that she thought this bad: one ought to merge into things.

Sunday March 12, 1922

So what if K.M. soars in the newspapers, & runs up sales sky-high? Ah, I have found a fine way of putting her in her place. The more she is praised, the more I am convinced she is bad. After all, there's some truth in this. She touches the spot too universally for that spot to be of the bluest blood.

Virginia Woolf, *The Diary of Virginia Woolf,*
Volume 1: 1915–1919 **and** *Volume 2: 1920–1924*

A S THE EVENINGS of February lengthened and the snow-drops bloomed, Margaret and Hilda saw even less of one another. Margaret's time was fully occupied with school work and visits to Westwood or to theatres and concerts with Zita, and Hilda, quite aware that she was being supplanted, concealed her natural feelings and even made excuses for her friend, reminding herself that Mutt had always been highbrow and now had found someone to share her tastes. Hilda had that impenetrable reserve which frequently accompanies a sunny temperament; her dislike of displaying her deeper feelings was almost neurotic, and when one of the young men with whom she went about was killed, she would fly into a rage, weep furious tears for a quarter of an hour, and then never mention his name again; hardly ever think of him; thrust the pain and anger deep, deep into the recesses of her mind and forget it.

On the rare occasions when Margaret telephoned to her or dropped in at the Wilsons', Hilda's manner was unchanged, but she herself never went to Margaret's home unless they were invited, and when she and Margaret met they only exchanged their usual affectionate banter and Margaret found it increasingly difficult to speak to her friend of the change that had taken place in her nature since Zita had opened to her the world of music and the doors of Westwood. I am so much happier, she would think, but she was compelled to admit that the ecstasy with which she listened to music and the thrill she experienced at a distant glimpse of Gerard Challis were too intense to be happiness.

Stella Gibbons, *Westwood* **(1946)**

Lizzie Stewart, 'A Quick Catch Up', *It's Not What You Thought It Would Be* (2021)

A N IMMENSE PITY for Olive sat in her heart, and she asked herself how far it was necessary to go in the path of self-sacrifice. Nothing was wanting to make the wrong she should do her complete; she had deceived her up to the very last; only three months earlier she had reasserted her vows, given her word, with every show of fidelity and enthusiasm. There were hours when it seemed to Verena that she must really push her inquiry no further, but content herself with the conclusion that she loved as deeply as a woman could love and that it didn't make any difference. She felt Olive's grasp too clinching, too terrible. She said to herself that she should never dare, that she might as well give up early as later; that the scene, at the end, would be something she couldn't face; that she had no right to blast the poor creature's whole future. She had a vision of those dreadful years; she knew that Olive would never get over the disappointment. It would touch her in the point where she felt everything most keenly; she would be incurably lonely and eternally humiliated. It was a peculiar thing, their friendship; it had elements which made it probably as complete as any (between women) that had ever existed. Of course it had been more on Olive's side than on hers, she had always known that; but that, again, didn't make any difference. It was of no use for her to tell herself that Olive had begun it entirely and she had only responded out of a kind of charmed politeness, at first, to a tremendous appeal. She had lent herself, given herself, utterly, and she ought to have known better if she didn't mean to abide by it. At the end of the three weeks she felt that her inquiry was complete, but that after all nothing was gained except an immense interest in Basil Ransom's views and the prospect of eternal heartache. He had told her he wanted her to know him, and now she knew him pretty thoroughly. She knew him and she adored him, but it didn't make any difference. To give him up or to give Olive up – this effort would be the greater of the two.

Henry James, *The Bostonians* (1886)

WHILE WAITING TO hear about job applications, I went to visit Pet at Essex University. She was lodged in a high grey tower and had to share a kitchen with thirteen other people, but she was breathless with excitement at her student life. She had a new group of friends. They all called her Petronella, not Pet, and she seemed to like this rediscovery of her true name. Most of them had bodies as pale and skinny as leeks, but Pet said, 'In fact, they're not people who can be bent or plucked; they're really angry.' She told me that their aim was to rise up against privilege and all the decades-long unfairnesses in British society and usher in a new age of social equality. When Pet said, 'I don't suppose you've ever thought about any of this, Marianne, have you?' I replied that when I'd worked on Bartlett's gift-wrap desk, I had understood that only a certain class of customer could afford to have their gifts professionally wrapped by me and that I had had moments of thinking this wasn't quite right. And Pet roared with mirth.

We went to an Indian restaurant with two of Pet's new friends, a boy called Orlando, who reminded me a little of Julius Templeman, and a girl called Savannah, who had beautiful, narrow hands adorned with bands of silver and a throaty voice. Through the harsh lighting in the restaurant, Orlando and Savannah smoked roll-ups and stared at my acne and I could feel them recoil from me before I'd had a chance to say anything at all. Pet saw this too and after we'd ordered a lot of unfamiliar food, she began to tell them what a loyal friend I'd been to her at school and how we'd gone riding together and galloped 'like Arabs' around a field of clover.

'You can't say "like Arabs", Petronella,' said Orlando. 'That's such insulting, racist language.'

'Och, fuck off, Orlando,' said Pet. 'Everybody knows about Arabian horses and their fearless riders. That was all I meant.'

'I know,' said Orlando. 'But you just can't say things like that any more.'

So then Pet and Orlando and Savannah began a big conversation about how people betrayed themselves by certain names and phrases they used, and I kept completely silent for a long time while little metal bowls of curry and lentils and coconut-flavoured rice were set down before us. I didn't feel much like eating any of this. I wanted to say that prejudice wasn't found only in language; that Orlando and Savannah had made their judgement about me on the basis of my bad skin and my posh voice, and that if they bothered to get to know me they might have understood that I was a brave and fearless rider, that I had once been lovable enough to steal the heart of the most beautiful boy in Berkshire and wild enough to lose my virginity in the back of a Morris Minor, wearing a home-made taffeta frock, but it seemed easier to keep silent. I didn't want to say anything that would embarrass Pet.

After the meal, as we made the long trek in the dark through the outskirts of Colchester to Pet's tower block, and Orlando and Savannah peeled off down some terrifying-looking cul-de-sac to visit a club, Pet said, 'So where are you now in your life, Marianne? D'you still feel lost?'

I found that I couldn't answer her. I just took her hand and felt the familiar warmth of it and we walked on under the sodium lights, with the traffic surging by. After a while, I said, 'I wish we were in Scotland, in a place you knew, living in a bothy, miles from every human habitation.'

Rose Tremain, *Absolutely & Forever* **(2023)**

INDIGO HAS A baby and I don't go to see it for a long time. It's not that I don't care about seeing her baby, it's that I don't care about seeing any baby. Also I know what will happen. I've been down this road before. Once I see the baby I will have *seen* the baby. I need to see the baby when it is little, so that someday when I see the baby when it is grown or at least not a baby anymore I can say, 'I remember you when you were *this* big.' It's all a setup for a later scene to occur at a holiday party, or in a cafe, or, realistically, on a street corner, two grown women nodding enthusiastically at the size of an uninterested child tugging on its mother's hand. Once you were small. Now you are big.

'Why haven't you come to see the baby yet?' says Indigo. A message she leaves on the phone. Non-combative, but making a point. Wheedling. Not a question she actually wants answered. 'I'll be home all day. I don't ever go anywhere. It's just me and the baby. So just come over. We'll be here.'

What will happen after I see the baby is that Indigo will become exceedingly busy with her life for a very long time. Say, five years or so. Then she will have time again to see me. Then she will desperately need to see me. Where has the time gone? What have I been doing? Oh, yes, parenting. But by then I will be a different version of me (or, worse, perhaps the same version) and she will be a different version of her and we will look at each other with different eyes. You had a baby and I didn't and here we are. Do you remember when . . .? Yes! Yes. Sure.

I text her back so I don't have to answer her specific question, the rhetorical status of it unclear. I say, 'I'll come on Saturday.' I break brunch plans with my mother, and I move my morning session with my therapist an hour earlier.

I know the minute I go to see that baby, my friendship with Indigo is over. I liked being friends with her. She was my most beautiful friend, physically, spiritually. She was always so healthy. She quit corporate America to become a yoga instructor and she stopped eating anything that came from a cow, and it showed in her tingling white teeth and her lustrous, enormous hair and her skin, which glowed a luxurious camel color. Any ailment I had, she could suggest a herbal remedy for it. Or a specific stretch. Indigo and me, doing backbends in her living room, my blood racing to my face, and I'm thinking: I always wanted a friend like this. I will miss those backbends, Indigo. They really did help with my stress.

*

'Have you been doing your meditation?'

'That's what Todd always asks,' she snaps. 'Of course I'm meditating. I meditate like a motherfucker.' She stops wrapping herself up, lets the scarf fall in her lap. 'I thought if I lost the baby weight it would help. Todd has always admired my physical self.' Indigo's hot yoga-teacher body. We had all admired it.

'You know that's not right,' I say. 'That's not what it is. It's never that, and anyway, even when you were pregnant you were still astonishing.' It's true, she glowed, and she had seemed thin forever until just before the baby was due, she popped a delicious bump. It wasn't her body, it wasn't her form, it wasn't her concern for her child.

It was Todd. It was his fault. He was having an affair. 'How did he have the time?' says Indigo. 'It doesn't take that long to stick your dick in someone,' I say. 'Sometimes, it's only a few seconds if you really want to get into it.' She chokes on air. 'Sorry,' I say. 'I shouldn't talk about your husband's dick like that.' Indigo says it doesn't matter. His dick was his dick; talking about it wasn't going to change the fact he was now putting it inside a marketing director in the cosmetics industry who abused lip liner and had graduated from Smith. 'How hard did you Google her?' I say. 'So hard,' she says. 'They met in Tunisia on one of his trips for his micro financing project. She was there on vacation. I saw pictures of the two of them together. Holding cocktails.' I gasp. 'With fruit wedges,' she says. 'Disgusting,' I say.

'I am trying to rise above.' She looks towards the sky for guidance.

I had thought I would never have Indigo in my life again. I had seen her once since she had her baby and that was all I ever expected. And now I could take pleasure in her downfall but I do not. Because here she was: bitter and edgy, and more like me. 'Whatever you need from me,' I say. 'Just ask.' I had been this way forever, or for at least as long as I could remember. I would welcome her to the fold if that was what she needed to hear. 'Your husband is a terrible man,' I say. My Indigo who taught me nasal breathing exercises to cool the mind and insisted I was beautiful every time I saw her, her hands on my wrists, rubbing up my arms to my shoulders and neck. 'Look at you,' she would say. 'Look at beautiful you.'

I am always merely in the state of just knowing her, I realize now. I bear witness to her life while I am in the thick of my own misery and joy and wastefulness and excess. Her life is architected, elegant and angular, a beauty to behold, and mine is a stew, a juicy, sloppy mess of ingredients and feelings and emotions, too much salt and spice, too much anxiety, always a little dribbling down the front of my shirt. But have you tasted it? Have you tasted it? It's delicious.

Jami Attenberg, *All Grown Up* (2017)

SHE MEANT TO tell Clare Kendra at once, and definitely, that it was of no use, her coming, that she couldn't be responsible, that she'd talked it over with Brian, who had agreed with her that it was wiser, for Clare's own sake, to refrain—

But that was as far as she got in her rehearsal. For Clare had come softly into the room without knocking, and before Irene could greet her, had dropped a kiss on her dark curls.

Looking at the woman before her, Irene Redfield had a sudden inexplicable onrush of affectionate feeling. Reaching out, she grasped Clare's two hands in her own and cried with something like awe in her voice: 'Dear God! But aren't you lovely, Clare!'

Clare tossed that aside. Like the furs and small blue hat which she threw on the bed before seating herself slantwise in Irene's favourite chair, with one foot curled under her.

'Didn't you mean to answer my letter, 'Rene?' she asked gravely.

Irene looked away. She had that uncomfortable feeling that one has when one has not been wholly kind or wholly true.

Clare went on: 'Every day I went to that nasty little post office place. I'm sure they were all beginning to think that I'd been carrying on an illicit love affair and that the man had thrown me over. Every morning the same answer: "Nothing for you." I got into an awful fright, thinking that something might have happened to your letter, or to mine. And half the nights I would lie awake looking out at the watery stars – hopeless things, the stars – worrying and wondering. But at last it soaked in, that you hadn't written and didn't intend to. And then – well, as soon as ever I'd seen Jack off for Florida, I came straight here. And now, 'Rene, please tell me quite frankly why you didn't answer my letter.'

'Because, you see—' Irene broke off and kept Clare

286

waiting while she lit a cigarette, blew out the match, and dropped it into a tray. She was trying to collect her arguments, for some sixth sense warned her that it was going to be harder than she thought to convince Clare Kendra of the folly of Harlem for her. Finally she proceeded: 'I can't help thinking that you ought not to come up here, ought not to run the risk of knowing Negroes.'

'You mean you don't want me, 'Rene?'

Irene hadn't supposed that anyone could look so hurt. She said, quite gently, 'No, Clare, it's not that. But even you must see that it's terribly foolish, and just not the right thing.'

The tinkle of Clare's laugh rang out, while she passed her hands over the bright sweep of her hair. 'Oh, 'Rene!' she cried, 'you're priceless! And you haven't changed a bit. The right thing!' Leaning forward, she looked curiously into Irene's disapproving brown eyes. 'You don't, you really can't mean exactly that! Nobody could. It's simply unbelievable.'

Irene was on her feet before she realized that she had risen. 'What I really mean,' she retorted, 'is that it's dangerous and that you ought not to run such silly risks. No one ought to. You least of all.'

Her voice was brittle. For into her mind had come a thought, strange and irrelevant, a suspicion, that had surprised and shocked her and driven her to her feet. It was that in spite of her determined selfishness the woman before her was yet capable of heights and depths of feeling that she, Irene Redfield, had never known. Indeed, never cared to know. The thought, the suspicion, was gone as quickly as it had come.

Clare said: 'Oh, me!'

Irene touched her arm caressingly, as if in contrition for that flashing thought. 'Yes, Clare, you. It's not safe. Not safe at all.'

'Safe!'

It seemed to Irene that Clare had snapped her teeth down on the word and then flung it from her. And for another flying second she had that suspicion of Clare's ability for a quality of feeling that was to her strange, and even repugnant. She was aware, too, of a dim premonition of some impending disaster. It was as if Clare Kendra had said to her, for whom safety, security, were all-important: 'Safe! Damn being safe!' and meant it.

Nella Larsen, *Passing* (1929)

M ISS LUCAS CALLED soon after breakfast, and in a private conference with Elizabeth related the event of the day before.

The possibility of Mr Collins's fancying himself in love with her friend had once occurred to Elizabeth within the last day or two: but that Charlotte could encourage him seemed almost as far from possibility as that she could encourage him herself; and her astonishment was consequently so great as to overcome at first the bounds of decorum, and she could not help crying out, —

'Engaged to Mr Collins! my dear Charlotte, impossible!'

The steady countenance which Miss Lucas had commanded in telling her story gave way to a momentary confusion here on receiving so direct a reproach; though, as it was no more than she expected, she soon regained her composure, and calmly replied, –

'Why should you be surprised, my dear Eliza? Do you think it incredible that Mr Collins should be able to procure any woman's good opinion, because he was not so happy as to succeed with you?'

But Elizabeth had now recollected herself; and, making a strong effort for it, was able to assure her, with tolerable firmness, that the prospect of their relationship was highly grateful to her, and that she wished her all imaginable happiness.

'I see what you are feeling,' replied Charlotte; 'you must be surprised, very much surprised, so lately as Mr Collins was wishing to marry you. But when you have had time to think it all over, I hope you will be satisfied with what I have done. I am not romantic, you know. I never was. I ask only a comfortable home; and, considering Mr Collins's character, connections, and situation in life, I am convinced that my chance of happiness with him is as fair as most people can boast on entering the marriage state.'

Elizabeth quietly answered 'undoubtedly;' and, after an awkward pause, they returned to the rest of the family. Charlotte did not stay much longer; and Elizabeth was then left to reflect on what she had heard. It was a long time before she became at all reconciled to the idea of so unsuitable a match. The strangeness of Mr Collins's making two offers of marriage within three days was nothing in comparison of his being now accepted. She had always felt that Charlotte's opinion of matrimony was not exactly like her own; but she could not have supposed it possible that, when called into action, she would have sacrificed every better feeling to worldly advantage. Charlotte, the wife of Mr Collins, was a most humiliating picture! And to the pang of a friend disgracing herself, and sunk in her esteem, was added the distressing conviction that it was impossible for that friend to be tolerably happy in the lot she had chosen.

Jane Austen, *Pride and Prejudice* (1813)

I REMEMBER ONLY THE one conversation that you and I had on the subject of Colin. This was after you and Eli split and Eli had left for London. You came to tell me you were moving to Connecticut: 'Why should you be surprised that I could love a person who might not suit your taste? I think he is a dear man.' 'I'm sure he is that, to you,' I said. 'I can see he is. If only that he likes me, which is a nice change from Eli.' 'Well, I intend to like Colin,' I promised you, and promised myself. 'I will. I'm going to like Colin for you.' 'And you'll come weekends,' you said, 'and you're coming to Provence with us next summer.'

I try to think backward: When did you stop inviting me? When did I begin to be envious, to regret having no places to not invite *you* to? I don't know that I blame you because I was never nice to Colin, nor about him. (In our emails, Eli and I refer to him as Mr Collins.) You knew that the week in London I stayed with Eli. Funny how, afterwards, we could no longer sign off with the easy old 'Love, Eli' and 'Love,

Lotte' – the word had become freighted. That was after you and Colin married, but of course I've wondered, sex being what it is, if it rankled. Rankles. Except that in all the years since then, you stay with me when you come up to town. We do the theatre and the parties Colin isn't keen on. And we talk. (Eli and I wonder what you and Mr Collins talk about besides the still-raging parking wars.)

You and I used to talk and talk. Wait. Hold on. I had to go and find Jane Austen. Here: this is Emma thinking about Mrs Weston, the friend 'interested in every pleasure, every scheme of hers, to whom she could speak every thought as it arose'. Bessie, that was you and me, until you learned to say, 'anyway', which being interpreted can only mean, 'When you stop telling me what you are telling me, we can get back to what I was saying.' And so now, dear Bessie, I think twice before speaking the thought as it arises, at a time of life when I'm likely as not to forget a name, forget the operative word. Bessie! Are you so sure you mightn't want to hear what I might want to say? Or, Bessie, does it feel to you as if I am not listening to what you are saying?

Lore Segal, 'How Lotte Lost Bessie', *Ladies' Lunch and Other Stories* (2023)

M EANWHILE, I HAVE caught up the threads of another friendship. Carrie Darling, when I was a young girl living in my own home, was my first intellectual friendship. She was the first 'professional' woman I had come across.

Fresh from Newnham and full of the fervour and enthusiasm of those early pioneers, saved from priggishness and pedantry by having earned her livelihood from fifteen years of age, by being at least three times engaged to be married before she went to college at twenty-eight – with, in fact, all the charms of a bohemian and a highly trained professional – she captivated my imagination. Her friendship was of the utmost value to me: she stimulated all that was good in me – my love of learning and intellectual ambition, all my moral enthusiasm, and to some extent checked the vulgar materialism brought about by life in second-rate fashionable sets. Her personality had a certain distinction and charm . . . All this charm is gone . . . For these thirteen years she has lived exclusively with inferiors. Eight years in a small Australian town with all its vulgarity and petty intrigues, five years in an Indian military station consorting with clergy and Eurasians, and, above all, five years' servitude to a husband who is her inferior in every respect – a mere elementary schoolteacher in training and a narrow evangelical prig by constitution . . . She has practically fled from him. Poor clever Carrie! The whole week we spent in one long tale of married misery. To me the friendship is no longer invigorating. I have lived in some ways a more strenuously 'professional' life than she has, I am satisfied by love, and overburdened with friendships. But there is the supreme value of faithfulness . . . to drop a friend or be dropped degrades life – makes life seem a horrid morass where anyone may be left to die uncared for. All ties should be made in their degree secure – to be broken only by mutual consent and for very sufficient reasons. The change

from youth to age, from success to failure, is no reason.
How I hate anarchism in all its forms!

**Beatrice Webb, 19 January 1896, *The Diary of
Beatrice Webb, Volume Two 1892–1905*, ed. Norman
and Jeanne Mackenzie (1983)**

O FTEN WHEN I went over to Sils's house, she would have
the side door unlocked and a salad or a cottage cheese
sandwich waiting for me on the kitchen counter. A salad! A
cottage cheese sandwich! How odd in memory to conjure it,
the dressed cucumbers and celery assembled as if by a wife
for her husband, or the sandwich, sweet and sloppy with
mayonnaise. I would take it, eat it, then go upstairs to her
room and sit next to her, strum the guitar with her, singing
harmony to folk songs like 'Geordie' or 'The Water is Wide I
Cannot Get O'er', feeling myself a goner in the minor-seven
chords, their sad irresolution stirring in me something lost
and heart-broken, though how could that be, I was only
fifteen. Still, something deeply sad had been born buried
in me, stirring occasionally inside like a creature moving in
sleep. Often I found myself concentrating on the frog painting, entering it with my eye, as if it were perhaps a dreamy
illustration from a real-life fairy tale, or a secret passageway
into another secret passageway. A joke into a secret joke
into a secret. When we were younger, Sils and I had always
looked for caves together, or some small undiscovered duck
pond with ducks. We'd go to the Grand Union and cheer

on the lobsters who managed to break free of their rubber bands. We'd build a half-tent out of three open umbrellas and we'd get underneath them and play cards. We'd walk miles to the county dump to see the bears. By the time we were twelve, we'd bike to the head shop and buy wisteria incense. Or we'd go downtown to the Orpheum, see an R-rated movie, occasionally a foreign one, which would mesmerize and perplex us. We'd eat Junior Mints and popcorn – each candy a sweet pillow on the tongue; each popped corn as big and complicated as a catalpa bloom. On a dare we might even drink the blueberry punch, which was the color of Windex and shot up the sides of the Jet-Spray cooler like some wonder of nature; no one else in our town had ever drunk it. That's what the man behind the counter always said. We would wash it down with water from the lobby fountain. Then we would sit in the dark, on the left, to watch the movie from an angle, eyes peeled for flesh. At thirteen, we would hang out at W. T. Grant's, buying bras and ice cream sundaes, and trying on men's sweaters, the bottoms of which, when we wore them at school, stretched out shapelessly, the hem warped and hanging around by our knees: that was the look we wanted. At fourteen, we would claim to be sleeping over at each other's house, and then we'd stay out all night, go to the railroad tracks, and from old mayonnaise jars drink liquor collected from our parents' own supply. Then we'd sleep in the family station wagon in the driveway, wake early, get donuts at Donna's Donuts at dawn when both the raised and glazed ones were still warm.

But increasingly now I was alone with my outings, wondering what it was like for Sils with her boyfriend Mike, what they did together, what were all the things I didn't yet even know to ask, and, now that she had gone to a new advanced place I hadn't, whether she liked me less.

*

There was a slight snap in the air from the lake, and Sils and I huddled under the blanket for warmth. Feeling the heat of her so close, I thought about how seldom we slept over these days, me in that sleeping bag at the foot of her bed, or she at the foot of mine, the routine intimacy of that, our talking out into the dark of our rooms, the cemetery quiet out the window and us with our jokes and sighs and then our sleep, side by side in duet, our breaths staggered like a round. Only once had we ever had a fight – she accused me of having deliberately developed a laugh like someone else, someone named Leslie Fish. She accused me of wanting to hang out with Leslie and be like Leslie, which summoned up such outrage on my part that I struck Sils in the arm and then rushed home in tears, waiting the week out until at last we were friends again.

It had been true about the laugh, and I never laughed like that again.

*

The few times I went home vacations, I would see Sils, but we were strangely awkward with each other. We looked different. She had layered her hair in a long wavy shag and was wearing a big leather jacket and palazzo pants. I had grown rounded and tall. We would sing in her room, but at the end of a song she'd strum the chords and we'd retreat shyly into silence. We didn't reprise our repertoire, all the songs we'd learned with Miss Field in Girls' Choir, or from the car radio, or her brothers' band. Instead we struggled with talk, though it all seemed to separate us. She had broken up with Mike and was now seeing a boy named Doug, who sold mobile homes. Months before her brothers had once again fled, with their band, to Canada. Was I going to college? She thought she might not, but might just stay in town and work for the post-office or something. Someday she hoped to move to Boston or Hawaii or Santa Fe.

'Oh,' I said. I'd somehow always thought we'd go to college together, to the same place; I couldn't imagine being totally without her.

*

I went into the bathroom. I touched the towels and towel bars and washcloths. I flicked on the light and opened the medicine cabinet: Q-Tips, nail files, and dark, beeswax soaps. I opened the pill bottles and took an aspirin and a Tylenol. I dabbed cologne on my wrists, stripped naked, then got into the shower, where I washed my hair with her shampoo – an apricot-walnut one that smelled like her. I stayed there for a long time – used her back-scrub brush and her creme rinse and let the bathroom fog up with steam. I lathered myself with a muddy scrap of beeswax soap I clawed out of the shower caddy. I felt close to her, in a larcenous way, as if here in the shower using her things, all the new toiletries she now owned, I could know better the person she'd become. All evening I'd been full of reminiscences, but she had seldom joined in. Instead she was full of kindnesses – draping her own sweater around my shoulders; bringing me tea. How could I know or hope that she contained within her all our shared life, that she had not set it aside to make room for other days and affections and things that now had all made their residence and marks within her? Of course, I knew there were no reassurances. Or, there were only reassurances. She had offered them. 'This place is just not the same without you,' she had said twice that afternoon. But I was greedy. Three was the magic number. I'd wanted her to say it one more time.

I got out, wrapped a towel around me, and went back to bed, where she lay still asleep, curved in a pale paisley, the sheet about her like an old tricot curtain. I slipped quietly under the covers, my hair wet, feeling the water bed give slightly beneath me like something gelatinous and alive.

'Did you just take a *shower?*' Sils suddenly murmured, surprising me.

'Yeah, I did.'

She kept her eyes closed, and simply readjusted her pillow for sleep. 'You were always a weird girl,' she said dreamily.

'I was?' I said. 'I was not.'

She gave a lazy laugh. 'You should invite me to where you live some day and see all the wacky things I'm going to do.'

'I will,' I said. 'I will.' Though I already imagined that by the time I got back to my new job and life, with all its distractions and busynesses, that I wouldn't know how. Or why. Despite all my curatorial impulses and training, my priestly harborings and professional, courtly suit of the past, I never knew what to do with all those years of one's life: trot around in them forever like old boots – or sever them, let them fly free?

Of course, one couldn't really do either. But there was always the trying, and pretending. And then there was finally someplace in between, where one lived.

I curled next to Sils, and closed my eyes. I slept the light, watery sleep of a sick person who has already slept off the day and then awakened to night, not knowing what to do.

Lorrie Moore, *Who Will Run the Frog Hospital?*
(1994)

A S FOR MYSELF, if I do become complacent and even a little delirious (as, with the utmost contempt for things and the fullest intention to remain sane and sardonic, I am sure I sometimes do) it is not because I feel self-satisfied in that Gordon loves me, for love is only one of the satisfactory things that may befall one, and to fulfil the least of one's ends means infinitely more, but it is the sheer astonishment and wonderment to find a love that is warm flesh and blood and caressing hands and brilliant shining eyes, instead of a few newspaper cuttings and a grave and some faded flowers and a memory. When I say 'love' here I mean love of the sexual sort – which leads me to say that you are quite wrong if you consider yourself any less *the* person than you were before. Gordon brought along a new set of experiences of great value, but he has very little part in the old kind (old because they came first, not because they are past, for they never pass) which belong to you. A relation based on some fact of sex – whether of husband, or of parents, or, I strongly suspect, of children, is not *necessarily* to me the best or most interesting sort of relation. About such matters I am quite unprejudiced, and though Gordon has come to play so important a part, and deeply as he interests me, and much as I love him, I think I speak the truth when I say that a world with Gordon, but without you, would be much more lonely than a world without Gordon but with you. I mean that as much as I meant it when I once said that if I had been given the choice to keep Roland or Edward, I would have kept Edward. And then I can never forget that you were *my* conquest – I sought you out and won you – whereas Gordon is merely the person who conquered me! . . . Be happy, my sweetheart; I can only repeat G's naive remark to me and say that you give so much happiness to other people that you surely must receive something in return. There are the Harrys, of course, but then we are not all Harrys; some of us are – not better – but luckier.

Au revoir, darling girl; I write again very, very soon.

My love and all greetings to your family.

Ever your V.S.V.D.L.

Vera Brittain to Winifred Holtby, 28 July, 1925

Darling little sweet,

How horrid of me to make you unhappy by being cross. And how humble and sweet you are in your reasoning . . .

Darling, I do love you. But you are quite, quite wrong if you think that either you or Gordon are complacent, or that I find your happiness painful. Why my dear love, what matters is that happiness – the golden day – should exist in the world – not much to whom it comes. For all of us it is so transitory a thing, how could one not draw joy from its arrival? I have known no greater pleasure – complete and soothing – (not like the wild dark joy of literary composition, which is more painful than agreeable) – no greater pleasure than in the knowledge that you and Gordon might be happy. This is not a sort of altruistic benevolence. It is a necessity. I can't enjoy my own pleasures so well if my beloved are not enjoying theirs – and positively, I can warm myself very comfortably at their fires. I like to be with you both – you give me exquisite joy. I never knew anyone who could make me giggle as Gordon can. They are chuckles of pure content without a backward thought. And as for you, my heart, do you not realise that I don't care twopence whereabout in the scale of your loves I come, provided that you love me enough to let me love you, and that you are happy? I don't want you to tell me whereabouts I come, to define and weigh and analyse – because a) one can't do it; b) I don't care. I simply don't care. I love you in a way that part of me has become part of you. When you are troubled, so must I be, whether I like it or not. When you are happy, part of me is happy, whatever else befalls. Only be happy, my sweet. Fulfil yourself, as you must with joys and pains and rich experience. I who am part of you, can only gain by your gains. This you must and shall believe. I do not want a shadow of doubt to cross your mind about this – for it would be a false doubt.

For myself, I have one of my own peculiar little private joys today – flowers in profusion, a lime tree outside my window, a broad, clear tablet and a ream of new paper.

Darling sweet, I love you. I also think that your husband is very nice. Give him my love. Of course he may read any of my letters that interest him sufficiently.

My sweet my pretty, I kiss your clear head. W.

Winifred Holtby to Vera Brittain, 29 July 1925

Letters like your last make me miss you more than ever. One of the few things Gordon has never understood – I suppose, in the nature of things, he could not understand – is how much I love you. One could hardly expect one's husband to understand the queer link that makes me able to give a freer devotion of the mind where there is no sexual connotation – just as I loved Edward better than Roland, though I didn't know it until I found, when they were both dead, that I missed him more. He gives delight to a side of me which is biologically beyond you – yet somehow to the rest of me you give more than he; we share more secrets, as it were. He hasn't your love for silly things, and he never says 'Tell me some more!' He is a most stimulating companion, yet it never does me as much good to discuss my books with him as with you, for instead of letting me tell him what I want to put and then commenting, he starts off by telling me what he thinks I ought to put! Much of it is good and useful, but it doesn't help me to develop my ideas in the same way.

Vera Brittain to Winifred Holtby, 19 November 1925

Sometimes I am afraid to come back; I dread the autumn, and that you'll be different after all these crowded experiences in Africa – or that you'll go away at the last moment, and leave me stranded in London without you or Gordon, fallen between two stools. Why do I think this? Why should you be different when I am not? There is no profounder psychological experience than marriage; you get to know so much that you can never unlearn whether you want to or not; it is more profound than travel, much more profound than lectures. Yet marriage has not changed me, I don't think. I count all the things that I wanted before I was married; if anything I want them more than ever . . . No, marriage (and a year is a test) hasn't altered me; it has only made me much, much more everything that I was before. So why should Africa have altered you? Perhaps your letters aren't as intimate? But then that's hurry, preoccupation. And you never were a very good letter writer. I have just read your letter of May 18th from Cape Town. Nice, but just a little impersonal. Do time and distance really make a difference, and are we too proud in imagining ourselves superior to them? At least I haven't torn myself to pieces over you as I did last year over Gordon during an even shorter absence. Yet he hadn't changed at all. Why should I worry about you, remembering that? But then you don't need me as he does.

Vera Brittain to Winifred Holtby, 16 June 1926

Of course I have not changed. How could I? Your small, fugitive figure goes with me in my thoughts, is so much a part of me that I question my feelings toward you as little as I question my own egotism. Perhaps like a loving husband, I have grown stale in my articulation. Oh, forgive me, my sweet, if I have proved so dull, so unworthy a husband. The fault lay in the pen, not the thoughts. How should I change? It is true that in one way I am self-sufficient; I can love; I can enjoy my life; see colours, hear music and voices; conceive ideas, taste new experiences, all with true eyes and all alone. It is true that I love other people, Mother, Jean McWilliam; that I find interest in almost every chance acquaintance – the people whom I met in Africa, or on the boat. But you are you. And because you are you, there is part of me with which, in Margaret's words to Faust, 'I need thee every hour' . . . Marriage or non-marriage has nothing to do with it. Were I married too, it would be the same. I want you to understand this, because other separations might lead to similar apprehensions.

Winifred Holtby to Vera Brittain, 17 July 1926

Sweetieheart, I don't think in my heart of hearts I ever doubted *you* weren't different; I really understood all the time that you were engrossed and overfull of work and travel. What really started me wondering, I think, was little postcards from your Mother forwarded by mine – and assumptions by mine that you wouldn't go to Geneva, that you wouldn't keep the flat, that you wouldn't fulfil the arrangement that I was basing all my plans on. In normal conditions one would take no notice of such things, but here, and after a year of facing assumptions on the part of every-body that because one is married one won't want to lead the same sort of life as one did before, it is different. (Unless I am with Gordon, I never tell people that I meet for the first time that I am married now. Over here, when people meet you and think you unmarried, their first question always is 'What's your job?' or 'What are you doing here?' But when they know you are married they ask: 'What is your husband?') Personally, I don't feel a scrap more married than I did two years ago; I still get a shock when the few people whom I have not trained to call me 'Miss Brittain' address

me as 'Mrs' and I have not lost one jot of my desire to do any
of the things I have always wished to do, and I think . . . I am
more ambitious than ever.

Vera Brittain to Winifred Holtby, 30 July 1926

9

OLD FRIENDS

The best mirror is an old friend

Attributed to George Herbert (1593–1633)

Jackie Kay ∼ *E. M. Delafield* ∼ *Carol Shields* ∼ *Margaret Drabble*
Amanda Craig ∼ *Barbara Pym* ∼ *Samuel Richardson* ∼ *Geoffrey Chaucer*
Toni Morrison ∼ *Katherine Philips*

We like to think that old friends are the best friends – and perhaps they are. Certainly, in this chapter, the aim is to celebrate them. If we're lucky, we grow older together, like trees in a forest, and luxuriate in that, with our shorthand and embarrassing stories. Only an old friend can reduce us to hysterical laughter (as Sula does Nel in Toni Morrison's novel); only an old friend can tell us that we do *not* suit brown (as Muriel does Dora in Barbara Pym's *Excellent Women*). But old friends can be so madly irritating, too – especially those who pop up unbidden, and whose status in our lives is akin to a rarely visited stately home (strictly heritage). E. M. Delafield captures this so well in *The Diary of a Provincial Lady*, when her 'dear old school friend', the well-named Cissie Crabbe, comes to stay. Delafield's elegantly clipped words – here are tightly pressed lips in prose form – make me laugh out loud.

Fiere

If ye went tae the topmost hill, fiere,
whaur we used tae clamb as girls,
ye'd see the snow the day, fiere,
settling on the hills.
You'd mind o'anither day, mibbe,
we ran down soon the hill in the snow,
sliding and oor way tae the foot,
lassies laughing thegither – how braw,
the years slipping awa; oot in the weather.

And now we're suddenly auld, fiere,
oor friendship's ne'er been weary.
We've aye seen the warld differently.
Whaur would I have been weyoot my jo,
my fiere, my fierce, my dearie O?
Oor hair it micht be silver noo,
oor walk a wee bit doddery,
but we've had a whirl and a blast, girl,
thru the cauld blast winter, thru spring, summer.

O'er a lifetime, my fiere, my bonnie lassie,
I'd defend you – you, me; blithe and blatter,
here we gang doon the hill, nae matter,
past the bracken, bonny braes, barley,

oot by the roaring sea, still havin blether.
We who loved sincerely; we who love sae fiercely,
the snow ne'er looked sae barrie,
nor the winter trees sae pretty.
C'mon, c'mon my dearie – tak my hand, my fiere!

Jackie Kay, *'Fiere'* (2011)

LETTER BY SECOND post from my dear old school-friend
Cissie Crabbe, asking if she may come here for two
nights or so on her way to Norwich. (Query: Why
Norwich? Am surprised to realise that anybody ever goes
to, lives at, or comes from, Norwich, but quite see that
this is unreasonable of me. Remind myself how very little
one knows of the England one lives in, which vaguely
suggests a quotation. This, however, does not materialise.)
Many years since we last met, writes Cissie, and she
expects we have both changed a good deal. P.S. Do I
remember the dear old pond, and the day of the Spanish
Arrowroot. Can recall, after some thought, dear old pond,
at bottom of Cissie's father's garden, but am completely
baffled by Spanish Arrowroot. (Query: Could this be one
of the Sherlock Holmes stories? Sounds like it.)
Reply that we shall be delighted to see her, and what a
lot we shall have to talk about, after all these years! (This,
I find on reflection, is not true, but cannot re-write letter
on that account.) Ignore Spanish Arrowroot altogether.

Robert, when I tell him about dear old school-friend's impending arrival, does not seem pleased. Asks what we are expected to do with her. I suggest showing her the garden, and remember too late that this is hardly the right time of the year. At any rate, I say, it will be nice to talk over old times – (which reminds me of the Spanish Arrowroot reference still unfathomed).

Speak to Ethel about the spare room, and am much annoyed to find that one blue candlestick has been broken, and the bedside rug has gone to the cleaners, and cannot be retrieved in time. Take away bedside rug from Robert's dressing-room, and put it in spare room instead, hoping he will not notice its absence.

November 15th. – Robert does notice absence of rug, and says he must have it back again. Return it to dressing-room and take small and inferior dyed mat from the night-nursery to put in spare room. Mademoiselle is hurt about this and says to Vicky, who repeats it to me, that in this country she finds herself treated like a worm.

November 17th. – Dear old school-friend Cissie Crabbe due by the three o'clock train. On telling Robert this, he says it is most inconvenient to meet her, owing to Vestry Meeting, but eventually agrees to abandon Vestry Meeting. Am touched. Unfortunately, just after he has started, telegram arrives to say that dear old school-friend has missed the connection and will not arrive until seven o'clock. This means putting off dinner till eight, which Cook won't like. Cannot send message to kitchen by Ethel, as it is her afternoon out, so am obliged to tell Cook myself. She is not pleased. Robert returns from station, not pleased either. Mademoiselle, quite inexplicably, says, 'Il ne manquait que ca!' (This comment wholly unjustifiable, as non-appearance of Cissie Crabbe cannot concern her in any way. Have often thought that the French are tactless.)

Ethel returns, ten minutes late, and says Shall she light fire in spare room? I say No, it is not cold enough – but really mean that Cissie is no longer, in my opinion, deserving of luxuries. Subsequently feel this to be unworthy attitude, and light fire myself. It smokes.

Robert calls up to know What is that Smoke? I call down that It is Nothing. Robert comes up and opens the window and shuts the door and says It will Go all right Now. Do not like to point out that the open window will make the room cold.

Play Ludo with Vicky in drawing-room.

Robert reads the Times and goes to sleep, but wakes in time to make second expedition to the station. Thankful to say that this time he returns with Cissie Crabbe, who has put on weight, and says several times that she supposes we have both changed a good deal, which I consider unnecessary.

Take her upstairs – spare room like an icehouse, owing to open window, and fire still smoking, though less – She says room is delightful, and I leave her, begging her to ask for anything she wants – (Mem.: tell Ethel she must answer spare room bell if it rings – Hope it won't.)

Ask Robert while dressing for dinner what he thinks of Cissie. He says he has not known her long enough to judge. Ask if he thinks her good-looking. He says he has not thought about it. Ask what they talked about on the way from the station. He says he does not remember.

November 19th. – Last two days very, very trying, owing to quite unexpected discovery that Cissie Crabbe is strictly on a diet. This causes Robert to take a dislike to her. Utter impossibility of obtaining lentils or lemons at short notice makes housekeeping unduly difficult. Mademoiselle in the middle of lunch insists on discussing diet question, and several times exclaims: 'Ah, mon doux St Joseph!' which I consider profane, and beg her never to repeat.

Consult Cissie about the bulbs, which look very much as if the mice had been at them. She says: Unlimited Watering, and tells me about her own bulbs at Norwich. Am discouraged.

Administer Unlimited Water to the bulbs (some of which goes through the attic floor on to the landing below), and move half of them down to the cellar, as Cissie Crabbe says attic is airless.

Our Vicar's wife calls this afternoon. Says she once knew someone who had relations living near Norwich, but cannot remember their name. Cissie Crabbe replies that very likely if we knew their name we might find she'd heard of them, or even met them. We agree that the world is a small place. Talk about the Riviera, the new waist-line, choir-practice, the servant question, and Ramsay MacDonald.

November 22nd. – Cissie Crabbe leaves. Begs me in the kindest way to stay with her in Norwich (where she has already told me that she lives in a bed-sitting-room with two cats, and cooks her own lentils on a gas-ring). I say Yes, I should love to. We part effusively.

Spend entire morning writing the letters I have had to leave unanswered during Cissie's visit.

E. M. Delafield, *The Diary of a Provincial Lady* **(1930)**

Mrs Flett's Old School Friend
Fraidy Hoyt and Daisy Goodwill Flett went to school together back in Indiana. They sat on the Goodwills' front porch in Bloomington and shared bags of Jay's Potato Chips. They went to college together too, and pledged the same sorority, Alpha Zeta, and ever since that time they've stayed in touch. That is, they've corresponded three or four times a year, and sent each other jokey presents on their birthdays and at Christmas. They haven't actually seen each other for years, but, finally, in August of 1947, Fraidy got herself on a train and went up to Ottawa for a week's visit.

While she was there she thought: here is Daisy Goodwill with a distinguished husband and a large well-managed house and three beautiful children. Daisy's got all that any of us ever wanted. Whereas I've missed out on everything, no husband, no kids, no home really, only a dinky little apartment, not even a garden! That garden's something else. She can get up in the morning and spend all day if she likes trimming and weeding and transplanting and bringing beauty into the world. While I'm sitting at work. Tied to a desk and to the clock. Missing out on this business of being a woman. Missing it all.

Or else Fraidy Hoyt thought: oh, poor Daisy. My God, she's

gone fat. And respectable. Although who could be respectable
going around in one of those godawful dirndl skirts – should
I say something? Drop a little hint? Her cuticles too. I don't
think she's read a book in ten years. And, Jesus, just look at
this guest room. Hideous pink scallops everywhere. I'm suffo-
cating. Four more days. And this crocheted bedspread, she's so
gee-dee proud of, no one has crocheted bedspreads any more,
it's enough to give you nightmares just touching it. I'd like to
unravel the whole damn thing, and I could too, one little pull.
These kids are driving me crazy, whining and sneaking around
all day, then dressing up like little puppets for the return of the
great man at the end of the day. Putting on a little play every
single hypocritical day of their lives.

And: what can I say to her? What's left to say? I see you're
still breathing Daisy. I see you're still dusting that nose of yours
with Woodbury Face Powder. I observe your husband is always
going off to 'meetings' in Toronto or Montreal, and I wonder
if you have any notion of what happens to him in those places.
I notice you continue to wake up in the morning and go to
bed at night. Now isn't that interesting. I believe your life is
still going along, it's still happening to you, isn't it? Well, well.

Carol Shields, *The Stone Diaries* (1993)

IN THEIR MID-FORTIES, after more than half a lifetime of
association, they share characteristics, impressions, memories,
even speech patterns: they have a common stock of knowledge,
they have entered, through one another, worlds that they would

not otherwise have known. They have pooled their discoveries, have come back from outer regions with examples of leaf, twig, fruit, stone, have turned them over together. They share much. The barriers between them are, they think, quite low.

As their professional worlds overlap, so do their diversions. They share, perhaps surprisingly, a love of walking, of the English countryside. This might have been expected from Alix, whose parents had patronised Youth Hostels long after their youth, and who like to boast of long pioneering rambles in the 1930s. But Esther too, essentially an indoor person, likes to walk. The countryside, she says defensively, is an aesthetic experience. She is knowledgeable about flowers, trees, even grasses. Liz, the most reluctant recruit to this wholesome pursuit, has become its most enthusiastic addict and of late tends to take upon herself the role of organiser . . .

They make an odd trio, to the eye of the observer. They refuse to dress seriously for their walking expeditions. Alix favours a pair of gym shoes, socks and a skirt: she does not like wearing trousers. Esther wears trousers, but they are not the right sort for walking in: velvet, loose silk, or striped cotton, with a smart little pair of somewhat indoor boots. Liz wears proper trousers, jeans or khaki land-girl's trousers from Laurence Corner Army Surplus, but she rather spoils the effect by the ill-assorted sunhat, Indian head squares, Liberty scarves and ski helmets with which she protects herself from the variable English weather, and by a pair of everlasting Dr Scholl's clogs which ought to be unsuitable for long tramps but which, according to Liz, serve very well. Off they trudge, with a picnic, happily, once or twice a year. Happily, innocently. Alix has a string bag, bought in an Oxfam shop, in which she is allowed to carry the map. Sometimes they speculate on the number of miles the bag has walked. Like Liz's clogs, it never perishes.

Men are not usually invited.

Margaret Drabble, *The Radiant Way* **(1987)**

THE THREE WOMEN who met for coffee in Via Nazionale every Saturday morning were united by age, exile, the love of dogs and their disinclination to discuss their infirmities.

'Enough of the organ grinding!' Marta declared if anyone complained of arthritic joints, failing eyesight, dizziness or debility. Between them, they had four breasts, five eyes and three hip replacements. These were the price of living long lives, as were one divorce, one widowhood and one husband with dementia. Age had not diminished them: quite the opposite. They had become more concentrated versions of themselves, just as a pot of soup does the longer it is simmered.

'One must not look back,' was Ruth's philosophy. 'To look back is to regret what can't be changed.'

'Dogs are happy because they live in the present, and so must we,' agreed Diana.

'*Evviva!*' said Marta. 'Let us live and love, for tomorrow we die.'

Amanda Craig, *The Three Graces* **(2023)**

'WHY, MILDRED,' SHE exclaimed, 'what have you done to yourself? You look different.'

No compliments, of course; Dora was too old and honest a friend ever to flatter me, but she had the power of making me feel rather foolish, especially as I had not realised she might find any difference in my appearance since the last time we met. I suppose I had taken to using a little more make-up, my hair was more carefully arranged, my clothes a little less drab. I was hardly honest enough to admit even to myself that meeting the Napiers had made this difference and I certainly did not admit it to Dora.

'You must be trying to bring William up to scratch,' she said, 'is that it?'

I laughed gratefully.

'There's not much you can do when you're over thirty,' she went on complacently. 'You get too set in your ways, really. Besides, marriage isn't everything.'

'No, it certainly isn't,' I agreed, 'and there's nobody I want to marry that I can think of. Not even William.'

'I don't know anyone either, at the moment,' said Dora.

We lapsed into a comfortable silence. It was a kind of fiction that we had always kept up, this not knowing anyone at the moment that we wanted to marry, as if there had been in the past and would be in the future.

'How's school?' I asked.

'Oh, Protheroe and I aren't on speaking terms,' said Dora vigorously. She was a small, stocky person with red hair, not at all like her brother, and could look very fierce at times.

'I'm sorry to hear that,' I said. 'But I should imagine Miss Protheroe is rather difficult to get on with.'

'Difficult! It's a wonder that woman keeps any of her staff.'

'What happened?'

'Oh, well, I let my form go into chapel without hats one morning, and you know how she is about that sort of thing. Of course I've no use for any of this nonsense . . .' I let Dora go on but did not really listen, for I knew her views on Miss Protheroe and on organised religion of any kind. We had often argued about it in the past. I wondered that she should waste so much energy fighting over a little matter like wearing hats in chapel, but then I told myself that, after all, life was like that for most of us – the small unpleasantnesses rather than the great tragedies; the little useless longings rather than the great renunciations and dramatic love affairs of history or fiction.

'What would you like to do this afternoon?' I asked. 'Shall we go shopping?'

Dora's face brightened. 'Oh, yes, that would be nice.'

Later, as were trying on dresses in the inexpensive department of a large store, I forgot all about the Napiers and the complications of knowing them. I was back in those happier days when the company of women friends had seemed enough.

'Oh, dear, this is too tight on the hips,' said Dora, her ruffled head and flushed face emerging through the neck of a brown woollen dress.

'I'm not sure that's your colour,' I said doubtfully. 'I've come to the conclusion that we should avoid brown. It does the wrong kind of things to people over thirty, unless they're very smart. When my brown coat is worn out I shall get a black or a navy one.'

'Now you're talking like a fashion magazine,' said Dora,

struggling with the zip-fastener. 'I've always had a brown wool dress for every day.'

Yes, and look at you, I thought, with one of those sudden flashes of unkindness that attack us all sometimes. 'Why not try this green?' I suggested. 'It would suit you.'

'Good Heavens, whatever would people at school say if I appeared in a dress that colour?' Dora exclaimed. 'I shouldn't know myself. No, I'll just ask for the brown in a larger size. It's just what I want.'

They had the dress in a larger size which was now a little too large, but Dora seemed perfectly satisfied and bought it. 'I don't know what's the matter with you, Mildred,' she complained. 'You never used to bother much about clothes.'

'Where shall we have tea?' I asked, changing the subject because I felt myself unable to give a satisfactory explanation.

'Oh, the Corner House!' said Dora, enthusiastically. 'You know how I enjoy that.'

Barbara Pym, *Excellent Women* (1952)

*A*nna to Charlotte Montague
You know not how I love her! – My own Soul is not dearer to me, than my Clarissa Harlowe! – Nay, she *is* my Soul – For I now have none – Only a miserable one, however – For she was the joy, the stay, the prop of my life. Never woman loved woman as we love one another. It is impossible to tell you half her excellencies. It was so my glory and my pride, that I was capable of so fervent a Love of so pure and matchless a creature. VI

Clarissa to Anna

What pain, my dearest friend, does your kind solicitude for my welfare give me! How much more binding and tender are the Ties of pure Friendship, and the Union of Like minds, than the Ties of Nature! Well might the Sweet Singer of Israel, when he was carrying to the utmost extent the praises of the friendship between his beloved friend, say, that the Love of Jonathan to him was wonderful; that it surpassed the *Love of Women!* What an exalted idea does it give of the Soul of Jonathan, sweetly attempered for the sacred band, if we may suppose it but equal to that of my Anna Howe for her fallen Clarissa! – But, altho' I can glory in your kind Love for me, think, my dear, what concern must fill a mind, not ungenerous, when the obligation lies all *on one side.* VI

Samuel Richardson, *Clarissa* (1748)

The Wife of Bath's Prologue

> My fifth housbonde – God his soule
> blesse! –
> Which that I took for love and no richesse,
> He som tyme was a clerk of Oxenford,
> And hadde left scole, and wente at hom to bord
> With my gossib, dwellynge in oure toun;
> God have hir soule! Hir name was Alisoun.
> She knew myn herte and eek my privetee,
> Bet then our parisshe preest, so moot I thee!
> To hir biwreyed I my conseil al.

For hadde myn housbonde pissed on a wal,
Or doon a thyng that should han cost his lyf,
To hir, and to another worthy wyf,
And to my nece, which that I loved weel,
I wolde han toold his conseil every deel.
And so I dide ful often, God it woot,
That made his face ful often reed and hoot
For verray shame, and blamed himself for he
Had toold to me so greet a pryvetee.*

Geoffrey Chaucer, 'The Wife of Bath's Prologue', *The Canterbury Tales* (c.1387–1400)

---

*   My fifth husband – God bless him! –
Who I married for love, not for riches,
Had been a clerk at Oxford,
And had left school and come home to board
With my closest friend, living in our town;
God save her soul! Her name was Alison.
And as I live and breathe, she knew the secrets of my heart
Better than our parish priest ever did,
Because I revealed them all to her, every one.
If my husband had pissed against a wall,
Or done a thing that might have cost him his life,
I would always tell her, and another woman I trusted,
And my niece, who I always loved a lot,
I'd tell them all the details,
And God knows,
Doing this made his face burn red
With the shame of it; and then he would blame himself
For having made the mistake of telling me so big a secret.

Trans: Rachel Cooke

NEL ALONE NOTICED the peculiar quality of the May that followed the leaving of the birds. It had a sheen, a glimmering as of green, rain-soaked Saturday nights (lit by the excitement of newly installed street lights); of lemon-yellow afternoons bright with iced drinks and splashes of daffodils. It showed in the damp faces of her children and the river-smoothness of their voices. Even her own body was not immune to the magic. She would sit on the floor to sew as she had done as a girl, fold her legs up under her or do a little dance that fitted some tune in her head. There were easy sun-washed days and purple dusks in which Tar Baby sang 'Abide With Me' at prayer meetings, his lashes darkened by tears, his silhouette limp with regret against the whitewashed walls of Greater Saint Matthew's. Nel listened and was moved to smile. To smile at the sheer loveliness that pressed in from the windows and touched his grief, making it a pleasure to behold.

Although it was she alone who saw this magic, she did not wonder at it. She knew it was all due to Sula's return to the Bottom. It was like getting the use of an eye back, having a cataract removed. Her old friend had come home. Sula. Who made her laugh, who made her see old things with new eyes, in whose presence she felt clever, gentle and a little raunchy. Sula, whose past she had lived through and with whom the present was a constant sharing of perceptions. Talking to Sula had always been a conversation with herself. Was there anyone else before whom she could never be foolish? In whose view inadequacy was mere idiosyncrasy, a character trait rather than a deficiency? Anyone who left behind that aura of fun and complicity? Sula never competed; she simply helped others to define themselves. Other people seemed to turn their volume

on and up when Sula was in the room. More than any other
thing, humor returned. She could listen to the crunch of sugar
underfoot that the children had spilled without reaching for
the switch; and she forgot the tear in the living-room window
shade. Even Nel's love for Jude, which over the years had spun
a steady gray web around her heart, became a bright and easy
affection, a playfulness that was reflected in their lovemaking.

Sula would come by of an afternoon, walking along with
her fluid stride, wearing a plain yellow dress the same way her
mother, Hannah, had worn those too-big house dresses – with
a distance, an absence of a relationship to clothes which empha-
sized everything the fabric covered. When she scratched the
screen door, as in the old days, and stepped inside, the dishes
piled in the sink looked as though they belonged there; the dust
on the lamps sparkled; the hair brush lying on the 'good' sofa
in the living room did not have to be apologetically retrieved,
and Nel's grimy intractable children looked like three wild
things insouciant in the May shine.

'Hey, girl.' The rose mark over Sula's eye gave her glance
a suggestion of startled pleasure. It was darker than Nel
remembered.

'Hey yourself. Come on in here.'

'How you doin'?' Sula moved a pile of ironed diapers from
a chair and sat down.

'Oh, I ain't strangled nobody yet so I guess I'm all right.'

'Well, if you change your mind call me.'

'Somebody need killin'?'

'Half this town need it.'

'And the other half?'

'A drawn-out disease.'

'Oh, come on. Is Medallion that bad?'

'Didn't nobody tell you?'

'You been gone too long, Sula.'

'Not too long, but maybe too far.'

'What's that supposed to mean?' Nel dipped her fingers into the bowl of water and sprinkled a diaper.

'Oh, I don't know.'

'Want some cool tea?'

'Mmmm. Lot of ice, I'm burnin' up.'

'Iceman don't come yet, but it's good and cold.'

'That's fine.'

'Hope I didn't speak too soon. Kids run in and out of here so much.' Nel bent to open the icebox.

'You puttin' it on, Nel. Jude must be wore out.'

'*Jude* must be wore out? You don't care nothin' 'bout my back, do you?'

'Is that where it's at, in your back?'

'Hah! Jude thinks it's everywhere.'

'He's right, it is everywhere. Just be glad he found it, wherever it is. Remember John L.?'

'When Shirley said he got her down by the well and tried to stick it in her hip?' Nel giggled at the remembrance of that teen-time tale. 'She should have been grateful. Have you seen her since you been back?'

'Mmm. Like a ox.'

'That was one dumb nigger, John L.'

'Maybe. Maybe he was just sanitary.'

'Sanitary?'

'Well. Think about it. Suppose Shirley was all splayed out in front of you? Wouldn't you go for the hipbone instead?'

Nel lowered her head into crossed arms while tears of laughter dripped into the warm diapers. Laughter that weakened her knees and pressed her bladder into action. Her rapid soprano and Sula's dark sleepy chuckle made a duet that frightened the cat and made the children run in from the back yard, puzzled at first by the wild free sounds, then delighted to see their mother stumbling merrily toward the bathroom, holding on to her stomach, fairly singing through the laughter. 'Aw. Aw. Lord. Sula. Stop.' And the other one, the one with the scary black thing over her eye, laughing softly and egging their mother on: 'Neatness counts. You know what cleanliness is next to . . .'

'Hush.' Nel's plea was clipped off by the slam of the bathroom door.

'What y'all laughing at?'

'Old time-y stuff. Long gone, old time-y stuff.'

'Tell us.'

'Tell *you?*' The black mark leaped.

'Uh huh. Tell us.'

'What tickles us wouldn't tickle you.'

'Uh huh, it would.'

'Well, we was talking about some people we used to know when we was little.'

'Was my mamma little?'

'Of course.'

'What happened?'

'Well, some old boy we knew name John L. and a girl name . . .'

Damp-faced, Nel stepped back into the kitchen. She felt new, soft and new. It had been the longest time since she had

had a rib-scraping laugh. She had forgotten how deep and down it could be. So different from the miscellaneous giggles and smiles she had learned to be content with these past few years.

'O Lord, Sula. You haven't changed none.' She wiped her eyes. 'What was all that about, anyway? All that scramblin' we did trying to do it and not do it at the same time?'

'Beats me. Such a simple thing.'

'But we sure made a lot out of it, and the boys were dumber than we were.'

'Couldn't nobody be dumber than I was.'

'Stop lying. All of 'em liked you best.'

'Yeah? Where are they?'

'They still here. You the one went off.'

Toni Morrison, *Sula* (1973)

Friendship's Mystery, To my Dearest Lucasia

1

Come, my Lucasia, since we see
That Miracles Men's faith do move,
By wonder and by prodigy
To the dull angry world let's prove
There's a Religion in our Love.

2

For though we were design'd t' agree,
That Fate no liberty destroyes,
But our Election is as free

As Angels, who with greedy choice
Are yet determin'd to their joyes.

3
Our hearts are doubled by the loss,
Here Mixture is Addition grown;
We both diffuse, and both ingross:
And we whose minds are so much one,
Never, yet ever are alone.

4
We court our own Captivity
Than Thrones more great and innocent:
'Twere banishment to be set free,
Since we wear fetters whose intent
Not Bondage is, but Ornament.

5
Divided joyes are tedious found,
And griefs united easier grow:
We are our selves but by rebound,
And all our Titles shuffled so,
Both Princes, and both Subjects too.

6
Our Hearts are mutual Victims laid,
While they (such power in Friendship lies)
Are Altars, Priests, and Off'rings made:
And each Heart which thus kindly dies,
Grows deathless by the Sacrifice.

**Katherine Philips (1632–64), 'Friendship's
Mystery, To my Dearest Lucasia'**

10
GOODBYES

I am glad to know as much as possible of all Her friends. I am not sorry that I do not find amongst them all any to who She Herself was more than She was and is to me.

Edith Simcox, 'Autobiography', after reading George Eliot's letters to Barbara Leigh Smith Bodichon (25 December 1881)

Mary McCarthy on Hannah Arendt ∼ *Rachel Cooke on Carmen Callil*
Anne Sexton on Sylvia Plath ∼ *Anne Preston on Hilary Mantel*
Edith Simcox on George Eliot ∼ *Virginia Woolf on Katherine Mansfield*
Anne Thackeray Ritchie on Margaret Oliphant ∼ *Helen Garner*
Elizabeth Bishop on Marianne Moore ∼ *Anne Stevenson on Frances Horovitz*
Charlotte Brontë

On 20 April 2023, a memorial service for the writer Hilary Mantel was held at Southwark Cathedral in London. It was, by any standards, a glorious event. Outside, the sun shone, hot for the time of year. Inside, the gathering was distinguished and starry. Among those reading and paying tribute that day were famous actors and celebrated novelists. When it was all over, there was champagne – and gossip, of a kind I think she might rather have enjoyed.

But the person whose words everyone remembered afterwards wasn't well known; few in the congregation had heard her name before. She was Anne Preston, a friend of Mantel's since childhood, and from the moment she began to talk you could have heard a pin drop. Here was the real thing: a person who had known Hilary for almost her whole life, and whose descriptions of her were neither overly worked up nor carefully trimmed with blandishments. All of their truth and authority lay in their simplicity and straightforwardness, and it was spellbinding to hear, as well as profoundly touching. Somehow, Preston had done that impossible thing: for a few moments, her old friend was an almost tangible spirit in that great, cavernous building; a more vivid presence by far than the photograph on the order of service, the videos that played on a loop on screens high above our heads.

Anne Preston's eulogy to Hilary Mantel is included in this chapter, along with several other accounts of friends deeply mourned, of which the most remarkable (in my eyes) is Mary McCarthy's of her friend, the philosopher Hannah Arendt, written a few weeks after her death in 1975. Would that all of us had someone like McCarthy to memorialise us: to capture all that we were, not only so beautifully, but so beadily (it is the noticing that counts). Verse lends itself to goodbyes, and there are two magnificent poems here. But in the end – and ends are what we're talking about – it is the death of Helen Burns in *Jane Eyre* that most touches my heart; it always has, and it always will, which is why it is the very last piece of writing in this book. Unbeliever that I am, I'm unable to read it without crying.

I DO NOT WANT to discuss Hannah's ideas here but to try to bring her back as a person, a physical being, showing herself radiantly in what she called the world of appearance, a stage from which she has now withdrawn. She was a beautiful woman, alluring, seductive, feminine, which is why I said 'Jewess' – the old-fashioned term, evoking the daughters of Sion, suits her, like a fringed Spanish shawl. Above all, her eyes, so brilliant and sparkling, starry when she was happy or excited, but also deep, dark, remote, pools of inwardness. There was something unfathomable in Hannah that seemed to lie in the reflective depths of those eyes.

She had small, fine hands, charming ankles, elegant feet. She liked shoes; in all the years I knew her, I think she only once had a corn. Her legs, feet, and ankles expressed quickness, decision. You had only to see her on a lecture stage to be struck by those feet, calves and ankles that seemed to keep pace with her thought. As she talked, she moved about, sometimes with her hands plunged in her pockets like somebody all alone on a walk, meditating. When the fire laws permitted, she would smoke, pacing the stage with a cigarette in a short holder, inhaling from time to time, reflectively, her head back, as if arrested by a new unexpected idea. Watching her talk to an audience was like seeing the motions of the mind made visible in action and gesture. Peripatetic, she would come abruptly to a halt at the lectern, frown, consult the ceiling, bite her lip, pensively cup her chin. If she was reading a speech, there were always interjections, asides, like the footnotes that peppered her texts with qualifications and appendices.

There was more than a touch of the great actress in Hannah. The first time I heard her speak in public – nearly thirty years ago, during a debate – I was reminded of what Bernhardt must have been or Proust's Berma, a magnificent stage diva, which implies a goddess. Perhaps a chthonic goddess, or a fiery one, rather than the airy kind. Unlike other good speakers, she was not at all an orator. She appeared, rather, as a mime, a thespian, enacting a drama of mind, that dialogue of me-and-myself she so often summons up in her writings. Watching her framed in the proscenium arch, we were not far from the sacred origins of the theatre. What she projected was the human figure as actor and sufferer in the agony of consciousness and reflection, where there are always two, the one who says and the one who replies or questions.

Yet nobody could have been further from an exhibitionist. Calculation of the impression she was making never entered her head. Whenever she spoke in public, she had terrible stage fright, and afterward she would ask only 'Was it alright?' (This cannot have been true of the classroom, where she felt herself at ease and among friends.) And naturally she did not play roles in private or public, even less than the normal amount required in social relations. She was incapable of feigning. Though she prided herself as a European on being able to tell a lie, where we awkward Americans blurted out the truth, in fact there was a little hubris there. Hannah's small points of vanity never had any relation to her real accomplishments. For example, she thought she knew a good deal about cooking and didn't. It was the same with her supposed ability to lie. Throughout our friendship, I don't think I ever heard her tell even one of those white lies, such as pleading illness or a previous engagement, to get herself out of a social quandary. If you wrote something she found bad, her policy was not to allude to it – an unvarying course of action that told you louder than words what she thought.

What was theatrical in Hannah was a kind of spontaneous power of being seized by an idea, an emotion, a presentiment, whose vehicle her body then became, like the actor's. And this power of being seized and worked upon, often with a start, widened eyes, 'Ach!' (before a picture, a work of architecture, some deed of infamy), set her apart from the rest of us like a high electrical charge. And there was the vibrant, springy, dark, short hair, never fully grey, that sometimes from sheer force of energy appeared to stand bolt upright on her head.

I suppose all this must have been part of an unusual physical endowment, whose manifestation in her features and facial gestures was the beauty I spoke of. Hannah is the only person I have ever watched *think*. She lay motionless on a sofa or a day bed, arms folded behind her head, eyes shut but occasionally opening to stare upward. This lasted – I don't know – from ten minutes to half an hour. Everyone tiptoed past if we had to come into the room in which she lay oblivious.

She was an impatient, generous woman, and those qualities went hand in hand. Just as, in a speech or essay, she would put everything in but the kitchen stove, as if she could not keep in reserve a single item of what she knew or had happened that instant to occur to her, so she would press on a visitor assorted nuts, chocolates, candied ginger, tea, coffee, Campari, whiskey, cigarettes, cake, crackers, fruit, cheese almost all at once, regardless of conventional sequence or, often, of the time of day. It was as if the profusion of edibles, set out, many of them, in little ceremonial-like dishes and containers, were impatient propitiatory offerings to all the queer gods of taste. Someone said that this was the eternal Jewish mother, but it was not that: there was no notion that any of this fodder was good for you; in fact most of it was distinctly bad for you, which she must have known somehow, for she did not insist.

She had a respect for privacy, separateness, one's own and hers. I often stayed with her – and Heinrich [Blücher, Arendt's second husband] – on Riverside Drive and before that on Morningside Drive, so that I came to know Hannah's habits well, what she liked for breakfast, for instance. A boiled egg, some mornings, a little ham or cold cuts, toast spread with anchovy paste, coffee, of course, half a grapefruit or fresh orange juice, but perhaps that last was only when I, the American, was there. The summer after Heinrich's death she came to stay with us in Maine, where we gave her a separate apartment, over the garage, and I put some thought into buying supplies for her kitchen – she liked to breakfast alone. The things, I thought, that she would have at home, down to instant coffee (which I don't normally stock) for when she could not be bothered with the filters. I was rather pleased to have been able to find anchovy paste in the village store. On the afternoon of her arrival, as I showed her where everything was in the larder, she frowned over the little tube of anchovy paste, as though it were an inexplicable foreign object. 'What is that?' I told her. 'Oh.' She put it down and looked thoughtful and as though displeased, somehow. No more was said. But I knew I had done something wrong in my efforts to please. She did not wish to be *known*, in that curiously finite and, as it were, reductive way. And I had done it to show her I knew her – a sign of love, though not always – thereby proving that in the last analysis I did not know her at all.

Her eyes were closed in her coffin, and her hair was waved back from her forehead, whereas *she* pulled it forward, some-times tugging at a lock as she spoke, partly to hide a scar she had got in an automobile accident – but even before that she had never really bared her brow. In her coffin, with the lids veiling the fathomless eyes, that noble forehead topped by a sort of pompadour, she was not Hannah any more but a composed death mask of an eighteenth-century philosopher. I was not moved to touch that grand stranger in the funeral parlor, and only in the soft yet roughened furrows of her neck, in which the public head rested, could I find a place to tell her good-by.[*]

Mary McCarthy on her friend Hannah Arendt,
New York Review of Books (1976)

---

[*] Arendt died on 4 December 1975, aged sixty-nine, by which time McCarthy had known her for more than thirty years.

I'D LOVE TO be able to say that it was Antonia White, or Rosamond Lehman, or one of the many other women writers she championed who brought us together. But that, alas, would be a lie. In the first instance at least, it is Padma Lakshmi, the TV cook who used to be married to Salman Rushdie, who must take the credit for my friendship with Carmen Callil.

The year was 2004, and I was at a book launch at the Polish Club in South Kensington, trying hard both not to look shy, and not to drink the dangerously terrible wine that was in my glass – a tricky proposition, given that the two acts were in direct opposition to one another. The weekend before, the *Observer* had run a disobliging profile I'd written of Lakshmi, with whom I'd spent a long and humiliating day in New York, and to my amazement, it was this that Carmen brought up when, as the party reached its noisy climax, we were unexpectedly introduced. 'Padma Lakshmi!' she all but shouted on hearing my name. And then, with even greater ferocity: 'My *heroine*!' For a few seconds, I was confused. Was she a . . . *fan* of Lakshmi? I took a step backwards, just in case. But, no. Her smile (she had the greatest smile in the world) was benign. It appeared to be me she was praising. I decided to drink the awful wine after all.

After this, we began to get acquainted: slowly at first, and then quickly. We had friends in common, which helped, and there was work to bind us, too: when her beloved Virago Modern Classics celebrated its 30th birthday in 2008, I went to her house to talk to her for a piece. But really, our relationship, and everything it eventually became, was mostly down to Carmen herself. She had – this cannot be overstated — an extraordinary capacity for friendship. Most people have half a dozen true pals, if they're lucky. But she had a hundred at least, and a way of making each one feel adored and important.

You were a heroine. You were a genius. You may even have been a heroine *and* a genius. My Liz, she would say, her voice an embrace even before her arms went around the person in question. My Deborah, my Nell, my Sophie. My Peter, my Colm, my Robert. She might well have read everything — it often felt to me as if she had — but she also loved company. Talk was her oxygen. When she asked you a question, it wasn't to be polite. It was because she wanted to hear your answer.

It goes without saying that I was in awe of her brilliant career as a publisher; of all the people she'd known (Rebecca West, for God's sake); of the way she connected the present to the past, a walking, talking library with a voice, even now, that was straight out of Melbourne (whether ecstatic or furious, she would screech like a parrot). The Virago Modern Classics, with their green spines and covers decorated with obscure paintings from even more obscure art galleries (friends gave her postcards as inspiration) had played a big part in my life, as they had in so many people's. And talking about books with her was an intense pleasure. One of the happiest memories I have is of the two of us, wedged into a couple of deckchairs in a garden in Saint-Emilion. (A tourist bus passed by this idyllic scene twice an hour, and I developed a routine in which I would pretend to be its driver pointing out the distinguished literary figure on the other side of the wall.) Carmen was reading Jonathan Coe's novel

Number 11, which I'd just finished, and I was desperate for her to do the same so we could argue about it – or not, as it turned out: she loved it, too.

In the end, though, there was more to it than books. Carmen was a singular person, which makes her easy to describe, but impossible properly to capture. She had a way of getting to the heart of things; an unlikely, erratic wisdom. But she was also incredible *fun*. If she was a workaholic, she was also a sybarite. She loved the sun, and could lie in it, like a lizard, for hours. She loved clothes, always looking fabulous in her – 'it's vintage now, darling' – Missoni coat. She loved food, especially tripe (delivered by her friend Simon Hopkinson), frisée (eaten with her fingers, usually), cheese and pavlova, of which she could easily devour three portions. Taking her out for sushi was like watching a sea lion eat a mackerel, an entire menu disappearing in seconds. She was the only person I've ever met who actually smacked her lips after eating something. And then there was wine (*never* Champagne). 'I haven't had a drink in *hours!*' she once announced plaintively, on finding her glass empty at dinner. This became, among a certain group of us, a catchphrase, deployed in case of thirst, whether extreme or not.

She loved games: online Scrabble, bridge with friends. She loved television. She loved the cinema. She loved music. She loved dogs; her terrier Effie was with her till the last. And she loved sport, especially cricket. In 2018, we went to Lord's together for a one-day Test (one of her quirks, of which there were many, was that she supported England, not Australia). We weren't undercover, it was very hot, and I sloped off at about three, feeling faint. But Carmen, 30 years older than me, stayed put. 'Goodbye, darling!' she said, somehow peeling her eyes from the pitch.

When she was 80, she had a grand party in the Long Room at Lord's. On the same night, England was playing Croatia in the semi-finals of the World Cup, which spelled misery for those who didn't want to miss it (a surprisingly high number of senior novelists were already wondering if they could run, unnoticed, back and forth to the nearest pub). Carmen, though, came to their rescue – and her own – by arranging for a huge screen to be set up next door. England lost, of course, but it was the best party ever, even if what Germaine Greer made of Kieran Trippier's goal isn't recorded.

She loved 'junking' (her term for rootling in antique markets), and she loved presents (giving and receiving) and took them seriously. She agreed with her friend, the agent Pat Kavanagh: it's not the thought that counts, it's the *present* that counts. The best present she ever gave me was a rolling pin on which are written '*les six commandments du mariage*'. The best present I ever gave her – or so she told me – was an old wooden kookaburra, originally a child's toy. Also, the sparkly necklace she wore on the day she got her DBE. As a republican, she pretended to be grumpy about becoming a dame, which happened in 2017. 'I went to the palace, YOU NITWIT,' she wrote, in reply to an email in which I'd innocently asked why she'd sent me a picture of herself in a hat (she'd sneaked off there, rather furtively). But she was pleased, really. It was an acknowledgement. She understood that.

Above all, she loved holidays, preferably to France, where she'd once owned a home. In the strange summer of 2020, when it briefly seemed as if the worst of the pandemic might be over, we flew to stay with friends on the Côte d'Azur. Heathrow Airport was hushed, the quiet only broken by an Australian woman talking at the top of her voice about Monoprix and how she absolutely had to get there to buy knickers. That week, somewhat glamorously, we went on a speedboat to the island of Porquerolles (people arranged treats for her, that's just how it was). Carmen sat up front, the wind blowing in her hair, surrounded by charming young men (the sons of our friends), a look of perfect delight on her face. We took turns holding on to her legs, in case she blew away.

The next holiday we planned – in August, I was to take her to the Languedoc, which she wanted to see again, perhaps for the last time – was cancelled. It was on the day before we were due to leave that she found out about the leukaemia.

*

Carmen once told me a story about her earliest days in London, when she was still trying to find her feet, struggling with the awful weather, the awful food and the awful men. She was staying with a cousin, and had a temp job at a newspaper, one of whose editors assaulted her after asking her out to lunch. Traumatised, she fled to King's Cross, getting on the first train she could. It was headed for Cambridge, and there, she wandered around, dazed, confused, hardly aware of her surroundings.

Her cousin was worried. Where was she? What to do? In those days, some newspapers still carried small ads on their front pages, and she decided to place one (it may have been in the *Evening News*, I forget). COME HOME WOMBAT, it said – Wombat being Carmen's cousin's nickname for her.

Carmen saw the ad, and to London she returned. I always thought Come Home Wombat should be the title of her autobiography, a book she was writing, but will now never finish.

In the days after she died, I kept thinking of this. Come home wombat, I said to myself whenever I cried, which was every five minutes. Where is she? What to do? Carmen used to say that it was easy to publish her authors: all that was required was to care passionately about what they did, and to stick up for them. She was my friend, not my editor, but I know all too well how it must have felt to be in her protection.

She was the only person besides my husband who read everything I wrote, who always let me know what she thought of it, and who (this is the important part) understood the effort it might have taken. Her emails and texts, encouraging and enthusiastic, would arrive every Monday almost without fail, and inevitably ended the same way: 'No need to answer this, I know you are busy.' Somehow, she gave me the ineffable feeling that she always had my back, and I wonder now what kind of writer – what kind of *person* – I will be without her. I hope it isn't a bad sign that I have found writing this so bloody hard. She was the best person I ever knew, and I will miss her forever.

Rachel Cooke on Carmen Callil, *Observer* **(2022)**

Sylvia's Death

for Sylvia Plath

O Sylvia, Sylvia,
with a dead box of stones and spoons,

with two children, two meteors
wandering loose in the tiny playroom,

with your mouth into the sheet,
into the roof beam, into the dumb prayer,

(Sylvia, Sylvia,
where did you go
after you wrote me
from Devonshire
about raising potatoes
and keeping bees?)

what did you stand by,
just how did you lie down into?

Thief! —
how did you crawl into,

crawl down alone
into the death I wanted so badly and for so long,

the death we said we both outgrew,
the one we wore on our skinny breasts,

the one we talked of so often each time
we downed three extra dry martinis in Boston,

the death that talked of analysts and cures,
the death that talked like brides with plots,

the death we drank to,
the motives and then the quiet deed?

(In Boston
the dying
ride in cabs,
yes death again,
that ride home
with *our* boy.)

O Sylvia, I remember the sleepy drummer
who beat on our eyes with an old story,

how we wanted to let him come
like a sadist or a New York fairy

to do his job,
a necessity, a window in a wall or a crib,

and since that time he waited
under our heart, our cupboard,

and I see now that we store him up
year after year, old suicides

and I know at the news of your death,
a terrible taste for it, like salt.

(And me,
me too.
And now, Sylvia,
you again
with death again,
that ride home
with *our* boy.)

And I say only
with my arms stretched out into that stone place,

what is your death
but an old belonging,

a mole that fell out
of one of your poems?

(O friend,
while the moon's bad,
and the king's gone,
and the queen's at her wit's end
the bar fly ought to sing!)

O tiny mother,
you too!
O funny duchess!
O blonde thing!

Anne Sexton, 'Sylvia's Death', first collected in
***Live or Die* (1966), taken from *Mercies: Selected Poems*,**
ed. Linda Gray Sexton (2020)

FROM AGE TWELVE, she and I walked to and from school
together every day, talking incessantly and laughing a
lot. We started doing our homework together in the front
room at Heyworth Avenue. She was unusual and interesting,
intelligent, irreverent, funny, full of self-belief and she knew
so much. She introduced me to Shakespeare around the age
of twelve. I think she may have first come across his works
through the elocution lessons she was sent to, along with our
friend Pamela. These were with the formidable Miss White
in her premises above the wool shop. At that age I would have
looked at the writing on the page, failed to understand a word
of it and gone back to reading *Anne of Green Gables*. But, perhaps
because they were speaking the words out loud, they both got
it right away. Hilary began to read entire plays. I clearly recall
being in her house and her reciting to me the Prologue to *Henry
V*, 'O for a muse of fire, that would ascend the brightest heaven

of invention, A kingdom for a stage . . .' etc. and that's when I began to understand too. And to love it.

We began to look at Shakespeare at school and she and I would sit on the hearthrug, either side of the gas fire, and read the plays aloud, taking alternate parts and occasionally pausing to sigh when we came to a line which particularly struck us, 'the isle is full of noises, sounds and sweet airs . . .'. When we finished our O levels Hilary, Pamela and I spent all the money we had earned in our holiday jobs on a trip to Stratford. We had two nights in a bed and breakfast and went to see four plays in three days. We became theatre groupies and usherettes at the University Theatre in Manchester, so that we could see every production multiple times.

Hilary introduced me to John Donne and Andrew Marvell, to the *Cautionary Tales* of Hilaire Belloc and to much else. She opened doors to new worlds for me. We made up fantasy characters and had them conversing. There was a Sir Filigree Petal who wore embroidered waistcoats and lived by Hampstead Heath. Also a pampered young woman called Matilda Esmerelda who was 'very, very rich'. We made each other laugh a great deal. I think every one of you here must have a mental picture of Hilary laughing uncontrollably and dabbing tears from her cheeks with her hanky.

Let's make a quick foray now into the history syllabus. I was not so enamoured of the subject as Hilary, but I clearly remember the essay on The Achievements of Charles V Holy Roman Emperor. I handed in a respectable fifteen sides in my medium sized handwriting saying he'd done this in Spain, that in the Low Countries, something else about the New World. Hilary meanwhile filled two and a half exercise books full of closely written script in her idiosyncratic black ink and, not only that, she dealt with his life's achievements year on year, demonstrating how many plates this poor guy was spinning at once and, some of you may be unaware, he reigned for forty years. She did well to keep it so brief. You can see how this technique of seeing history from Charles' perspective might play out for her in later works. She didn't write her history essays during our evenings together, by the way. I think she stayed up nights getting those done.

What to me is really significant about those times and our lovely companionship was that we both were keeping significant secrets about our home lives from one another. In my house there was violence, volatility and rage and for her there was huge underlying tension and the damaging, bizarre facade of secrecy that she was expected to maintain about her family circumstances, which you will have read about in her autobiographical works. The odd thing is that we both knew something of each other's secrets from outside sources, but with great delicacy and some kind of intuitive teenage wisdom, we chose never to speak of them. I think what we'd done was to create, in her front room, a world of friendship and words and drama and beauty, fantasy and cheerfulness which was a place of safety for both of us. I think if we had spoken of the shadows in our lives then we would have burst that fragile bubble and the bad things would have rushed in and swamped us. It felt like a valuable thing we had been able to do for each other. We only spoke of these matters as we made our escapes to university, which was for her also an escape into her other place of greater safety, her relationship with Gez, which endured these fifty years.

She went on to create worlds on worlds, she carried a muse of fire within herself, she ascended the brightest heaven of invention, she had a kingdom for a stage and princes to act and monarchs to behold the swelling scene. She moved through the ghosts of history and the shadow world she created in her fiction as though born to it. And indeed she was born to it.

In the documentary *Return to Wolf Hall* she recollects listening to her Grandma Kitty and Auntie Annie sitting in the little house in Hadfield. She says 'They never ran out of words. They would sit either side of the fire and they would just talk and the conversation never flagged. That fluency was implanted in me. I carried off to school an enormous vocabulary and the habit of sustaining a story. It was a free gift given to me.' I see her, between life and death, her mother Margaret behind her, behind them Grandma Kitty, Auntie Annie, Grandad, Auntie Margaret, the great uncles who fought in the First War, then Catherine O'Shea who came from Ireland to Hadfield to work in the mills and all the nameless shadowy others there, all feeding each other with memories and stories and jokes and passing their great oral tradition forward to Hilary, who honoured them always . . . the consummate craftsman and weaver of spells.

**Anne Preston, Eulogy for Hilary Mantel,
Southwark Cathedral (2023)**

IN FRIENDSHIP GEORGE Eliot had the unconscious exact-ingness of a full nature. She was intolerant of a vacuum in the mind or character, and she was indifferent to admiration that did not seem to have its root in fundamental agreement with those first principles she held to be most 'necessary to salvation'. Where this sympathy existed, her generous affection was given to a fellow-believer, a fellow-labourer, with singularly little reference to the fact that such full sympathy was never unattended with profound love and reverence for herself as a living witness to the truth and power of the principles thus shared. To love her was a strenuous pleasure, for in spite of the tenderness for all human weakness that was natural to her, and the scrupulous charity of her overt judgements, the fact remained that her natural standard was ruthlessly out of reach, and it was a painful discipline for her friends to feel that she was compelled to lower it to suit their infirmities. The intense humility of her self-appreciation, and the unfeigned readiness with which she would even herself with any sinner who sought her counsel, had the same effect upon those who could compare what she condemned in herself with what she tolerated in them. And at the same time, no doubt, this total absence of self-sufficiency had something to do with the passionate tenderness with which commonplace people dared to cherish their immortal friend . . .

Edith Simcox, 'George Eliot: A Valedictory Article', *The Nineteenth Century* (1881)

KATHERINE HAS BEEN dead a week, & how far am I obeying her 'do not quite forget Katherine' which I read in one of her old letters. Am I already forgetting her? It is strange to trace the progress of one's feelings. Nelly said in her sensational way at breakfast on Friday 'Mrs Murry's dead! It says so in the paper!' At that one feels – what? A shock of relief? – a rival the less? Then confusion at feeling so little – then, gradually, blankness & disappointment; then a depression which I could not rouse myself from all that day. When I began to write, it seemed to me there was no point in writing. Katherine wont read it. Katherine's my rival no longer. More generously I felt, But though I can do this better than she could, where is she, who could do what I can't! Then, as usual with me, visual impressions kept coming & coming before me – always of Katherine putting on a white wreath, & leaving us, called away; more dignified, chosen. And then one pitied her. And one felt her reluctant to wear that wreath, which was an ice cold one. And she was only 33. And I could see her before me so exactly, & the room at Portland Villas. I go up. She gets up, very slowly, from her writing table. A glass of milk & a medicine bottle stood there. There were also piles of novels. Everything was very tidy, bright & somehow like a dolls house. At once, or almost, we got out of shyness. She (it was summer) half lay on the sofa by the window. She had her look of a Japanese doll, with the fringe combed quite straight across her forehead. Sometimes we looked very steadfastly at each other, as though we had reached some durable relationship, independent of the changes of the body, through the eyes. Hers were beautiful eyes – rather doglike, brown, very wide apart, with a steady slow rather faithful

& sad expression. Her nose was sharp, & a little vulgar. Her lips thin & hard. She wore short skirts & liked 'to have a line around her' she said. She looked very ill – very drawn, & moved languidly, drawing herself across the room, like some suffering animal. I suppose I have written down some of the things we said. Most days I think we reached that kind of certainty, in talk about books, or rather about our writings, which I thought had something durable about it. And then she was inscrutable. Did she care for me? Sometimes she would say so – would kiss me – would look at me as if (is this sentiment?) her eyes would like always to be faithful. She would promise never never to forget. That was what we said at the end of our last talk. She said she would send me her diary to read, & would write always. For our friendship was a real thing we said, looking at each other quite straight. It would always go on whatever happened. What happened was, I suppose, faultfindings and perhaps gossip. She never answered my letter. Yet I still feel, somehow that friendship persists. Still there are things about writing I think of & want to tell Katherine. If I had been in Paris & gone to her, she would have got up & in three minutes, we should have been talking again. Only I could not take the step. The surroundings – Murry & so on – & the small lies & treacheries, the perpetual playing & teasing, to whatever it was, cut away much of the substance of friendship. One was too uncertain. And so one let it all go. Yet I certainly expected that we should meet again this summer, & start fresh. And I was jealous of her writing – the only writing I have ever been jealous of. This made it harder to write to her; & I saw in it, perhaps from jealousy, all the qualities I disliked in her.

THE VIRAGO BOOK OF FRIENDSHIP

For two days I felt that I had grown middle aged, & lost some spur to write. That feeling is going. I no longer keep seeing her with her wreath. I dont pity her so much. Yet I have the feeling that I shall think of her at intervals all through life. Probably we had something in common which I shall never find in anyone else. (This I say in so many words in 1919 again & again.) Moreover I like speculating about her character. I think I never gave her credit for all her physical suffering & the effect it must have had in embittering her.

**Virginia Woolf, *The Diary of Virginia Woolf,*
Volume 2: 1920–1924**

I HAVE WISHED IN this little address to recall these four well-known Sibyls of my early youth – George Eliot, Mrs Gaskell, Currer Bell, Mrs Oliphant. Of all these, Mrs Oliphant's life is the one most familiar to me, and with my remembrance of her I will conclude. Her presence is still vivid for all who knew her, that white-haired, bright-eyed lady, sitting in her sunny room at Windsor, with her dogs at her feet, with flowers round about, with the happy inroads of her boys and their friends, with girls making the place merry and busy, and that curious bodyguard of older friends, some-what jealous and intolerant of any affections of later date than their own. It was good to see her among them all, ever serene in attention and interest, the most noteworthy mistress of the house, welcoming courteously, speaking definitely and to the point with her pretty racy Scotch accent and soft tones.

Her work was never-ceasing, but it scarcely interfered with her hospitable life among her associates.

I knew her abroad as well as at home. I was once staying in a hotel at Grindelwald with the Leslie Stephens. Mrs Oliphant and her young people were there also, and our parties joined company. We used to dine together, walk together; I used to see her at her daily task, steadily continuing, notwithstanding all the interruptions of nature and human nature – the changing lights on the mountains, the exclaiming of youthful excursionists, the many temptations to leave her task. I was always struck, when I saw her writing, by her concentration and the perfect neatness of her arrangements – the tiny inkstand of prepared ink, into which she poured a few drops of water, enough for each day's work, the orderly manuscript, her delicate, fine pen . . . When she had finished, she would come out in the evening for a saunter along the valley with Leslie Stephen and the rest of us. She was one of those people whose presence is even more than a *pleasure*, it was a stimulus; she was kindly, sympathetic, and yet answering with that chord of intelligent antagonism which is so suggestive and makes for such good talk.

She used to tell me a great deal of her past life at that time, but with a certain reserve also, and it was not until I read the Autobiography published after her death that I realised what her great cares had been.* I could then understand why she had been so scornful of mental difficulties which seemed real enough to some of us, and why she always spoke bitterly of

---

* Margaret Oliphant (1828–97) had six children. Three died in infancy. After this, she became a widow. She lost her remaining daughter in 1864; the elder of her two remaining sons died in 1890, the younger in 1894.

problems of thought – she who had so many practical troubles to encounter. The impression of that special time is very
vivid still – the busy clatter of the Swiss village close at hand,
the great surrounding mountains, the terrace where we used
to sit together under the clematis in full flower, and her eyes
shining as she talked on and on. I remember her once saying,
when I exclaimed at something she told me, 'Temperament
has a great deal to do with our lives, and mine is a hopeful
temper and has carried me on through terrible trials.'

Some time after our visit to Grindelwald, I wrote to her
to ask for a literary contribution for a friend, an editor who
was ill and in great need of help. Mrs Oliphant immediately
sent a story, a charming, long, cheerful story, which (as I
discovered later) had been written by her son's sick-bed, and
which she gave as a gift with her bountiful hand at a time
when she hardly knew where to turn for money. What friend
in trouble was ever dropped or ignored by her?

**Anne Thackeray Ritchie, 'A Discourse on
Modern Sibyls', collected in *From the Porch* (1913)**

I DIDN'T KNOW THEN, as Bessie and I lay on my bed and rea-
soned about fate and the universe, that Nicola's mad dream
of flying her carers down to Melbourne and putting them up
at the Windsor Hotel would come true, and that in ten days
she would return to Sydney for good with Mr Hathaway's
titanium post flawlessly implanted in her spine.

I didn't know yet how many times I would fly to Sydney to

play my small part in the remains of her care, or how often, when I buzzed at Iris's apartment, the door would be opened by Harriet from Yass, her round, weather-beaten face sweating and wild with fatigue, or by Marion the Buddhist, white, composed and stoic after a five-day stint without relief. I had not prepared myself to sleep on the floor beside Clare from Byron, when Iris, half out of her mind, pulled on a backpack and fled north, on foot, along the coast of New South Wales.

I could not imagine the urge to start drinking that would seize me every time I entered the high-airy rooms of the apartment and found Nicola enthroned on the sofa where, propped against its hard padded arm, she woke and slept and laughed and coughed, commanding the stewing of Chinese herbs, planning brown rice fasts and drastic alkaline diets, turning her face up each morning to the sun that streamed in through the uncovered windows. Nor could I foresee that one day, with her swollen legs propped on a stack of cushions, she would announce brightly, 'I've suddenly realised why I feel so terrible – I must be anaemic.' Or how dull my life at home would seem between my visits to Sydney, how I would write to her on a postcard: 'I miss you. I'm bored. I'd rather be scrubbing shit off Iris's bathroom tiles.' For this too would be required of me: like her other carers, whom I came to love in the intimacy of our labour, I would have to help carry her to the lavatory, where I learned to wash her arse as gently as I had washed my sister's and my mother's, and as some day someone will have to wash mine.

I might have guessed that she would resist the hospice until the contents of her lungs began to bubble up into her nose and throat, until everyone around her was deranged with exhaustion, fury and despair. She relented only when Marion said to her, 'Don't regret the things you haven't done. That's the past. Let it go. Rejoice: you're our teacher now.'

But for all my anxious readiness I was still shocked by the summons. It reached me at Writers' Week in Adelaide. On the plane to Sydney everything I looked at – strangers' hair, the weave of their garments – glowed with forceful value. When I tiptoed into her hospice room, preparing to be solemn, she took my hand with her slow, puffy one and croaked, under the oxygen cannula, 'Did you nick off from the festival? Any gossip?' I told her how the big names had scrambled to see the Nobel Laureate get his Australian citizenship in a tent and gleeful laughter rose off her in a shimmer. Feebly she squeezed my fingers and murmured the last thing she said to me: 'Don't go, will you.'

I did not foresee that two Buddhists would chant her out of there: that with Clare and Iris I would crouch shuddering in a corner of the dim hospice room and listen to the thrilling alto drone of the women's voices, calling on all compassionate beings to come to that place, to come to Nicola, who like each of us in this life had been sunk deep in the mud of unbearable suffering; for whom the light of this life had set, who was entering a place of darkness, a trackless forest; who had no friends, who had no refuge, who was poised on the lip of a precipice, a frightful chasm into whose echoing spaces she would plunge and be swept away by the mighty wind of karma, the hurricane of karma. I glanced up from this scalding vigil and saw her sister's face in profile against a black curtain, patient and stark, as grand in the remnants of its beauty as was the face that lay gasping on the pillow.

Nor could I foresee that at her memorial celebration, days after her ashes had been scattered in the presence of those who had been closer to her than I, a beautifully clad woman with the order of service in her hand would address me thus, in a voice with a nasal, frosty edge: 'I'm Verity. I was at school with Nicola. I see you're to speak, and I was curious to know – what exactly was your connection to her?'

I had no idea that, before she left my house, Nicola would write me a valedictory letter of such self-reproach, such tenderness and quiet gratitude, that when I came across it, months later, in its clever hiding-place, I was racked with weeping, with harsh sobs that tore their way out of my body, as she had fancied her toxins would rush from hers.

Helen Garner, *The Spare Room* (2008)

I FIRST MET MARIANNE Moore in the spring of 1934 when I was a senior at Vassar College, through Miss Fanny Borden, the college librarian . . .

The day came when Miss Borden told me that she had heard from Miss Moore and that Miss Moore was willing to meet me in New York, on a Saturday afternoon. Years later I discovered that Marianne had agreed to do this with reluctance; in the past, it seems, dear Miss Borden had sent several Vassar girls to meet Miss Moore and sometimes her mother as well, and every one had somehow failed to please. This probably accounted for the conditions laid down for our first rendezvous: I was to find Miss Moore seated on the bench at the right of the door leading to the reading room of the New York Public Library. They might have been even more strict. I learned later that if Miss Moore really expected *not* to like would-be acquaintances, she arranged to meet them at the Information Booth in Grand Central Station – no place to sit down, and, if necessary, an instant getaway was possible. I was very frightened, but I put on my new spring suit and took the train to New York. I had never seen a picture of Miss Moore; all I knew was that she had red hair and usually wore a wide-brimmed hat. I expected the hair to be bright red and for her to be tall and intimidating. I was right on time, even a bit early, but she was there before me (no matter how early one arrived, Marianne was always there first) and, I saw at once, not very tall and not in the least intimidating. She was forty-seven, an age that seemed old to me then, and her hair was mixed with white to a faint rust pink, and her rust-pink eyebrows were frosted with white. The large flat black hat was as I'd expected it to be. She wore a blue tweed suit that day and, as she usually did then, a man's 'polo shirt', as they were called, with a black bow at the neck. The effect was quaint, vaguely Bryn Mawr 1909, but stylish at the same time. I sat down and she began to talk.

It seems to me that Marianne talked to me steadily for the next thirty-five years, but of course that is nonsensical. I was living far from New York many of those years and saw her at long intervals. She must have been one of the world's greatest talkers: entertaining, enlightening, fascinating, and memorable; her talk, like her poetry, was quite different from anyone else's in the world. I don't know what she talked about at that first meeting; I wish I had kept a diary.

Happily ignorant of the poor Vassar girls before me who hadn't passed muster, I began to feel less nervous and even spoke some myself. I had what may have been an inspiration, I don't know – at any rate, I attribute my great good fortune in having known Marianne as a friend in part to it. Ringling Bros. and Barnum & Bailey Circus was making its spring visit to New York and I asked Miss Moore (we called each other 'Miss' for over two years) if she would care to go to the circus with me the Saturday after next. I didn't know that she *always* went to the circus, wouldn't have missed it for anything, and when she accepted, I went back to Poughkeepsie in the grimy day coach extremely happy.

Elizabeth Bishop, 'Efforts of Affection: A Memoir of Marianne Moore' (*c.*1969), collected in *Elizabeth Bishop: Prose* (2011)

Orcop: In Memoriam: Frances Horovitz, 1938–83

Driving south from Hereford one day in March
memorable for trickling piles of snow, with sideshows,
drift upon drift of snowdrops lapping the hedgerows,
we sighted the signpost and, on impulse, turned up
the winding, vertical road to Orcop. The church,
further away from the village than I remembered,
was no less an image of you than I remembered
with its high-pitched, peasant roof and wooden steeple
on a slope with yew trees and a painter's view –

ploughed red soil, a pasture, a working barn –
that set it apart from the ordinary, just as your field stone,
when we found it, set you apart from the good people
labelled in polished marble, buried around you.
As in your life, though never aloof, you were alone.
I remembered how, when quietly you entered a room
in one of those woven dresses you used to wear,
heather or lavender, all senseless chattering would
    cease,
shamed by your dignity. I remembered your beautiful
    things:
your pots, your books, your cat, silver as your cross,
your delicate drawings. Yes, I remembered you
    exactly.
And there you were, still – beautiful, exceptional,
    subtle –
in a landscape of lichen I had to read like Braille
to find your name. I heard the first blackbird, then a
    thrush.
Later, as we left, the children we'd seen playing
among the graves when we arrived resumed their
    game,
using your stone, a hump from another century,
to hide behind, while one, the smallest, counted
    slowly.

Anne Stevenson, 'Orcop: In Memoriam: Frances Horovitz, 1938–83' (2006), *Collected Poems* **(2023)**

M Y FAVOURITE SEAT was a smooth and broad stone, rising white and dry from the very middle of the beck, and only to be got at by wading through the water; a feat I accomplished barefoot. The stone was just broad enough to accommodate, comfortably, another girl and me, at that time my chosen comrade – one Mary Ann Wilson; a shrewd, observant personage, whose society I took pleasure in, partly because she was witty and original, and partly because she had a manner which set me at my ease. Some years older than I, she knew more of the world, and could tell me many things I liked to hear: with her my curiosity found gratification: to my faults also she gave ample indulgence, never imposing curb or rein on anything I said. She had a turn for narrative, I for analysis; she liked to inform, I to question; so we got on swimmingly together, deriving much entertainment, if not much improvement, from our mutual intercourse.

And where, meantime, was Helen Burns? Why did I not spend these sweet days of liberty with her? Had I forgotten her? Or was I so worthless as to have grown tired of her pure society? Surely the Mary Ann Wilson I have mentioned was inferior to my first acquaintance: she could only tell me amusing stories, and reciprocate any racy and pungent gossip I chose to indulge in; while, if I have spoken truth of Helen, she was qualified to give those who enjoyed the privilege of her converse a taste of far higher things.

True, reader; and I knew and felt this: and though I am a defective being, with many faults and few redeeming points, yet I never tired of Helen Burns; nor ever ceased to cherish for her a sentiment of attachment, as strong, tender, and respectful as any that ever animated my heart. How could it be otherwise, when Helen, at all times and under all circumstances, evinced for me a quiet and faithful friendship, which ill-humour never soured, nor irritation never troubled? But Helen was ill at present: for some weeks she had been removed from my sight to I knew not what room upstairs. She was not, I was told, in the hospital portion of the house with the fever patients; for her complaint was consumption, not typhus: and by consumption I, in my ignorance, understood something mild, which time and care would be sure to alleviate.

I was confirmed in this idea by the fact of her once or twice coming downstairs on very warm sunny afternoons, and being taken by Miss Temple into the garden; but, on these occasions, I was not allowed to go and speak to her; I only saw her from the schoolroom window, and then not distinctly; for she was much wrapped up, and sat at a distance under the verandah.

One evening, in the beginning of June, I had stayed out very late with Mary Ann in the wood; we had, as usual, separated ourselves from the others, and had wandered far; so far that we lost our way, and had to ask it at a lonely cottage, where a man and woman lived, who looked after a herd of half-wild swine that fed on the mast in the wood. When we got back, it was after moonrise: a pony, which we knew to be the surgeon's, was standing at the garden door. Mary Ann remarked that she supposed some one must be very ill, as Mr Bates had been sent for at that time of the evening. She went into the house; I stayed behind a few minutes to plant in my garden a handful of roots I had dug up in the forest, and which I feared would wither if I left them till the morning. This done, I lingered yet a little longer: the flowers smelt so sweet as the dew fell; it was such a pleasant evening, so serene, so warm; the still glowing west promised so fairly another fine day on the morrow; the moon rose with such majesty in the grave east. I was noting these things and enjoying them as a child might, when it entered my mind as it had never done before: —

'How sad to be lying now on a sick bed, and to be in danger of dying! This world is pleasant – it would be dreary to be called from it, and to have to go who knows where?'

And then my mind made its first earnest effort to comprehend what had been infused into it concerning heaven and hell; and for the first time it recoiled, baffled; and for the first time glancing behind, on each side, and before it, it saw all round an unfathomed gulf: it felt the one point where it stood – the present; all the rest was formless cloud and vacant depth; and it shuddered at the thought of tottering, and plunging amid that chaos. While pondering this new idea, I heard the front door open; Mr Bates came out, and with him was a nurse. After she had seen him mount his horse and depart, she was about to close the door, but I ran up to her.

'How is Helen Burns?'

'Very poorly,' was the answer.

'Is it her Mr Bates has been to see?'

'Yes.'

'And what does he say about her?'

'He says she'll not be here long.'

This phrase, uttered in my hearing yesterday, would have only conveyed the notion that she was about to be removed to Northumberland, to her own home. I should not have suspected that it meant she was dying; but I knew instantly now! It opened clear on my comprehension that Helen Burns was numbering her last days in this world, and that she was going to be taken to the region of spirits, if such region there were. I experienced a shock of horror, then a strong thrill of grief, then a desire – a necessity to see her; and I asked in what room she lay.

'She is in Miss Temple's room,' said the nurse.

'May I go up and speak to her?'

'Oh no, child! It is not likely; and now it is time for you to come in; you'll catch the fever if you stop out when the dew is falling.'

The nurse closed the front door; I went in by the side entrance which led to the schoolroom: I was just in time; it was nine o'clock, and Miss Miller was calling the pupils to go to bed.

It might be two hours later, probably near eleven, when I – not having been able to fall asleep, and deeming, from the perfect silence of the dormitory, that my companions were all wrapt in profound repose – rose softly, put on my frock over my night-dress, and, without shoes, crept from the apartment, and set off in quest of Miss Temple's room. It was quite at the other end of the house; but I knew my way; and the light of the unclouded summer moon, entering here and there at passage windows, enabled me to find it without difficulty. An odour of camphor and burnt vinegar warned me when I came near the fever room: and I passed its door quickly, fearful lest the nurse who sat up all night should hear me. I dreaded being discovered and sent back; for I must see Helen, — I must embrace her before she died, — I must give her one last kiss, exchange with her one last word.

Having descended a staircase, traversed a portion of the house below, and succeeded in opening and shutting, without noise, two doors, I reached another flight of steps; these I mounted, and then just opposite to me was Miss Temple's room. A light shone through the keyhole and from under the door; a profound stillness pervaded the vicinity. Coming near, I found the door slightly ajar; probably to admit some fresh air into the close abode of sickness. Indisposed to hesitate, and full of impatient impulses – soul and senses quivering with keen throes – I put it back and looked in. My eye sought Helen, and feared to find death.

Close by Miss Temple's bed, and half covered with its white curtains, there stood a little crib. I saw the outline of a form under the clothes, but the face was hid by the hangings: the nurse I had spoken to in the garden sat in an easy-chair asleep; an unsnuffed candle burnt dimly on the table. Miss Temple was not to be seen: I knew afterwards that she had been called to a delirious patient in the fever-room. I advanced; then paused by the crib side: my hand was on the curtain, but I preferred speaking before I withdrew it. I still recoiled at the dread of seeing a corpse.

'Helen!' I whispered softly, 'are you awake?'

She stirred herself, put back the curtain, and I saw her face, pale, wasted, but quite composed: she looked so little changed that my fear was instantly dissipated.

'Can it be you, Jane?' she asked, in her own gentle voice.

'Oh!' I thought, 'she is not going to die; they are mistaken: she could not speak and look so calmly if she were.'

I got on to her crib and kissed her: her forehead was cold, and her cheek both cold and thin, and so were her hand and wrist; but she smiled as of old.

'Why are you come here, Jane? It is past eleven o'clock: I heard it strike some minutes since.'

'I came to see you, Helen: I heard you were very ill, and I could not sleep till I had spoken to you.'

'You came to bid me good-bye, then: you are just in time probably.'

'Are you going somewhere, Helen? Are you going home?'

'Yes; to my long home – my last home.'

'No, no, Helen!' I stopped, distressed. While I tried to devour my tears, a fit of coughing seized Helen; it did not, however, wake the nurse; when it was over, she lay some minutes exhausted; then she whispered –

'Jane, your little feet are bare; lie down and cover yourself with my quilt.'

I did so: she put her arm over me, and I nestled close to her. After a long silence, she resumed, still whispering –

'I am very happy, Jane; and when you hear that I am dead, you must be sure and not grieve: there is nothing to grieve about. We all must die one day, and the illness which is removing me is not painful; it is gentle and gradual: my mind is at rest. I leave no one to regret me much: I have only a father; and he is lately married, and will not miss me. By dying young, I shall escape great sufferings. I had not qualities or talents to make my way very well in the world: I should have been continually at fault.'

'But where are you going to, Helen? Can you see? Do you know?'

'I believe; I have faith: I am going to God.'

'Where is God? What is God?'

'My Maker and yours, who will never destroy what He created. I rely implicitly on His power, and confide wholly in His goodness: I count the hours till that eventful one arrives which shall restore me to Him, reveal Him to me.'

'You are sure, then, Helen, that there is such a place as heaven, and that our souls can get to it when we die?'

'I am sure there is a future state; I believe God is good; I can resign my immortal part to Him without any misgiving. God is my father; God is my friend: I love Him; I believe He loves me.'

'And shall I see you again, Helen, when I die?'

'You will come to the same region of happiness: be received by the same mighty, universal Parent, no doubt, dear Jane.'

Again I questioned, but this time only in thought. 'Where is that region? Does it exist?' And I clasped my arms closer round Helen; she seemed dearer to me than ever; I felt as if I could not let her go; I lay with my face hidden on her neck. Presently she said, in the sweetest tone –

'How comfortable I am! That last fit of coughing has tired me a little; I feel as if I could sleep: but don't leave me, Jane; I like to have you near me.'

'I'll stay with you, dear Helen: no one shall take me away.'

'Are you warm, darling?'

'Yes.'

'Good-night, Jane.'

'Good-night, Helen.'

She kissed me, and I her, and we both soon slumbered.

When I awoke it was day: an unusual movement roused me; I looked up; I was in somebody's arms; the nurse held me; she was carrying me through the passage back to the dormitory. I was not reprimanded for leaving my bed; people had something else to think about; no explanation was afforded then to my many questions; but a day or two afterwards I learned that Miss Temple, on returning to her own room at dawn, had found me laid in the little crib; my face against Helen Burns's shoulder, my arms round her neck. I was asleep, and Helen was – dead.

Her grave is in Brocklebridge churchyard: for fifteen years after her death it was only covered by a grassy mound; but now a grey marble tablet marks the spot, inscribed with her name, and the word 'Resurgam.'

Charlotte Brontë, *Jane Eyre* **(1847)**

Acknowledgements

I OWE THE GREATEST debt to my publisher, Lennie Goodings, who understood immediately what I wanted to do with this book, saw all the fun and the beauty, and who has helped me so much since. Thank you to her, and to everyone at Virago: Katy Bridgen, Nithya Rae and especially my dear Zoë Hood. Thank you also to Rachel Thorne, who tirelessly helped me secure all the permissions I needed, however elusive.

I don't know if an agent should also be a pal, but as unprofessional as I am, to me Peter Straus is the greatest friend a writer could ever have. Thank you, Peter, for everything.

The irony isn't lost on me that while I was working on this book, I sorely neglected my friends. Sorry to all of them, for that. But I'm back now: bring me your jokes, your gossip, and your tales of woe. All of you! Thank you to my family, too. I'll visit soon, I promise. Edith Johnson, I'm still waiting for you to send me the best bits of *First Term at Malory Towers*.

Thank you to Sarah Donaldson, Jane Ferguson, Lisa O'Kelly, Lucy Rock, and Paul Webster: close colleagues at the *Observer* without whom I would not have survived the last few years. So many of the books I have reviewed for Ursula Kenny, the *Observer*'s literary editor, have fed into my thinking for this project; it wouldn't exist without her. The chapter called 'Solidarity' I hereby dedicate to my 24-hour work support group: Catherine Bennett, Hadley Freeman, Amelia Gentleman, Lucy Mangan, Isobel Montgomery, Susanna Rustin and Sonia Sodha. You are the bravest and the best.

Thank you to my neighbour, Sue Brealey, for giving me a vital copy of Professor Todd's magisterial survey, and to the staff of the London Library for saving me when the British Library closed at the worst possible moment. Special, heart-felt thanks to Sophie Lyne and Stephen Browett for having regularly whisked this workaholic away on holiday.

Most of all, thank you to Anthony Quinn, whose friend-ship and abiding love takes many forms, but for the purposes of this book was best and most usefully expressed via the astonishing library that exists inside his head. He is the com-panion of my heart.

Bibliography

The Bible (King James Version)

Arnim, Elizabeth von, *The Enchanted April* (1922; Penguin, 2012)

Austen, Jane, *Emma* (1815; Penguin, 2006)

—*Love and Freindship* (1790; Penguin, 2014)

—*Persuasion* (1817; Penguin, 2006)

—*Pride and Prejudice* (1813; Penguin, 2006)

Baker, Ida, *Katherine Mansfield: The Memories of LM* (1971; Virago, 1985)

Barnard, Josie, *The Book of Friendship* (Virago, 2011)

Blain, Virginia (ed.), with Grundy, Isobel, and Clements, Patricia, *The Feminist Companion to Literature in English* (1990, Batsford)

Brittain, Vera, *Testament of Friendship* (1940; Virago, 2012)

Brontë, Charlotte, *Jane Eyre* (1847; Penguin, 2006)

—*Letters* (collected and published Clarendon Press, 2004)

—*Shirley* (1849; Penguin, 2012)

Burnett, Frances Hodgson, *A Little Princess* (1905; Collins, 2014)

—*The Secret Garden* (1911; Collins 2017)

Burney, Fanny, *Journals and Letters* (Penguin, 2006)

Carlyle, Jane Welsh, and Carlyle, Thomas, *The Collected Letters of*, ed. Ian Campbell, David Sorenson et al., 44 vols (see carlyleletters.dukeupress.edu)

Chaucer, Geoffrey, *The Canterbury Tales* (1387–1400; Penguin, 2005)

Colette, *Break of Day* (1928; FSG, 2002)

Delafield, E. M., *Diary of a Provincial Lady* (1930; Penguin, 2014)

Dickinson, Emily, *The Complete Poems* (Faber, 2016)

Dunbar, Robin, *Understanding the Power of Our Most Important Relationships* (Little, Brown, 2021)

Eichenbaum, Luise, and Orbach, Susie, *Between Women: Love, Envy and Competition in Women's Friendships* (1987; Arrow, 1994)

Eliot, George, *Middlemarch* (1871–72; Penguin, 2011)

—*Selections from George Eliot's Letters*, ed. Gordon S. Haight (Yale, 1985)

Ellis, Sarah Stickney, *The Daughters of England: Their Position in Society, Character and Domestic Habits* (Fisher, Son & Co., 1842)

—*The Women of England: Their Social Duties, and Domestic Habits* (Herman Hooker, 1839)

Enright, D. J., and Rawlinson, David (eds), *The Oxford Book of Friendship* (Oxford University Press, 1991)

Gaskell, Elizabeth, *Ruth* (1853; Penguin, 2004)

Gissing, George, *The Odd Women* (1893; Penguin, 2007)

Hardy, Thomas, *Tess of the d'Urbervilles* (1891; Penguin, 2003)

Holtby, Winifred, *The Crowded Street* (1924; Persephone, 2008)

James, Henry, *The Bostonians* (1886; Penguin, 2009)

Jansson, Tove, *Fair Play* (1989; Sort of Books, 2007)

Lurie, Alison, *Boys and Girls Forever: Reflections on Children's Classics* (Chatto & Windus, 2003)

Mangan, Lucy, *Bookworm: A Memoir of Childhood Reading* (Vintage, 2019)

Mansfield, Katherine, *Letters and Journals*, ed. C. K. Stead (Penguin, 1977)

Marcus, Laura, *Between Women: Friendship, Desire, and Marriage in Victorian England* (Princeton, 2007)

Maud, Constance, *No Surrender* (1911; Persephone, 2011)

Mayor, F. M., *The Rector's Daughter* (1924; Persephone, 2021)

Montgomery, L. M., *Anne of Green Gables* (1908; Puffin, 2014)

Morgan, Robin (ed.), *Sisterhood is Powerful* (Vintage, 1970)

Nicholson, Virginia, *Singled Out: How Two Million British Women Survived Without Men After the First World War* (Penguin, 2008)

Philips, Katherine, *The Collected Works of Katherine Philips: The Matchless Orinda, Volume I: The Poems*, ed. Patrick Thomas (Stump Cross Books, 1990)

Porter, Roy, and Tomaselli, Sylvana (eds), *The Dialectics of Friendship* (Routledge, 1990)

Richardson, Henry Handel, *The Getting of Wisdom* (1910; Text, 2012)

Richardson, Samuel, *Clarissa, or The History of a Young Lady* (1748; Penguin, 1985)

Ritchie, Anne Thackeray, *From the Porch* (Smith, Elder & Co., 1913)

Rossetti, Christina, *Complete Poems* (Penguin, 2001)

Rowe, Dorothy, *Friends and Enemies: Our Need to Love and Hate* (HarperCollins, 2001)

Shakespeare, William, *As You Like It* (1599?; Penguin, 2015)

Shattock, Joanne, *The Oxford Guide to British Women Writers* (OUP, 1993)

Simcox, Edith, 'George Eliot: A Valedictory Article', *The Nineteenth Century* (1881; Sampson, Low, Marston and Co., 1877–1900)

—A Monument to the Memory of George Eliot: Edith J. Simcox's *Autobiography of a Shirtmaker* ed Constance M Fulmer and Margaret E Barfield (Routledge, 1997)

Todd, Janet, *Women's Friendship in Literature* (Columbia University Press, 1980)

Webb, Beatrice, *The Diary of Beatrice Webb, Volume Two 1892–1905*, ed. Norman and Jeanne Mackenzie (Virago, 1983)

Wharton, Edith, *A Backward Glance* (1934; S&S, 1998)

Wollstonecraft, Mary, *A Vindication of the Rights of Men* (1790; Oxford World's Classics, 2008)

Woolf, Virginia, *A Room of One's Own* (1928; Penguin, 2019)

—*Mrs Dalloway* (1925; Vintage, 2016)

Permissions

Opening epigraphs

Virginia Woolf, epigraph from *The Diary of Virginia Woolf, Volume 2, 1920–24,* ed. Anne Oliver Bell, Wadsworth, 1980. Reproduced with permission of Granta Books.

Robin Morgan, epigraph from 'Letter to a Sister Underground, 1970' in *Sisterhood is Powerful,* ed. Robin Morgan, Vintage, 1970. Reproduced by kind permission of the author.

Dorothy L. Sayers, epigraph from *Gaudy Night,* Hodder & Stoughton, 1935. Reproduced with permission of David Higham Associates.

Shirley Conran, epigraph from *Lace,* Canongate, 2012, copyright © Steiden Enterprises NV, 1982. Reproduced with permission of Simon & Schuster LLC. All rights reserved.

Definitions

Emily Dickinson, poem 'Nature assigns the Sun' published in *The Poems of Emily Dickinson,* ed. Thomas H. Johnson, Cambridge, Mass.: The Belknap Press of Harvard University Press, copyright © 1951, 1955 by the President and Fellows of Harvard College. Copyright © renewed 1979, 1983 by the President and Fellows of Harvard College. Copyright © 1914, 1918, 1919, 1924, 1929, 1930, 1932, 1935, 1937, 1942, by Martha Dickinson Bianchi. Copyright © 1952, 1957, 1958, 1963, 1965, by Mary L. Hampson. Reproduced with permission. All rights reserved.

Childhood

Antonia White, excerpt from *Frost in May*, Virago, 2018, copyright © The Literary Executors of Antonia White, 1933. Reproduced with permission of Virago, an imprint of Little, Brown Book Group, Carmelite House, 50 Victoria Embankment, London, EC4Y 0DZ; and Curtis Brown Group Ltd, London, on behalf of The Estate of Antonia White.

Margaret Atwood, excerpt from *Cat's Eye*, Virago, 2009, copyright © Margaret Atwood, 1988. Reproduced with permission of Bloomsbury Publishing Plc.

Emilia McKenzie, illustrated pages from *But You Have Friends*, Top Shelf Productions, 2023, pp.8–14, copyright © Emilia McKenzie. Reproduced with permission from Top Shelf Productions / IDW Publishing.

Excerpt from 'Dear Cathy & Claire', published in *Jackie*, 2006. Reproduced with kind permission of DC Thomson & Co Ltd.

Curtis Sittenfeld, excerpt from *Prep: A Novel*, Black Swan, copyright © Curtis Sittenfeld, 2005. Reproduced with permission of The Random House Group Limited; and Random House, an imprint and division of Penguin Random House LLC. All rights reserved.

Barrie Mitchell, illustrated pages from 'The Four Marys' published in *Bunty*, 1979. Reproduced with kind permission of DC Thomson & Co Ltd.

Toya Wolfe, excerpt from *Last Summer on State Street*, Merky Books, 2022, copyright © Toya Wolfe, 2022. Reproduced by permission of The Random House Group Limited.

Enid Blyton, excerpt from *Malory Towers: First Term*, Hodder Children's Books, 2019, copyright © 1946. Reproduced with permission of Hodder & Stoughton Ltd (Enid Blyton Estate), Carmelite House, 50 Victoria Embankment, London, EC4Y 0DZ.

Elizabeth Jane Howard, excerpt from *Slipstream*, Macmillan, an imprint of Pan Macmillan, 2002, copyright © Elizabeth Jane

First Encounters

Loneliness & Longing

Frenemies & Falling Out

Vera Brittain, letter excerpts to Winifred Holtby published in
Between Friends, ed. Elaine and English Showalter, Virago, 2022,
copyright © The Literary Executors of the Vera Brittain Will Trust,
1970. Reproduced with permission of the Vera Brittain Literary
Estate.

Winifred Holtby, letter excerpts to Vera Brittain published in *Between
Friends*, ed. Elaine and English Showalter, Virago, 2022, copyright ©
Kingston upon Hull City Council, Literary Executor for the Estate of
Winifred Holtby.

Old Friends

Jackie Kay, poem 'Fiere', published in *Fiere*, 2011, copyright © Jackie
Kay, 2011. Reproduced with permission of The Wylie Agency (UK)
Limited.

Carol Shields, excerpt from *The Stone Diaries*, World Editions, 2020,
copyright © Carol Shields, 1993. Reproduced with permission of
the Carol Shields Literary Trust; and Viking Books, an imprint of
Penguin Publishing Group, a division of Penguin Random House
LLC. All rights reserved.

Dame Margaret Drabble CBE, excerpt from *The Radiant Way*,
copyright © Margaret Drabble, 1987. Reproduced with permission
of United Agents Ltd (www.unitedagents.co.uk) on behalf of Dame
Margaret Drabble CBE.

Amanda Craig, excerpt from *The Three Graces*, Abacus, 2023.
Reproduced with permission of Virago, an imprint of Little, Brown
Book Group, Carmelite House, 50 Victoria Embankment, London,
EC4Y 0DZ.

Barbara Pym, excerpt from *Excellent Women*, copyright © 1952.
Reproduced by kind permission of the Estate of the author.

Toni Morrison, excerpt from *Sula*, Chatto & Windus, 1998,
copyright © Toni Morrison, 1973, 2004 and renewed 2002 by Toni
Morrison. Reproduced with permission of The Random House
Group Limited.

Goodbyes

Mary McCarthy, excerpt on her friend Hannah Arendt, copyright ©
The Mary McCarthy Literary Trust. Reproduced with permission of
A.M. Heath & Co Ltd.

Rachel Cooke, excerpts from 'Virago founder Carmen Callil
remembered by her friend Rachel Cooke: 'Of course she was
difficult', *The Observer*, 23/10/2022. Reproduced with permission.

Anne Sexton, poem 'Sylvia's Death', published in *Mercies: Selected
Poems*, ed. Linda Gray Sexton, Penguin, 2020, copyright © Linda
Gray Sexton. Reproduced with permission of SLL/Sterling Lord
Literistic, Inc.

Anne Preston, the Eulogy for Hilary Mantel, 2022. Reproduced with
kind permission of Anne Preston.

Virginia Woolf, excerpts from *The Diary of Virginia Woolf, Volume 2,
1920–24*, ed. Anne Oliver Bell, Wadsworth, 1980. Reproduced with
permission of Granta Books.

Helen Garner, excerpt from *The Spare Room*, Canongate, 2019.
Reproduced with permission of Canongate Books Limited through
PLSClear; and Text Publishing.

Elizabeth Bishop, excerpt from 'Efforts of Affection: A Memoir of
Marianne Moore', published in *Prose* by Elizabeth Bishop, Chatto &
Windus, 2011, copyright © The Alice H. Methfessel Trust, 2011.
Reproduced with permission of The Random House Group Limited.

Anne Stevenson, poem 'Orcop, In memoriam: Frances Horovitz,
1938–1983', published in *Collected Poems* by Anne Stevenson, Bloodaxe
Books, 2023. Reproduced with permission of Bloodaxe Books, www.
bloodaxebooks.com.

Author index